ENDORSEMENTS & PRAISE
VOL. 1.

"Curtis, I not only like your book; I love it!"
Edwin Meese III
White House Counselor to President Ronald Reagan
U.S. Attorney General, President Ronald Reagan
Legal Affairs Secretary & Chief of Staff for Governor Ronald Reagan
Author WITH REAGAN: The Inside Story, Regnery Gateway

"Curtis, I do like your chapter on me—it is interesting!" "I like your chapters."
"They tell the story correctly." "I told you it had to be interesting—well, it is
interesting!" *"Good!"*
Lyn Nofziger
White House Communications Director President Ronald Reagan.
Consultant Communications Director Governor Ronald Reagan.

"Curtis Patrick, thanks for your help in making much of this happen. Best
Regards, always." (in his book "AT THE ABYSS" An Insider's History of the Cold War)
"REAGAN: WHAT WAS HE REALLY LIKE? is an incredibly detailed account
of the early Reagan years, beautifully written by a man who was there, and who
thus made the later years possible."
Signed, Tom / Thomas C. Reed
Special Assistant to President Reagan for National Security Policy
U.S. Air Force Secretary, President Gerald Ford.

"Dear Curtis, As usual, you are doing the Lord's work in advancing the truth
about our great leader and friend. How may we assist?"
Judge Wm. P. Clark, Jr.
Secretary of the Interior
National Security Advisor to President Ronald Reagan
CA Supreme Court Justice
Rancher & Cowboy

"A great addition to the scholarship on Reagan. It is especially important as I think you really capture the compelling essence of Reagan's character and political convictions. At base, Reagan comes across, not as an ambitious political zealot—which many liberal critics assert—but a man of genuine beliefs and personal warmth."
Dr. Eric Herzik
Chair Department of Political Science
University of Nevada, Reno

"Great book! Better than many of us, you knew the 'Prez' Ronald Reagan. Congratulations. A real treasure!"
Verne Orr, PhD
U.S. Air Force Secretary President Reagan
Dean Emeritus, College of Business & Public
Management, University of La Verne, CA

"A gripping reminder of the days before the presidency."
Richard B. Whitaker, author, Las Vegas, NV

"Curtis, I want to compliment you on writing a very interesting, engaging presentation of RR's political beginnings."
Frank Stermole, PhD, Golden, CO

"Curtis, Thank you for your book. I couldn't put it down! It is a treasure to have the benefit of your experiences and insight. I'm glad you took the time to put it down on paper."
Sincerely, Doug / Douglas W. Patterson, C.P.A. / P.C. Lake Tahoe, NV

"Thank You! Congratulations, Curtis! Your book about the REAL Ronald Reagan is so rich and full of valuable wisdom, it should be included in all leadership studies regardless of any student's field. How elegantly RR conducted himself and his work, that you chronicled so well, is a winning format."
Buck Ware, Reagan's CA Advance Team, business owner, retired Bigfork, Montana.

"Curtis, I had no idea of your early involvement with the Gov's. campaign. Your insight and historical perspective, not to mention your excellent writing style, are most impressive. I'm looking forward to Vol.2!"
Best Wishes, Bill / William J. Raggio, Senate Majority Leader & longest serving Member of NV State Senate (37 years). Carson City / Reno, NV

"To say that I was thrilled to receive a signal copy of your book about Ronald Reagan would be an understatement. Thank you for allowing us to hear from those who worked so closely with the Gov. and Pres. Who better to tell us what he was 'really' like. Thank You."
Ed Worthington, Fairless Hills, PA

"Dear Curtis, I finished your Reagan book & enjoyed it very much. Valuable insight!"
Regards, Doc / Dr. Joseph W. Johnson, ("Physician to the Stars") Henderson / Las Vegas NV

"This book is great! It makes me yearn for the Reagan years again. The author, Curtis Patrick, did a wonderful job of presenting intimate glimpses of President Reagan, as remembered by himself and many of his colleagues."
Linn of Pine Valley Ranch, Milford, MI

"Patrick, You wrote on the flyleaf of the book, REAGAN: WHAT WAS HE REALLY LIKE? Vol.1 that you sent me, 'Thanks!' No! It is my privilege to say 'Thanks.' What a great account of the early Reagan years. Thank You!!!"
Nita Wentner Ashcraft, N.CA Vice Chairman Finance 1966 RR for Gov., Napa, CA

"Curtis, Thank you very much for REAGAN: WHAT WAS HE REALLY LIKE? Marvelous contribution to his legacy. I remember many of the contributors and have fond memories of those days."
Herb Temple, Former Adjutant Gen. State of California. Lt. Gen. U.S. Army Ret., Palm Desert, CA

"Kudos for this book, it gave me insights of Ronald Reagan the many others in print have not. The most unusual Table of Contents are an easy read and informative. Thank you for this book. You made me laugh. I'm now more knowledgeable and I miss our beloved President even more!"
Shirley Randall, Archive Assistant, The Reagan Ranch Center,
Young America's Foundation, Santa Barbara, CA

"Dear Mr. Patrick, What a rare pleasure meeting you! Douglas County Lincoln Day Dinner proved to be a roaring success due to your presence. Your enthusiasm about your life, and writing about Ronald Reagan was spell-binding. We've had so many wonderful comments about your presentation!"
Maggie Benz, Chair Douglas County Republican Central Committee, Minden, NV

REAGAN

What Was He Really Like?
VOL. 1.

To: Mike Thanks!
Best Regards

Curtis Patrick

Curtis Patrick

NEW YORK

REAGAN
What Was He Really Like?
VOL. 1.

by Curtis Patrick

ISBN 978-1-60037-909-3 (paperback)
ISBN 978-1-60037-910-9 (EPub)
Library of Congress Control Number: 2011922091

Published by:

MORGAN JAMES PUBLISHING
The Entrepreneurial Publisher
5 Penn Plaza, 23rd Floor
New York City, New York 10001
(212) 655-5470 Office
(516) 908-4496 Fax
www.MorganJamesPublishing.com

Cover Photo by
Don Dornan
Sherman Oaks, CA

Interior Image Restoration by
Brian G Barlow & Michael Barlow

Additional Editing by
Michael Barlow
contact@michaelbarlow.info

Cover Design by:
Rachel Lopez
rachel@r2cdesign.com

Interior Design by:
Bonnie Bushman
bbushman@bresnan.net

In an effort to support local communities, raise awareness and funds, Morgan James Publishing donates one percent of all book sales for the life of each book to Habitat for Humanity.
Get involved today, visit
www.HelpHabitatForHumanity.org.

DEDICATION

To Ronald & Nancy Reagan

Who gave me the rare opportunity to participate in a series of life-changing events which later changed the world. They gave me their trust and confidence and made me a part of their lives, for which I am deeply grateful.

Curtis Patrick

TABLE OF CONTENTS

"Mr. Amerine has done more to ease my concerns about flying than anybody!"

- Mr. and Mrs. Amerine were owners of Amerine Turkey Farms.
- Mervin was a former B-29 Superfortress Recon pilot during WWII.
- Appointed by Governor Reagan to Civil Aeronautics Board, served eight years.

The "Turkey Bird" was a DC-3 owned by the Amerines for use in their turkey farm business. They provided the plane and their services as pilot and stewardess free of charge to Candidate Reagan and flew him all over California during his first gubernatorial campaign. Until that time, Reagan hated to fly. When not flying Reagan, his staff and members of the press to various appearances, the plane was used to ferry up to 48,000 live baby turkeys to different destinations.

"From our very first day together, I was drawn to this great citizen by his loyalty, integrity, and discretion – all revealed in both minor moments and in crisis!"

- Cabinet Secretary
- Governor Reagan's Chief of Staff
- Judge, CA Superior Court
- Associate Justice, CA Court of Appeal
- Justice, CA Supreme Court
- President Reagan's National Security Advisor
- Secretary, Dept. of the Interior under President Reagan
- Rancher, cowboy

Interviewee: *Tom Ellick*

"*Here* was a man we could work with! Here was a man who would trust us and we could trust *him*!" (State Senator Bill Green, Chairman of the Legislative Black Caucus, to Tom Ellick regarding Ronald Reagan.) Ellick comments, "It's a *tribute* to the man and the very *approachable, honest, straightforward* guy that he was. People *loved* him and you can understand why!"

- TV documentary film producer
- Public relations consultant
- Special Assistant to the Reagan Cabinet
- Planning & Policy Development: "Selling" of New Programs Through the Media
- Liaison with California State Legislature

Interviewee: *Patricia Gayman*

"He was a very private person. Reagan was not a pretentious person. Sometimes staff made RR seem *ostentatious*. He was not! Even a number of his Demo enemies had respect for him. His *humor* had to be the major thing. He disarmed them. It was clearly his own humor; it wasn't stuff that anybody wrote for him."

- Staffer for U.S. Senator George Murphy in Washington, D.C., 1964-65
- Staffer for Sandy Quinn scheduling 1966 Reagan for Governor campaign, Los Angeles, CA headquarters
- Schedule Secretary/Scheduling Director to Governor Reagan for eight years

Interviewee: *O. James Gibson, Ph.D.*

"In the *worst* of times he had a sense of humor – to help carry him through! He was an *intellectually* bright man. I thought Reagan did an *excellent* job as governor – first and second terms!"

- Researcher at BASICO for 1965-66 Reagan for Governor campaign
- Appointed to Planning & Research Unit

- Author of famous "Black Books" and 1967 Dissertation entitled "The Creative Society" (comparing Reagan's campaign promises with his accomplishments after taking office)

Interviewee: *Jackie Habecker*

"There is no question, he was a real human being who was interested and cared about others, especially when he went around to say 'Goodbye and thank you' when his second term was over. That's pretty unusual. I do not find this a perfunctory act! I think of all of those personal notes he wrote, primarily to Mrs. Reagan, but to others as well… so thoughtful."

- Governor Reagan's Reception Desk Secretary/Gatekeeper/Greeter.

She was the "first impression" for the Governor's office in the State Capitol Building. She began her career as a Clerk-Typist in 1945 and served seven governors during her career.

Interviewee: *Ken Hall*

"He was such a wonderful, down-to-earth kind of a person. I don't know that I have *ever* met a person in high office who ever had *less* of an ego than Ronald Reagan."

- Assistant Legislative Liaison to Governor Reagan
- Special Assistant to the Governor for Education, interfaced with all of the Governor's staff and Governor Reagan
- Appointed Chief Deputy Director, State Dept. of Finance (a Cabinet position), served 1971-74

Interviewees: *Pat Dunnebeck Ingoglia and Sal Russo*

"We were just children," said Pat Ingoglia. "I know, we were babies," agreed Sal Russo, as they reminisced about the first time they volunteered to help Ronald Reagan run for governor.

- Pat volunteered at UCLA for Young Americans for Freedom
- Sal volunteered at U.C. Berkeley for Goldwater for President

Later, they both volunteered to do anything, any kind of work to get Reagan elected governor. Both were appointed to the Governor's staff to handle numerous tasks for Cabinet officers as Staff Secretaries and Assistants to the Governor.

Later, Sal was appointed Deputy Chief of Staff to Gov. George Deukmejian. He also held a key White House position dealing with personnel. He heads a successful political consulting firm in Sacramento, CA.

Interviewees: *Nevada State Senator Lawrence Jacobsen, U.S. Senator Paul Laxalt, and Rex Hime*

Former Senator Paul Laxalt said of his and Reagan's first major environmental effort together, "I guess our reward for these efforts is being able to view beautiful Lake Tahoe – still blue, still clear – and say, 'We had a little bit to do with saving it'."

Key state leaders involved with Lake Tahoe and other environmental issues who influenced Reagan on his first action on developing strong environmental policies.

Interviewee: *Curtis Mack*

"I wasn't one that was on the 'inside' – I was the 'go-fer' on the staff and that was fine with me. I didn't have to be *next* to him. I felt comfortable with who he was and what he was doing. I wanted to help him!"

- First active volunteer go-fer in Southern California headquarters for 1966 Reagan for Governor campaign
- Became a paid Staff Assistant for the Ronald Reagan Committee
- Associate of Lyn Nofziger's private political consulting firm
- Executive Director, Citizens for the Republic, C.F.T.R. President Reagan's Political Action Committee
- Appointed Assistant Secretary of Commerce (NOAA)
- President, L.A. World Affairs Council
- Appointed to the President's Commission on White House Fellowships
- Associate Professor, Pepperdine University
- Retired at rank of Colonel, U.S. Air Force Reserves

"*Honesty,* the one word that sums up the essence of Ronald Reagan. There's one thing that people seem to forget about him and that is, he was a *brave* man. He instilled confidence in people because he had confidence in himself —he wasn't a fearful man or a fearful politician."

- Newspaperman, reporter – Copley Newspapers, San Diego, CA
- Hired by Spencer-Roberts & Associates to be Press Director, but could not shed image of Press Secretary to 1966 Reagan for Governor Committee
- Appointed Communications Director to Governor Reagan
- Started his own political consulting firm in Sacramento, CA
- Helped found Citizens for the Republic – Reagan's national "testing-ground" operations
- Appointed White House Communications Director by President Reagan
- Author of political nonfiction and western novels
- Chairman Emeritus of The Clandestine Activities Committee
- Quintessential rascal, wizard of "one-liners"

"RR was absolutely *Numero Uno* in [his wife] Nancy's life … all the time … and *she* was with him! They were totally *wound* into each other, to the exclusion of everybody else. This was a totally *interdependent* relationship. … Reagan was *gracious* and funny! He had people in stitches all the time—and he was a *total* gentleman. … You always knew where Reagan stood. He never equated *disagreement* with *disloyalty*. … Even after working fourteen and eighteen hour days, I could hardly wait to get to work the next morning!"

- KPIX-TV (San Francisco, CA) news anchor
- Assistant Press Secretary under Lyn Nofziger
- Special Assistant to Nancy Reagan
- Deaver & Hannaford Public Relations during Reagan's "hiatus" period. In 1980, created first Press/Media contact in Washington, D.C. for Reagan's presidential campaign
- East Wing Transition Team

- International Election Observer
- U.N. Conference on Women, Kenya, Africa
- President's Advisory Committee Trade Negotiations; Member/Delegate to symposiums, conferences, conventions, meetings, and missions worldwide, 1981-1994

Interviewee: *Dale Rowlee*

"From my viewpoint, there wasn't much about Ronald Reagan *not* to like. There may have been idiosyncrasies, but nothing you would dislike! But he sure functioned on his own – his *own* philosophies, his own attitudes – he was very *genuine* about that. He was a very *forthright* individual."

- Career California Highway Patrol officer based in Sacramento, chosen as Governor Reagan's Northern California Driver
- Personal Security and Transportation Coordinator for Reagan's two terms as Governor
- Accompanied Governor Reagan on official and personal trips to many locations worldwide
- Reagan's friend and confidant

Interviewee: *Stu Spencer*

"He was probably the best candidate I've ever dealt with. I've dealt with a lot of good candidates, but he was *exceptional!* Why? Number one, he had a core, he had a *sense*, he had a *belief* system. His ego *never* got in his way!"

- Volunteer - Young Republicans (East Los Angeles)
- 1958, founded Spencer-Roberts & Associates Campaign Consultants;
- Campaign Director - 1966 Reagan for Governor campaigns; Campaign Consultant - 1980 and 1984 Reagan for President campaigns; Spencer-Roberts achieved premier status in campaign management on a national and international level

Interviewees: *Bob and Urania Tarbet*

Urania Tarbet said of her late husband, "Bob was so thrilled when he was assigned to work for Reagan! He would come home at night and talk about what 'good people' he was working with. He was excited that he was surrounded by 'good people.' It came down from the top—it started with Reagan and Nancy! Because Bob and I were so close, he saw this same *great* closeness, this love affair, in RR and Nancy."

- Originally a Pacific Telephone & Telegraph Co. communications representative assigned to 1966 Reagan for Governor Campaign, General Election
- Established and oversaw Governor Reagan's Telecommunications task force
- Extensive skill in handling unusual communication tasks requiring his traveling with both Ronald and Nancy Reagan on a regular basis
- Director of all Reagan communications at the 1968 GOP Convention, Miami Beach, FL., assisted by his wife, Urania, as a volunteer. Bob became a trusted friend and confidant of the Reagans.

Interviewees: *Dave and Mary Tomshany*

"Nothing phony about the guy, anywhere, anyway, anyhow—it was just that he was totally human—typical Midwestern upbringing; this guy… people could relate to easily!"

- Dave organized and accompanied Candidate Reagan on exploratory trip around California in 1965 in Dave's Mustang convertible
- Established first advance team for campaign
- Assistant Campaign Director Reagan for Governor Committee/Director of Field Operations, Spencer-Roberts & Associates
- Independent campaign consultant in Southern California
- Mary volunteered and contributed time and talent to the early campaign

"It was a labor of *love* ... He treated me fine! Just like I was a friend. He never said, *'Do this! Do that!'* He never issued *any* orders. ... From my personal experience, and I don't know how he was as president, but he was very easy to work for."

Motorcycle/traffic officer, Los Angeles Police Dept. Volunteered as personal security for Candidate Reagan during first campaign, as Governor-Elect, and as Governor (when requested), including both in-state and out-of-state travel.

"The *essence* of Ronald Reagan —Courtesy, Integrity, Congruency, and Practical Intelligence. In private, even after long days on the campaign trail, he was always the same person everyone saw on T.V. Profound *decency*."

- Co-owned and ran family and corporate-oriented company picnic and outdoor events park in Southern California. Volunteered time, talent and money
- Lead / Key Advance Man, 1966 Reagan for Governor Campaign, Southern California
- Handled very complicated public events / myriad details with greatest of ease
- Assisted staff and Reagan family during Interim-government period / Inauguration

"I never saw a real hatred for Ronald Reagan. I was very much impressed with him then—because he was so likeable!"

- Freelance professional photographer, provided photos to AP, UPI, and worldwide news organizations
- Traveled extensively with Reagan, including to GOP conventions
- Special Exhibit: Photographs of Governors in California Capitol

Interviewee: *George Young*

"The press portrayed Ron as a puppet and a *tool* of his handlers. He simply was not! He was one tough *nut* to handle. He was focused and knew what he believed in—and what he wanted to portray. I marveled at how advanced Reagan was in his thinking!"

- Worked for Spencer-Roberts, traveled throughout Southern California with Reagan as Director of Headquarters Operations for Reagan's first gubernatorial campaign and at 1968 GOP Convention in Miami, FL
- Retired from Spencer-Roberts and now is an independent consultant in Los Angeles, CA

FOREWORD

"Curtis, you have captured the *true* Ronald Reagan at the genesis of his political career. You have done a fantastic bit of investigation and you have drawn from true witnesses the feeling, the heart and the mind of Ronald Reagan in those most important hours and days of his formation—his political and governmental world. Things that were his *principles*. The beginning of the *vision* that he needed. He wasn't looking for Washington—Washington came to him; but it was on the basis of the principles that he taught us in Sacramento. You were certainly *key*, incident to all of that; for which the rest of the Reaganauts are most grateful!"

Bill

Wm. P. Clark, Jr.
February 3, 2006
Paso Robles, CA 93446

Bill Clark held the following positions:
Chairman Ventura County RR for Governor Campaign, 1966
Cabinet Secretary Governor Ronald Reagan
Executive Secretary (Chief of Staff) Governor Ronald Reagan
Superior Court Judge, CA
Associate Justice California Court of Appeals
Associate Justice California Supreme Court
National Security Advisor President Ronald Reagan
Secretary of the Interior
Rancher & cowboy

ACKNOWLEDGMENTS

Joan Patrick, my brilliant, loving wife, who stood by me through the darkest days of infirmity and despair and through each tiny victory to help produce the most accurate, in-depth, account of our beloved boss, president and friend.

Andrea Lower, Eleanor Mills, Lyn Nofziger, Joanne Drake, Wren Powell, Erica Jolles and, dear friends, William P "Bill" Clark, Jr. & Joan Clark, who gave me their prayers, trust, confidence and love.

The Ronald Reagan Presidential Library, Simi Valley, CA, Duke Blackwood, E.D., Kirby Hanson & Holly Holdridge Bauer. Always supportive and helpful! The California Years exhibit, for which Volume 1. & Volume 2. are written, is outstanding and growing.

A *must see,* along with the awesome AIR FORCE ONE exhibit!

The following persons who dug into their personal collections, files, attics and basements to locate, donate and loan literally hundreds of candid *never-before-published* photos of Ronald and Nancy Reagan, Patti and Skipper, members of the candidate's / governor's staff and assorted guests, friends, V.I.P.'s & government officials from all over the world: Dennis Warren, Bob & Urania Tarbet, Dale & Bonnie Rowlee, Patricia Dunnebeck Ingoglia, Nancy Clark Reynolds.

Buck Ware, who painstakingly compiled a large album of excellent color photos he had taken (only God knows when he had time to do *that*) of candidate Reagan on the 1966 Campaign trail, with many of us in security and advance, along with actors, actresses and even undercover agents of our opponents, at dozens of venues, including rallies, speaking engagements, parades, boisterously friendly crowd scenes and interminable reception lines, which he personally had advanced. He then applied a whimsical caption to each one, placed them into the albums and presented them to a handful of "The Insiders" and the Reagans, and was kind enough to allow me to share them with you, the Readers, in both Volume I and Volume II.

Dr. O. Jim Gibson, who parted with his most prized possession, other than his Claremont home; his Doctoral Dissertation on Ronald Reagan's "Creative Society," in which Gibson presents an historic, factual chronology of the 1966 campaign, the promises Reagan made and how he *kept* them, during his two terms as governor.

Thomas C. Reed, for his confidence in me to try to ferret out every grain of truth from the murky depths, and for granting me permission to utilize in my interview, thousands of words from his own personal files and manuscript entitled SNAPSHOTS FROM AN EARLY REAGAN ERA-1958-1970.

The Sun City Anthem Author's Club, Henderson, NV, whose members helped me understand the genre and art of writing non-fiction, introduced me to innovative methods of editing and publishing, and were bold enough to give constructive criticism while remaining friends.

All of my Interviewees who graciously shared their inner-most anecdotes, thoughts, stories and secrets about the Reagans.

Due to the fact that we had more than nine hundred pages in the manuscript, a Special "Thank You" must be given to those Interviewees, my colleagues, whose stories will not appear in Volume I, but are stretching their patience to wait for the publication of Volume II. This was a tough call, choosing which ones went into which volume. The issue: We didn't want to cut a word out, after editing, and it was just too cumbersome / unwieldy all squeezed into one volume; it didn't do justice to all of the hard work we put into this project. The Interviewees who will appear in Volume II are: Clyde Beane, Wendy Borcherdt, Robert Carleson, Esther Rushford Greene, Hon. Paul Haerle, Rex Hime, Dr's. Howard & John House, Hon. Bob & Norma Lagomarsino, Susan Dewsnup Madden, Hon. Edwin Meese III, Karen Hansen Munro, Hon.Verne Orr, Hon. Thomas C. Reed, Alex Sherriffs (PhD.), Reed Sprinkel, Kay Valory and Richard Wirthlin (PhD.)

STATE OF CALIFORNIA
EXECUTIVE DEPARTMENT

Know All Men By These Presents:

That I, RONALD REAGAN, Governor of the State of California, do hereby appoint

CURTIS PATRICK

Special Assistant to the Executive Secretary

In Witness Whereof, I have hereunto set my hand and caused the Great Seal of the State to be affixed at Sacramento, this   second day of   January   nineteen hundred and   sixty-seven.

Governor of the State of California

By the Governor

Secretary of State

By   *Burt Clinkston*
                                                        Deputy

Author's Official Commission from Governor Reagan.

Nancy Reagan greets the Patricks during festivities & Christening of CVN-76 Aircraft
Carrier Ronald Reagan, the Navy's newest, March 2001 in Newport News, VA.

INTRODUCTION

"What was Ronald Reagan *REALLY like?*" The single most frequently asked question follows when people hear that I worked for the Reagans from the beginning of his first campaign for governor and for several years later in his California administration during the 1970's and on special projects into the '80's and '90's. After reading many books on Ronald Reagan, from academic, historical or personal perspectives, I found some were interesting, some boring, some factual, and some *fictional,* down to and including the footnotes.

The purpose of *this* book is to present to the reader *intimate* glimpses of Ronald Reagan, as remembered by many of my colleagues and me, in a factual, enjoyable and relaxed format. Each chapter tells the memories of one or two individuals.

Anxious to learn more of the inside story of how the Reagans lived, worked and functioned? Read any chapter in any order, then browse through the dozens of photographs of my colleagues and me doing all manner of things with the Reagans. Breathe in the *essence* of this remarkable man and his loving wife, Nancy. Soak up the "team spirit" which permeated our lives whenever we were "on-the-move" with the Reagans, whether on the way to the State Capitol Building on a busy legislative morning, or, off for a horseback ride through the rye grass and Poppy covered rolling foothills of the California Gold Rush Country.

Both Volume I and Volume II consist of anecdotes and *first-person* recollections and stories from individuals who were my interviewees and, more importantly, my colleagues and friends. Many were members of Ronald Reagan's original 1965-1966 Campaign for Governor. Some came aboard soon after the election and were appointed to fill key positions in the Governor's Cabinet and to head up the state agencies and departments. You will also find a sprinkling of professionals who had personal associations with the Reagans. For the most part, except in a few cases, these interviewees have *never* been recorded or published before.

This work is not a cursory glimpse; it gets *very* specific. A thrill came to me each time, either the interviewee or I would recall some exciting moment we had shared while working for the Reagans. One vignette would generate another. It was almost a miracle, after all of this time, the *camaraderie,* the *excitement,* the *spirit* was never lost!

Reagan has been gone from the Office of the Governor of California for over thirty Years. Hundreds of books, magazine articles, essays, op-eds, newspaper features and stories have been written about this *uncommon* man and his life. NONE, that I could see, thoroughly discussed his metamorphosis from actor and General Electric spokesman, union president and stem-winding speaker out on the "stump" all over America speaking for the principles in which he believed; then making the transition from a tough campaign for the highest office of one of the most pivotal states in the union, after winning by a landslide—through the eyes of the people who *made it happen!*

These stories and anecdotes are told by the boys and girls, men and women, many who were in the *"trenches."* Many of us began in 1963 and '64 in colleges and universities, coffee shops, bars, discussion groups, Rotary and other service clubs, YR's, chambers of commerce; all over California. We were listening and responding to the powerful and moving words of the actor-turned-spokesman for his conservative beliefs in his now famous speech entitled: "A Time For Choosing." Later on, this speech was fine-tuned by Reagan, all by himself, and delivered on behalf of Senator Barry Goldwater of Arizona , in his failed 1964 campaign for president.

This book was written to help tell the stories of the interaction between Reagan and the *unsung heroes,* some of whom have already passed away. Their personal stories reveal why they dropped everything, worked nights, studied at their colleges and worked their jobs, sometimes day *and* night, as they tried to do whatever needed to be done to help start up the "boomlet" that was to become RR's 1966 campaign. Their common thread: They were high-principled individuals with a strong love of country, an insatiable work-ethic, an honest-spirit —*and*—an abiding love for Ronald Reagan. Sometimes these people would not agree with Reagan's views on certain issues and spirited arguments ensued!

The relationship between the volunteers, staffers, secretaries, "go-fers," campaign managers, advance-people and Reagan is *key* to the understanding of this man. It is important for everyone who is interested in the history of Ronald Reagan to hear from those who were *intimately* involved in Reagan's everyday life. They helped mold and set the tone for the goals he set for himself and the people of California. RR, as our leader, was able to accomplish many of his goals with this strong, dedicated team; all of which led to his ability to be a better governor and, ultimately, to be a better president. Most of those team members worked under a common bond of trust in each other and themselves, spawned from the top and returned ten-fold to the Reagans. These people were dedicated, not only to making the dream of a better government, with less interference in people's private lives come true, but also, to making Ronald Reagan *happy!* He was happiest when he succeeded. He inspired each of us to do better and to be *better* people and *better* citizens. They proved their dedication by working their hearts out helping RR accomplish his goals.

Other books have been written by and about many of the top-level staff members, some of whom went to Washington with President Reagan. This is a chronicle of those who were there in the *beginning,* some who rose to key positions in California, worked hard to protect and promote Reagan's legacy through the hiatus years and went on to Washington or into successful business positions. During the past eleven years they have kindly allowed me to record their Oral Histories and publish new stories that have *not* been told. Some have already passed on, before publication. They, like Bob Tarbet, Dr. Alex Sherriffs, Lyn Nofziger, Robert Carleson and especially, Cap

Weinberger, (whose story was too late to be chronicled here), were friends, colleagues, mentors and collaborators on this book project. They are part of the band of *unsung heroes* known as "The Reaganauts" (aka "Reaganites"). Except for his wife Nancy, there was not one individual who could take credit for or stand above the others in helping RR achieve his successes and learn to govern well, while miraculously weaving his way through the political mine-fields.

Volumes I and II reveal new information on "turning-point" crises which faced Reagan as a candidate in his first campaign and later as governor. They also contain revelations of the secret plan, with *never-before-published* insider photos, hatched by Appointments Secretary, Thomas C. Reed and renowned political operative F. Clifton White to capture the GOP presidential nomination for Reagan at the 1968 Republican National Convention in Miami Beach. Reagan's communications system, a component of that clandestine plan now fully revealed, may have been one of the first in history to employ the use of high-tech electronics and space-age technicians on vacation from a top secret division of a Defense Department firm and the Intelligence Division of a major metropolitan police department. These were dedicated *volunteers!*

The glamour of the White House had an allure which is unsurpassed, but this is about people involved in the winning of the Statehouse in Sacramento, Ca, when we believed it was *impossible!* Some of those odds were strongly stacked against us. Using chicanery and dirty tricks, our opponent, who had the entire state government at his disposal, used his own campaign people along with (we were informed by reliable sources) certain state departments to try to derail our advance operations and our candidate's speaking schedule. This challenge to wrest the governorship away from an entrenched politician like Edmund G. "Pat" Brown, was out there in the ether waves! This was a win we never counted on. True, some of our leadership, namely Stu Spencer and Bill Roberts and a few others, felt the contrast between our candidate and Brown was so heavily weighted in *our* favor—that we couldn't lose. But, to those of us out there on the streets, in those "trenches," it was like winning the Gold Medal at the Olympic Games! The new Lt. Governor-elect, Bob Finch, summed it up beautifully in what became a banner headline the morning after the election—**"HOW SWEET IT IS!!!"**

My goal was to present never-before seen or heard *INTIMATE* glimpses into the *essence* of Ronald and Nancy Reagan during the sprouting, nurturing and blossoming of RR's political career.

The following statement embodies everything I've tried to present in the two volumes of REAGAN: WHAT WAS HE *REALLY* LIKE? in a simple, concise, accurate way, and Mayor Giuliani said it with such conviction, it brought many in the very diverse, multigenerational crowd to a standing ovation!

LEADERSHIP

Mayor Rudy Giuliani spoke to several thousand people at the *Get Motivated: Lessons in Leadership* seminar at Mandalay Bay Hotel & Convention Center in Las Vegas, Nevada on September 27, 2005; four years and seventeen days after 9-11. He gave his example of a *Leader.*

"My mentor, my hero is Ronald Reagan. He had a set of beliefs, *strong* beliefs. He didn't care what public opinion polls showed or said. He stuck with his ideas and beliefs, no matter what the polls said. He set goals and kept on trying. He was an optimist! He envisioned success! Courage is the management of fear—he did that.

You have to *love* people. You have to *like* people. You have to care for people. Reagan loved people, and they could tell it."

Ronald Reagan was my hero, too. C.P.

CAPITOL
REPORT
from the office of the governor

VOL. 1, NO. 16   SACRAMENTO, CALIFORNIA   JULY 17, 1968

Governor Reagan's First 18 Months   —Special Edition—

When Governor Ronald Reagan took office on January 1, 1967, he was immediately faced with the biggest single financial crisis California state government has ever known.

Under the previous governor's budget, the state was spending nearly one half billion dollars more than it was taking in. The old administration had resorted to a fiscal gimmick called "accrual," the last in a series of similar devices which had been used since 1959 to provide one-shot windfall revenue accelerations, making it possible to finance budgets without increasing taxes. In essence, these incredible gimmicks had allowed the state to use nearly 15 months income to finance only 12 months of expenditures.

There no longer was enough money for the new administration to pay the state's bills. Nor was there any responsible alternative, but to seek new taxes.

Governor Reagan resolved at the outset to balance the budget without tax gimmicks.

His very first action was to seek every possible economy in the operation of state government. The new administration immediately established as a goal a 10 percent across-the-board cut in spending in all departments. In fact, the Governor's Office itself was the first to achieve this goal.

After every possible economy was put into effect, the administration found itself in the position of being forced to ask for a tax increase in order to pay off the inherited debt and get the state back in the black.

(Continued on Page 2)

8

This special edition of Capitol Report is devoted exclusively to the accomplishments of a man and his administration over the past 18 months.

In these pages, we have endeavored to set forth the record of achievement — and the quality of leadership — by and from a government which is determined to be responsive to the needs of the people it serves, while, at the same time, making the best possible use of the taxpayers' money.

—The Editor

The First Eighteen Months

(Continued from Page 1)

Governor Reagan not only reduced the previous administration's hold-over 1967-68 budget by $127.6 million, but blue penciled $43.5 million out of the final budget as submitted by the legislature.

The action was drastic, but absolutely necessary to put the state back on a sound fiscal footing.

"Cut Squeeze and Trim"

Since that time, the governor's "cut, squeeze and trim" mandate has reached virtually every area of state government over which he exercises meaningful control. On this basis, the governor has kept growth down to an average of 4.8 percent per year during fiscal 67-68 and 68-69. Seen another way, Reagan administration economies have cut growth trends in state government spending —— established by the previous governor —— by fully 40 percent.

Even now — 18 months after taking office, and during which time the state's population was increasing by 675,000 — the new administration is still operating with fewer employees than were authorized by the former administration.

Task Force Recommendations

Some 2,000 specific recommendations for bringing economics to state government were submitted to Governor Reagan by a blue-ribbon task force of business and professional men who contributed six months of their time —— at no cost to the taxpayer —— to study the operations of California government.

Of the 1,700 specific recommendations for efficiencies and economies which apply directly to the departments in the administration, 439 have already been implemented, providing a potential one-time savings of $17 million and potential annual savings of $108.5 million.

Many of the recommendations are under study and are being progressively implemented as they become practicable.

Fully implemented, the recommendations have the potential of bringing savings to state government totaling as much as $600 million over the next 10 years.

Control Over Only $600 Million

By coincidence, the $600 million figure represents the amount of state funds in the current $5.7 billion budget

over which Governor Reagan exercises meaningful control. The balance is represented by activities which are either statutorily established, supported by voter-authorized bonds or by special user fees, or which are administered by groups not responsible to the governor.

The fiscal 1968-69 budget submitted to the governor by the legislature was $10 million higher than that originally sent to state lawmakers by the administration earlier this year. Governor Reagan blue-penciled some $16 million from the legislature's version when the budget was signed June 29.

Higher Education Priority

The new budget provides substantial increases for support of the University of California and the state colleges — three times more money per university student and twice as much per state college student as the average yearly increase per student over the past 10 years.

In fact, had higher education received the same budgetary alignment as all other departments of state government, the university budget would have been $11.7 million less than was actually allocated. The state colleges would have received $28.1 million less.

In line with the administration's emphasis on the importance of higher education, the university and the state colleges clearly received top priority in the current budget.

This priority was made possible, in part, by projected administrative savings totaling $66 million for 1968-69 in the state's medical assistance program (Medi-Cal). Such action by the administration during 1967-68 saved the state some $42 million.

Medi-Cal Flexibility

The governor has urged the legislature to pass an administration bill designed to provide sufficient flexibility to administer Medi-Cal. If this flexibility is not granted, the governor has warned that the program's soaring cost will continue to cause the state serious financial problems in the years to come.

Another area where costs are rapidly outstripping the state's ability to pay is in the field of public assistance, or welfare.

Governor Reagan has offered specific proposals to the legislature in order to

bring the rate of increase in public assistance programs down to a reasonable level. The only alternative is perpetual tax increases.

At the same time, the governor has repeatedly stressed his belief that the only purpose of welfare should be to help the individual get off it.

"To avoid and reduce the need for welfare," he has said, "is much more rewarding than to perpetuate an unworkable program that robs citizens of the initiative to make a place for themselves in society.

"This administration is determined to break the chain of dependency being forged by misguided welfare programs. Even the most effective welfare is no substitute for employment."

In line with the philosophy of the administration, Governor Reagan has asked the state's lawmakers to completely revamp California's welfare system. He has proposed adoption of additional measures to cut red tape, simplify welfare procedures, and make the program more understandable to recipients and taxpayers alike.

The administration is continuing to seek not only administrative improvement of the present system, but innovative approaches to the problem of welfare which weld together all available resources, both public and private. For example, a pilot program has been launched in Fresno to employ the most modern management techniques to effect close coordination of federal, state, local and private agencies in a concerted effort to reduce not only unemployment and public dependency, but potential public dependency.

Tax Reform

The vital need for an overhaul of California's tax system has long been recognized by individuals both inside and outside state government.

Governor Reagan, noting that "genuine tax reform is one of the most important benefits we can bring the people of California," has created a special commission headed by Controller Houston I. Flournoy and asked the commission to submit specific recommendations for revising the state's crazy-quilt tax structure by next January 1.

The governor has characterized the taxpayer as "the too-often forgotten man who today is working two and one half hours out of every eight-hour day just to pay his taxes. He is the source from which the blessings of tax supported programs flow. Before we can provide any government services, we

(Continued on Page 3)

Governor Reagan and his cabinet in session

The Accomplishments Of The First Eighteen Months

(Continued from Page 2)

must first take the money from him. WE MUST be fully concerned with the measure of his gain and the size of his loss."

The commission on tax reform will make recommendations regarding property tax relief, the personal income tax, sales taxes, bank and corporation taxes, the inheritance tax and others.

The Reagan administration has already sponsored legislation to provide $155 million in property tax relief to California homeowners and another $35 million in personal income tax relief to the state's overburdened middle income taxpayer who has a large family, as well as $22 million in property tax relief for the state's senior citizens.

Other Legislation

In other areas of legislation, the administration has sponsored bills to:

—Remove the appointment of judges from partisan politics. This legislation would rewrite state law to insure that in the future no governor could appoint any judge except on the basis of competence and merit. The essential elements of the measure have voluntarily been adhered to by Governor Reagan since taking office.

—Guarantee each member of organized labor the right to a secret ballot on all matters affecting union policy.

—Protect young people from smut and pornography.

—Protect citizens from the drunken driver by setting presumptive limits for

determining the influence of intoxicating liquor.

—Provide the Human Relations Agency the flexibility needed to effectively administer the Medi-Cal program.

—Impose greater penalties for assaults on University of California and State College campus police.

—Permit the use of evidence obtained by electronic or mechanical devices in criminal cases, provided that a warrant is obtained by a court authorizing use of such equipment by law enforcement agencies.

Unfortunately, a Democratic Party-controlled legislature has seen fit to ignore the need for passage of a number of forward-looking administration bills due, for the most part, to strictly obstructionist and partisan considerations.

The Reagan administration is now in the process of releasing a series of "creative papers" designed to delineate the major problem areas in our society, to seek the causes and provide constructive solutions.

The studies — dealing with the subjects of human relations, law and order, education, public assistance and the quality of life in today's environment — emphasize the roles and responsibilities of private citizens in meeting the challenges of today.

"Creative Papers"

In line with the governor's creative society concept, the papers also stress

the importance of cooperation between the independent and private sectors with all levels of government.

Each creative paper lists a myriad of practical proposals to meet the objectives it outlines as necessary to help solve our problems.

In the "human relations" paper, for example, Governor Reagan calls on Californians to attend to the legitimate grievances of minority race citizens, "not by shrill exaggerations or false promises . . . but by involvement and honest leadership" by all segments of our society. Twenty three separate suggestions are listed to accomplish these objectives.

The "law and order" paper stresses the need for a "total and sustained fight against lawlessness" and reaffirms "the right of every citizen to the full protection of the law . . . the responsibility of every citizen to uphold and obey the law." The study outlines dozens of ways the crime problem can be alleviated. It emphasizes that crime, "in all its forms, must be the concern of the entire community, "including such diverse organizations as chambers of commerce, neighborhood groups, ministerial and church associations, law enforcement and even the news media.

Education Proposals

The forthcoming creative paper on "education" looks at the problems facing California's elementary and second-
(Continued on Page 6)

PAGE 4

CAPITOL REPORT—JULY 17, 1968

Reorganization Plan Provides For Improved Communications

One of Governor Reagan's major accomplishments is his reorganization of the executive branch of state government.

This plan has, in fact, been in effect since the early days of the administration.

It streamlines the executive branch by providing better coordination and improved communications between the governor and his administrative departments.

Under the plan, the departments are grouped, insofar as practicable, under four cabinet-level secretaries representing the areas of Business and Transportation, Resources, Human Relations and Agriculture and Services. These secretaries, plus the director of finance, the governor's executive secretary and cabinet secretary, comprise the governor's cabinet which meets often to advise the governor on major policy and program matters.

The cabinet secretaries, in turn, serve as the primary communications link for transmission of policy problems and decisions between the governor and the operating departments.

In contrast, under the previous administration, virtually every department of state government reported unilaterally to the governor which led to uncoordinated and duplicate services.

Under Governor Reagan's reorganization, the cabinet-level secretaries are able to function in essentially a policy-making role, leaving the every-day operating decisions to the department heads.

Cabinet decisions are now communicated promptly, effectively and accurately throughout the executive branch. Now, departmental decisions requiring the governor's attention can be resolved in 24 hours or less.

In sum, it has been tried, it works and works well. It has provided the governor with an organizational structure through which he and his administration are able to effectively handle the complex affairs of state government.

In The Governor's Study

Task Force Savings

Here are some examples of savings to state government resulting from implementation of task force recommendations submitted to the administration by the Governor's Survey on Efficiency and Cost Control:

—The Department of Parks and Recreation formed a Division of Information to encourage greater public use of state operated recreational areas. This will augment annual state revenues by as much as $500,000 from increased admissions.

—The Office of State Printing standardized publication procedures and materials at a potential one-time saving of $113,000.

—The Department of General Services, by taking over all leasing and space planning functions of the state, expects to be able to reduce total office space requirements of the departments by some 25 percent over the next 10 years at an average savings to taxpayers of $7.5 million per year.

—Establishment of an integrated warehouse system using stringent inventory management controls will enable the state to reduce its continuing inventory investment from $30 million to $17.5 million. The plan also will reduce operating costs by $3 million per year.

—By not filling 600 positions which had previously been authorized for the Department of Water Resources, the administration effected salary savings of $300,000 during fiscal 1967-68. Estimated salary savings from this action will total $4.4 million in the current fiscal year.

—A proposed new 10-story Highway Patrol building in Sacramento was cancelled at a savings to the state of some $4 million. The task force discovered that the building would not be needed until 1980. The immediate savings were reallocated to the state's highway construction program.

This decision triggered development of new and more reasonable space allocation standards for state employees. The result has been that construction of other buildings has been delayed or postponed. In addition, two new high-rise buildings to house offices of the state's Human Relations Agency—authorized and already under construction by the previous administration—were closely scrutinized for space utilization. These two buildings were originally planned to house only 2,100 employees. Under Governor Reagan's approach, they will now contain 3,100 personnel, an increase of 47 percent, at no loss in operating efficiency.

10   REAGAN   *What Was He Really Like?*

Administration Achievements In Minority Area

In an effort to help solve problems which beset members of the state's minority communities, the Reagan administration is working closely with the independent, private and local governmental sectors of California toward the goal of assuring the opportunities and rights guaranteed by our system of government.

This effort is based on the premise that our system can and must provide justice and equal opportunity for all.

Many of the state's minority citizens have legitimate grievances. For them, especially the Negro and the American of Mexican descent, the road to opportunity and prosperity has been particularly difficult.

In Governor Reagan's words:

"It is imperative, and morally right, that we attend to these grievances; that we correct whatever injustices may exist; that we remove unnatural barriers; and that we guarantee equal rights to all of our citizens, regardless of color and creed.

"This administration will do all that it can to see that every citizen has the opportunity to become whatever his manhood and his vision can combine to make him.

"We cannot guarantee every citizen success, but we must guarantee every citizen an equal place at the starting line and his right to try to succeed.

"However, just as it is the function of government to lead in solving these problems, so it is the responsibility of government to keep order and maintain the law. The mob cannot solve these pressing problems. It cannot build a better world. And, those who lead the mob surely double-cross the very people they pretend they are trying to help.

"Society can have law and order without freedom. But no society, and no man, can have real freedom without law and order. Every lawabiding citizen — regardless of color — has the right to expect that his government will insure the safety of his person, his home and his family. And, every homeowner, every businessman, every resident of every community, has the right to expect his government to protect his property against the criminal, the arsonist, the rioter and the looter. No man should be above the law, no man should be beneath it.

"I know that at least 98 percent of our minority citizens feel the same way."

Governor Reagan is working to close several gaps which exist in the area of race relations. One of these gaps, the "expectation gap," has resulted from promises to the minority community which cannot be kept, promises which stimulate great expectations but few results, promises which delude, but do not produce.

Another gap is the "communications gap" between the majority and minority communities.

The Reagan administration is working diligently to close both these gaps, not with promises, but with action, through down-to-earth programs.

Governor Reagan — without publicity or fanfare — has held meetings with neighborhood leaders from minority communities throughout the state — to listen to suggestions and complaints. The meetings will continue.

"The problems won't be solved overnight. The road is long and hard. But, between us, we can find the answers," he has said.

Governor Reagan recently appointed six minority race persons as his personal representatives to work in the state's six neighborhood service centers. These centers are located in disadvantaged areas of the state and provide a number of important state services, including public health, welfare and employment.

—A Negro and a Mexican-American hold key positions on the governor's capitol staff as his community relations secretaries.

—A Negro executive appointee heads up the overall state service center program for the governor.

—A Negro directs the State Office of Economic Opportunity.

—Another Negro heads the State Department of Veterans Affairs.

—A Mexican-American works as Governor Reagan's personal representative out of the Los Angeles office.

In fact, during the first 18 months of the Reagan administration, the governor has appointed more members of minority groups to executive and policy-making positions than any other administration in the history of California state government.

(Continued on Page 6)

Governor Reagan answers questions at weekly press conference

Governor Reagan addresses a Republican rally

Minority Achievements

(Continued from Page 5)

The administration is pushing for greater participation by industry and labor in apprenticeship programs and attempting to correct inequitable laws as well as supporting programs and policies which must be developed in the minority communities.

Governor Reagan signed over 200 bills dealing with minorities and others in low income levels during the last session of the legislature.

A "Summer-Jobs-For-Youth" campaign headed by the governor in cooperation with business, labor, and all levels of government has already resulted in more than 40,000 jobs for California young people — many from disadvantaged areas of the state.

The State Department of Conservation has hired 700 youth — most of them also from disadvantaged areas — to help fight fires this summer in California's tinder-dry forests and wildlands.

Space has allowed the listing of but a handful of the many accomplishments made by the administration in this vital area.

The words of Governor Reagan sum up the administration position:

"We can, and we intend to provide adequate education . . . job training and jobs for our youth and untrained adults."

Accomplishments Of The First Eighteen Months

(Continued from Page 3)

ary schools as well as the state colleges and university system. It spells out a number of practical ways to raise teaching standards, improve administration, overhaul school financing and apply technological innovations to the educational process.

In the paper, the governor reaffirms his strong stand that the campus must not be used as a staging area for insurrection but must be a place where our young people can study in safety, on the grounds and in classrooms paid for with taxpayers' money.

The rights of ordinary students and faculty members must be protected, for they are not the exclusive preserve of dissidents and disrupters, he says.

Under the state's present tax structure, students from families with relatively high income pay exactly the same as those from poor families.

For this reason, the governor has proposed an "Equal Education Plan" which provides grants-in-aid and loans for qualified students from low income families. The plan specifies that part of the funds derived from tuition must be set aside for needy students to pay for the legitimate expenses of their education.

CAPITOL REPORT
Founded October 1967

Published twice each month at Sacramento, California in the Governor's Office, Room 1020, State Capitol. Subscription: Two dollars annually. Telephone 445-8054

Contents may be reprinted or reproduced without permission.

Chapter One

FLIGHT OF THE "TURKEY BIRD"

Mervin & Nancy Amerine

"Mr. Amerine has done more to ease my concerns about flying than anybody!"

Governor Reagan once declared to a group of visitors in his Capitol office, when Merv Amerine dropped by.

During WWII Mervin Amerine flew B-29 Superfortress bombers. He and his fellow airmen of the 3rd Photo-Reconnaissance Squadron took some of the original photos before and after the Atomic bombing of Hiroshima and Nagasaki, Japan.

Twenty-some years later, during Ronald Reagan's 1966 Campaign for Governor of California, Amerine with his wife, Nancy as stewardess, flew the actor who had refused to fly—Ron Reagan—to previously unreachable campaign stops in as many out-of-the-way towns and hamlets in the boonies of the huge state as possible—with Reagan seated in the co-pilot's seat at the controls, in what has been described as Donald Douglas's greatest aeronautical achievement—a lumbering DC-3—# N-63440! A refinement of the DC-2—the DC-3 was originally designed and built in 1935, and was the first commercial airliner to fly passengers and make a profit. The Reagan 1966 Campaign transport plane, N-63440 was not built in the 1950's as an airliner as we were originally told, but was constructed, as our research later proved, at Douglas Aircraft Co. in Long Beach, California in 1943 for the U.S. Army Air Corps as a C-47, for troop and cargo transport, and was easily interchangeable.

This tail-dragging, shiny classic with the huge, twin, radial engines, however, had one more unique feature: Normally, it was used to haul up to forty-eight thousand *live* baby **turkeys** at a time, all over the country.

These pioneers in the breeding, raising and mass-delivery of turkeys in North America decided, 'out of the blue', *cold-turkey,* that they wanted to help this uncommon man whom they had never met, Ronald Reagan, run for Governor of California. Merv had been watching RR for some time as he grew into a dynamic speaker.

"We had just come back from the midwest after delivering another load of baby turkeys." Merv then mused, I thought, 'What am I going to do to help Mr. Reagan get elected governor?' "This was the Winter of 1965 /'66." "I had heard parts of a speech or two that he had made. I was a life-long Republican and I was tired of Democrats." "I thought, I'll take one of these three DC-3's of mine. I had all of these seats, twenty-eight, put away in a hangar at our little airport in Oakdale (CA Central Valley) and we'll fly Mr. Reagan wherever he needs to go for his campaign." " So I told Nancy about it when I got back." And she said, 'Yeah, and you're going to go to the moon, huh?'

Then Nancy chimed in to confirm she had also said, 'Oh, you are, huh?'

Merv said he didn't know anybody connected with the campaign—*anybody!*

"I just took my Airline Pilot's credentials and license, went up to San Francisco to the Reagan for Governor Campaign Committee headquarters" (at that time it may have been the Northern CA offices of Spencer-Roberts & Associates, frequented by Northern CA Chairman Tom Reed who would have thought this was a most fortuitous gift from the heavens). The words: 'Airline Transport Pilot DC-3' were written across the license.' Merv said, "I presented these, told the staff about my airplanes down at Oakdale, California, and told them I'd like to help them out flying Mr. Reagan, wherever he needed to go." Nita Wentner Ashcraft, former Vice Chairman of Finance for the Northern California Campaign, confirmed this in 2006. "Now Ronald Reagan didn't like to fly. He refused to fly—until this campaign started!" "Then he realized he had to fly (due to the size and shape of California) with San Francisco up here so far from Los Angeles." "Amerine not only presented his credentials but also mentioned his county Reagan chairman where he had come from and he knew a number of people who were easily checked out and who knew Reagan people. We accepted him right after his visit," Wentner said. "I remember the jokes about how Merv would have to clean out the *turkey poop* to get ready for the next campaign flight."

Wentner spent many hours with Reagan driving him around northern California. "We decided to go up the coast one time, and I had a 1964 Lincoln Town Car and Ron loved it. This was before he announced as a candidate for governor. We'd go to little towns and GOP Central Committee meetings—when he said that he wanted to make a tour of the state to see whether people would accept an *actor.* That was his big problem! He was putting his 'toe-in-the-water.'

I asked Nita how he was received.

"Oh!" "Curtis!" "Like a movie star—with the *aura.* " "People knew him—he had name recognition. It was immediate; with everyone. His days in television helped."

I probed deeper: Without trying to think of the exact words which you and he used, how did he treat you—how did he respond to you?

"He was an absolute *gentleman* with a great sense of humor! Never as a boss to an employee. No, no, no! Just a *genuinely* nice person. He had an **heroic** aura about him! Therefore, when Mervin Amerine came into the office and presented his "Turkey Bird"—We accepted!"

"It wasn't just Amerine and his airplane who were in awe of RR, Paul Haerle, an attorney, Marin County Reagan Chairman and later to become Appointments Secretary, following Tom Reed, and still later, an Associate Justice of the California Court of Appeals, came to his first meeting, along with other business people, with a check in his hand to help give the fledgling campaign a 'jump-start,'" Nita said. (See Paul's chapter in Vol.2.)

The "Turkey-Bird" takes off: filled with press, media crews, advance-staff and candidate Reagan; sometimes at the controls.

"Well, I can remember the first place that I picked candidate Reagan up was in a little town called Calistoga up in the heart of the Napa Valley. We met—walked around the airplane, talked about the airplane, where we were goin' that day, got in, cranked her up and away we went! I knew that the runway at Calistoga was short (about 1,000 feet long / modern jet airliners need eight to ten thousand feet of runway) gravel and asphalt and used mainly by people who were flying gliders and sail-planes. And to this day they still hook their little gliders to 'tug' planes and tow them into the air to catch the thermals coming up from the ridges ringing the manicured, verdant vineyards of the Napa Valley."

I asked Merv how he got permission to land and takeoff on that short little field.

Merv said, "I called the glider clubs and told them, 'Hey, I plan to come in there with a DC-3.'" And they said, 'Hey, you're *crazy!*' I said, 'No I'm not, I fly in and out of Oakdale all the time and we've only got a little over a thousand feet of runway here so I'm not concerned about your airport.' "All I can remember is; at the end of the runway was the *main street* in Calistoga! So, when I got ready to take off, I remember looking back and —Boy!—I really had that dust *roiling up*—(clouds of dust from the props on those thundering, thousand-horsepower, radial engines which sounded like a dozen crop- dusting bi-planes all revving their engines at the same time)—but I never heard anything (adverse or negative) so I got away with it! I had pulled my gas load way down so the airplane was lighter than normal, so that I could get airborne quicker."

I asked Merv how he thought the candidate's advisors and campaign consultants had been able to talk Ronald Reagan into agreeing to do this; because he didn't want to fly in *anything*. He wanted to drive, take a bus or the train. The only thing that we could come up with was the fact that Merv had impeccable flying credentials, with years of experience in all types of multi-engine aircraft and that the DC-3's had a reputation for being some of the toughest planes in the air; both as cargo-transports and commercial passenger liners. The military loved them, i.e., The C-47's flying over the 'Hump' in Indochina in WWII.

Pertaining to the 'stamp-of-approval,' Merv, the handsome, no-nonsense, quintessential pilot found an affinity with Reagan from their first encounter in the California Wine Country.

He said, "We got along just great from the moment we met. I don't remember anything *special.*" Referring to the reason he, Nancy Amerine and the "Turkey Bird" were accepted almost immediately.

It may have been Reagan's optimism, after meeting the Amerines.

Merv said, "I can remember, Mr. Reagan rode in the co-pilot's seat—he wondered about this and that on the control panel—we just chatted and talked like we're talkin' right now."

"After he was elected governor, we were at a meeting in his office in the Capitol one day—I happened to be there and I don't know why he happened to say this but when he saw me he said, *'Mr. Amerine has done more to ease my concerns about flying than anybody!'* "He really got a kick out of it!" "We'd be comin' in to land and we were just like—seasoned pilots and old friends—I mean—there he was just sitting right up there in the cockpit with me—he was only three feet away from me on the other side of the cockpit—watching everything that went on—*all* the procedures." I'd say, 'Now, we're going to make a power change—I'd tell him why—that we're going to go back to level flight, to a cruise speed and I'm going to reduce my power.' "I'd pull the throttles back slowly—change the RPM, and that didn't bother Mr. R. a bit. And that old DC-3 would just be pluggin' along—like a Caterpillar tractor. There has never been another plane built like it—and there never will be, again!"

I reminded Merv that he carried numerous members of the media and the working press along with three or four members of the candidate's staff, including myself; on most flights. Sometimes the plane was full.

Merv said, "*You* remember, Curtis, it got to be kind of a joke—but it was just part of the process, too: If I happened to make a landing that was a little better than the normal bounce—why, everybody aboard would *gobble* (shrill) like turkeys and clap and then go '*gobble—gobble—gobble!*'"

Yes! It was wild, I recalled; a live turkey call from twenty-eight people in unison.

"Unfortunately, I never got a recording of that—but I should have," Merv said. He went on, "But I sure remember the *gobbling* that came forward from the back end of the plane; if I made a nice, smooth landing."

It was priceless and **loud** and put everyone in a jovial mood. I questioned Merv about landing in those little towns all over the back-country of California, since a lot of folks came out to the airports and landing strips to see us when we would arrive or depart.

"Oh, Yeah!" "There'd be people who'd come out to see the landing and takeoff operations—and get a chance to get a little closer to the candidate—or maybe chat with him for a second. Going back for a moment, after this takeoff from Calistoga, we went to San Andreas (the heart of the Mother Lode Gold Country on the Western slope of the High Sierra) where RR had an evening speech to make at the fairgrounds. Almost any place you could go with a (smaller) general aviation airplane; you could go with that DC-3."

"It was night by the time the speech was over—it was dark when we took off— it may have been one of the few times I took him back to Los Angeles, where he went home to rest for a few days from the rigors of the campaign trail. We'd land as close as we could to where he wanted to go—home, of course—so we would land at Santa Monica Airport by the old Douglas plant."

Then, the Amerines would have to fly the "Turkey Bird" back to their home base in Oakdale, CA, way to the north. They would work 24 / 7 usually at NO charge—it was their donation to the campaign—and they *never* complained!

I asked how he and Reagan got along, throughout their relationship.

"We hit it off right away! Right from the very first we liked each other. Of course, he had an outgoing personality and I have too: I've got a little Irish in me.

That helped a lot about easing any tension. I was comfortable and felt confident with my airplane—it's ability and my ability."

"The DC-3 we actually flew the campaign in, I had purchased from an airline that was re-tooling with more modern equipment and it was retiring it's DC-3,'s. The purpose of the whole thing was to make it possible for us to place our product, day old baby turkeys, into the national market and you could not hatch them in California and truck them any distance; so the airplane just fit in perfectly. These turkeys were relatively light and I can remember several times I had almost fifty-thousand baby turkeys on board. I could go from a people-hauling configuration to cargo configuration in about half an hour."

It was still an amazing twist of fate, for our transportation plans, when the Amerines came along—thinking back over our thirty-nine year friendship: We on the Reagan staff found it fascinating and a *vital* link to our success! We just found it was a wonderful way to get the entire press corp, their bags, typewriters, cameras and other paraphernalia, the candidate, staff and our necessary equipment around California. It was certainly *unique*. I thought it was important to tell Merv and Nancy, after a thirty-year hiatus, 'We in the advance and scheduling staff spent a great deal of time, in 1965 and early 1966, discussing how we were going to get the candidate around the state. Then you came along and I thought, This man is **never** going to fly in *that* plane. And *you* two made it happen!' 'Thanks!'

Merv grinned and said, "And—after it was all over—I think he really enjoyed it!

After that Calistoga to San Andreas flight, he got out of the plane, we shook hands and that was *it!"* 'It was obvious, RR was hooked, sold and confident,' I recalled to Merv.

"We were in Eureka (the wet north coast of CA) The schedule called for an evening speech, at a men's club, in Eureka—then after that we were going to take Mr. Reagan back to his home in L.A.; about a three and a half hour trip in the DC-3. One of the fellas on board that time was with one of the liberal newspapers or magazines and he was a little negative about this whole operation—so I let him fly the airplane a little bit—'chewed the fat' with him—and made a *friend* out of him.

I put him right up there in the co-pilot's seat. The reporter loved it, and could go back and tell the folks at home he had flown a DC-3!"

Governor Reagan depended on Merv Amerine over the years, as a friend and an expert in his field, having learned of his history in aviation beginning in their days in the cockpit aboard the "Turkey Bird.," and he recognized that Amerine had managed airports in the Central Valley, in addition to running his four-ship, turkey transport, airline.

Shortly after taking office, the governor appointed Amerine to the California Aeronautics Board, where he served for nearly eight years and became its chairman.

The Reagans invited the Amerines to both the 1980 and 1984 Presidential Inaugurations and they were even guests at the White House at some of the Thanksgiving Day "Save the Turkey" ceremonies, replete with live turkeys receiving Presidential Pardons.

Chapter Two

A PILLAR OF STRENGTH &
THE VOICE OF REASON

Wm P. 'Bill' Clark, Jr.

"The essence of Ronald Reagan was that he treated us, not as 'footmen' nor employees, but rather as *partners* in a gigantic team that he invigorated by his vision."

"As an example, if he heard that a staff meeting was running late at the end of the day, and it was time for him to go (home) to 45ᵗʰ St.; he'd stick his head in the door and tell us, *"Alright, you guys and gals, get home to your spouses and your kids; the day is over."* And we'd laugh and say, 'Yes, Governor, just give us five more minutes!'

And he'd say, *"You promise only five?"* And we'd say, 'Sure!' "And we'd normally be there an hour or two more, after he left for home. He always worried that we were, maybe, spending too much time in the office and not enough time in our home life."

"It was a marvelous *partnership,* as he called it, *teamwork,* that lead to saving at least some aspects of our culture; both in this country and worldwide, as we look back today (2006)."

"From our very first day together, I was drawn to this great citizen by his loyalty, integrity and discretion—all revealed in both minor moments and in crises." Bill Clark appeared to have been born on a horse from the first day I met him. I grew up on a ranch and Bill reminded me of the many down-to-earth, no-nonsense cattle ranchers, farmers and grass roots Americans whom I had met over the years in this great country; outside of the large, heavily-populated, mainstream cities. Bill rose like an eagle to a mountain top to accept a number of top jobs and special assignments in his private and public life.

He became a lawyer before and without graduating from law school, he was appointed Governor Reagan's cabinet secretary, his chief of staff, a District Court judge, Associate Justice of the California Supreme Court, later National Security Advisor to President Reagan and even Secretary of the Interior of the U.S.; but he always remained a true-to-life cowboy with their intrinsic hard-working ethics and focus. He was my mentor and example in the Governor's Office; because he was so much like RR.

When I asked Bill for an interview, he gladly consented and said he'd do me one better, he'd put some thoughts down on paper regarding our early days with Ronald Reagan, then send them to me for inclusion in this book. I sent him a list of questions, and we talked on the phone and I met with him and his wife, Joan, at his cattle ranch in the oak dotted rolling hills with the ocean breezes at Paso Robles, CA.

Bill's response:

"I first became acquainted with the citizen-politician Ronald Reagan when he telephoned me in 1965 requesting I run for office as a new Goldwater Republican. Yes, I was a member of a five-generation California family of Jeffersonian Democrats until 1964, when Joan and I jumped their fence upon realizing the unfortunate transformation of the Democratic Party, as did our friend, Ronald Reagan, remember: RR's now-famous line, *"I didn't leave the party, it left me!"* "Ron phoned requesting that I consider entering the political race for the State Assembly against an entrenched, or maybe embedded, liberal democrat in Ventura County. This was one of many calls I received to come to the aid of the party, the GOP. After considering it with Joan, and thinking of my young law practice and five young children, I declined the invitation but told my new acquaintance, Ronald Reagan, that if something occurred in the future involving himself to please reach me and I would make my first entry into the political thicket. Several months later, that call came. He told me that he was seriously considering running for governor of California, Sacramento being the State Capital, and he asked me to assist him. I subsequently became Ventura County Chairman of the Reagan for Governor Committee, working with Katherine Haley."

"Among the fifty-eight California counties Ventura finished both the primary and the general near the top of all counties, in numbers of votes for Reagan. Along the campaign trail. Ronald Reagan and I became close and trusted friends, both on and off our horses."

"The morning after the Ambassador Hotel Victory Celebration, he called to ask that I proceed to Sacramento with Caspar Weinberger, Hugh Flournoy and Ivan Hinderocker to determine the state of affairs and to decide exactly what we had won. Upon reporting back to RR concerning the fiscal problems we had been left by Governor Pat Brown, the Governor-elect asked," (tongue-in-cheek) *"May we ask for a vote recount?"*

"I shall now attempt to speak to the first months of the new administration, particularly relating to your area of responsibility in security and transportation. You were such a vital part of the process and a trusted player, Curtis."

"In the first days, we determined we were working with a great leader in our new Governor Reagan: underestimated, understated and selfless." "His key expression, his guidepost for all of us: *We can accomplish anything in building the Creative Society if we don't worry about who will receive the credit!*"

Security:

"I recall sitting in the Corner Office (inside the 'Horseshoe' of the Governor's Complex) with several of you, the room being comparable to the Oval Office at the White House. Suddenly, both of the double doors swung open with a resounding crash and we realized, in shock, we were being confronted by two or more men with drawn pistols leveled at our heads. Several thoughts came to mind: were we being kidnapped by some foreign power or criminal element, or was this a joke?"

"We were stunned into silence and momentary paralysis. When things were sorted out, the explanation become both clear and near laughable. Inadvertently, our new governor's left knee had hit an unknown *panic* button located under the left side of Ron's desk, alerting the State Capitol Police to immediate and imminent danger in the new chief executive's office. We simply had not been told in the interim-government briefings of this little gadget left behind by Governor Brown."

"I suggested that we review the entire security system to include study of the training given those three men who had burst in on us. The result? As well-intentioned as these officers were, these good men had received far less than adequate training in the use of weapons, apprehension, protocol or other elements of good police protection. A training program was instituted under you and Ed Meese, our Clemency and Extradition Secretary, later elevated to a new and broader responsibility, Legal Affairs Secretary."

Actually, it was Ed Meese who created the governor's new security plan while Security Chief, Art Van Court and I helped coordinate it.

Cinco de Mayo:

"Early in the first year of the gubernatorial era, 1967, Governor Reagan accepted the invitation from the Hispanic community in Los Angeles to lead the Cinco de Mayo parade, one of the largest gatherings of its kind in California. He was scheduled to ride in an open convertible with the mayor, I believe it was Mayor Sam Yorty, at the time.""But the community was pretty upset by what it heard and read about their new governor, particularly the misinformation and cartoons delivered by the Los Angeles Times, especially concerning welfare reform. Three days prior to the 5th of May parade, the chief of the political section of the L.A.P.D. phoned me to say that they possessed reliable information that at a certain intersection on Broadway that the governor and the mayor would be bombarded with a barrage of garbage, and who knows what else?

The chief advised that the governor *not* appear so as to avoid certain embarrassment".

When informed of this message, the governor said, *"Bill, I'm certainly not going to back away from this threat." "Let's think about it for a moment." "What if I were to ride a horse, rather than sit in the back of a fancy convertible with the mayor?"*

"I thought, certainly not unlike our good governor himself, the Mexican people love horses and would not allow anyone to throw anything but flowers towards a *caballo*. I phoned my horseman father for his good counsel. He in turn phoned Adolfo Camarillo in the town of the same name and asked to borrow his famous stallion, 'Captain,' for the occasion. To heart-felt cheers from a fantastic crowd, our governor proudly rode his borrowed stallion that beautiful May day through the streets of East Los Angeles, winning many hearts in that community. I must add that when the mayor and his convertible reached the appointed intersection, he bravely withstood the programmed garbage attack."

Deficit Challenge:

"Early in 1967 our new governor ordered us to study alternatives for making up the overwhelming budget deficit left by the Brown Administration. In closed-door sessions we discussed—but had not yet reached the point of making— recommendations for cutting costs and increasing revenues when we first experienced 'media leakage.' One alternative among many included increased fees and tuition from the nine campuses of the University of California System; but it was only an option for discussion and study."

"However, as happens in these sensitive areas, an aggressive news reporter received word, reported increased tuition as an accomplished fact, and the word became national news, resulting in anger and action from academia. Media flashed word throughout the state that Governor Reagan planned to increase the fees and tuition at all campuses of the University of California System for the purpose of bridging the deficit gap. Faculty senates and student groups immediately moved into action to challenge any such move. Of course, attempting to explain that a rise in tuition had been only discussed among *many* revenue raising options, and that no decision had been reached, were found totally unacceptable by both academia and students."

"Demonstrations were organized and the largest of these called for a mass march by students and faculty on the State Capitol building the following Saturday, as thousands were expected to parade to challenge the governor personally. Fortunately, Governor Reagan was scheduled to be out of Sacramento the entire weekend to meet with Governor Tom McCall in Oregon. Our Governor's staff was pleased that the long-scheduled meeting would remove Reagan from the firing line. However. Ronald Reagan, being *Ronald Reagan*, hastily determined to change the weekend schedule by stating, *"I am NOT going to Oregon, I wouldn't miss this opportunity for anything!"* "He called Governor McCall and deferred their first full meeting together to another date. However, Governor Reagan asked that the schedule change not be publicized. Accordingly, on Saturday, midmorning, some five thousand students and faculty marched down the mall to the west steps of the Capitol Building in the knowledge that the governor would be out of the state and thus unable to respond to the planned allegations on the part of the students and faculty members."

"Their leader mounted the capitol steps using a P.A. system to rally the angry crowd. The governor and several of us staff waited patiently in the corner office of the Governor's Complex, listening to the student leader's rhetoric—demagoguery at its best—or its worst."

I reminded Bill that I was out front taking the 'pulse' of the crowd and sending reports back to Van Court, the CHP and a member of the Military Department who were with him, Meese, Nofziger and the governor.

"Finally, that genius of great timing stood up, with that catbird smile of his, and said, *"Let's proceed!"* "We walked down the long hall, through the rotunda, and stepped out from behind the speaker who, of course, could not see the uninvited guests standing at his back. But the crowd could see and 'oooo'd! and 'ahhhed!' until the student leader was forced to turn around to see what had occurred behind him. Stunned—he passed the hand-mike to the well-prepared governor. Again, Governor Reagan had won the hour and the day by having created the opportunity to explain his policy options to our young citizens. Most went away reluctantly satisfied."

Spirituality:

"Ronald Reagan was a very spiritual person, but not necessarily in a formal religious sense. In other words, I was convinced in the time we spent together, particularly in times of crisis, that the governor was in frequent communication with God, but not necessarily in a church or formal setting." "One of his favorite Lincoln quotes was, 'I'm driven to my knees daily in the overwhelming conviction that I have no place else to go.'

"His spirituality frequently shown spontaneously such as during our first trip from Sacramento to Washington aboard a TWA plane destined for Baltimore's Friendship Airport. Approximately one hour before landing, the captain came back to state he had just received word that Dr. Martin Luther King had been assassinated, and that I might wish to inform our governor."

"I turned around to tell the governor of this fact, expecting him to say something in response. He said nothing from behind his sorrowful facial expression. He said nothing further until we landed. In the interim, I noted that he sat silently in his assigned seat, looking down toward his feet, his lips silently *praying...*"

Conclusion

"From our very first day together, I was drawn to this great citizen by his loyalty, integrity and discretion—all revealed in both minor moments and in crisis!"

Loyalty:

"Ronald Reagan displayed a constant deep loyalty to his God, country and family at all times. No one in his or her right mind would challenge me on this!"

Integrity:

"His thoughts, words and actions all spoke the truth."

Discretion:

"He approached people and problems with clear common sense, never having to backtrack. Of course, we made mistakes for which he was always ready and able to concede and to even apologize."

In conclusion, I sincerely believe that Ronald Wilson Reagan will be ultimately shown by historians as the *greatest* of presidents in our time.

Chapter Three

MEDIA MAGIC

Tom Ellick

"*Here* was a man we could work with!" "*Here* was a man who would trust *us* and we could trust *him*!" Statement by State Senator Bill Green, Chairman of the Legislative Black Caucus, to Tom Ellick, recalling good meeting with Reagan and good relations, thereafter."It's a *tribute* to RR." "It's a tribute to the *man* he was, and, the very *approachable, honest, straightforward* guy that he was." "People *loved* him and you can understand why!"

Tom Ellick was a film producer, lobbyist and government relations consultant for the California Trucking Association when he first came in contact with Ronald Reagan.

Governor Pat Brown had been very close to the Trucking Association, which had agreed to fund and produce a film for Brown, to show off the governor and his administration in a *good light*, to assist in his re-election campaign.

"I had *no* involvement in politics, at that point, I was a registered Republican—but this was a *client* and they offered me a very nice amount of money to write, produce and film—this motion picture. So, I wrote the film and I worked with Jack Burby, who was Pat Brown's Press Secretary, and he helped me in getting footage of the governor in his office and Senator Randolph Collier, who was then Chairman of the Senate Transportation Committee, and, a very key guy to the trucking industry. Hubert Humphrey came out, when he was vice president, along with Governor Brown and—bottom line—we produced a very effective film—and I was able to get actor Barry Sullivan, who was a big Democrat and a friend of the governor's, to narrate it for me—and we produced it—and delivered it—and they were *very* pleased with it!"

"And, of course, at that time, I began to be more and more aware of Ronald Reagan and the fact that the head of the Trucking Association, was saying, 'Well, maybe we ought to hedge our bets, here.' I said, "Well, it's a little late for that." "I basically walked away from it—other than the fact that I was still doing some lobbying for the Association in Sacramento."

Tom was also doing P.R. work, using television interviews for other clients in Sacramento and San Francisco, where he had worked with Nancy Clark Reynolds at KPIX-TV. He had *voted* for Reagan, but had not *worked* in the campaign.

Tom was living in Sacramento and stopped by the Governor's Office one day to say 'Hello' to NCR, who had just been brought aboard the Press Unit by Lyn Nofziger, after the inauguration.

Lyn offered Tom a job as an assistant in media operations, and thus he went to work, hands-on, one-on-one, with the *new* governor, almost immediately.

"So, I went to work for the Reagan Administration. The first time I met the governor, Lyn took me into a Cabinet meeting. I was seated off to the side of the 'big' room—and all of the other folks were sitting around the long table."

"The governor was presiding over the meeting and I was very impressed with the manner in which he handled people, how he listened, how he would ask good questions —and how, when he didn't get what he thought was a straight answer—I remember, at one point, he took his glasses off and threw them on the table and said, *"God Damn it!" "If I want to do—whatever—I'll do it."* " Someone said something like, 'Well, we can't do *that.'* Then Reagan said, *"Why do we keep getting hit over the head by this all the time?"*

"I think it may have had to do with RR's controversial proposal to 'shut down' many of the state's mental hospitals and return the patients to their own communities"

"I remember, he was very unhappy with the answer he received, because he apparently had asked that question before and wasn't satisfied." I thought, 'This is an interesting guy.' "I liked him. After the Cabinet meeting, Lyn took me into the back office to the Governor's Study and gave me the *personal* introduction."

"The governor was very *warm*," and Lyn said, 'Tom is going to be working with *me* and he is going to be doing some liaison with the different Cabinet Officers— doing some liaison with the different government agencies, so that we can put the Governor's Office 'spin' on what comes out of the Department of Motor Vehicles— what comes out of whatever agency.' "So I did *that.* I had the title of Special Assistant to the Cabinet."

"I would go over and Lyn introduced me to the different Cabinet secretaries and to the P.R. people in each of the government agencies and departments and I would work with them and they would give me a 'Heads Up' if there was a good story coming out of Motor Vehicles or coming out of the Department of Conservation or whatever—and—when I felt we could do it—I put a little message in it, that the governor had something to do with this—or that—or whatever—and I would give him some credit for the accomplishments of the administration. And, it got a little testy at times, because some of the cabinet secretaries wanted *their* names to be on it." And I would have to say, 'Well, you know, Mr. Secretary, with all due respect, we all work for the governor and this is something that we ought to give *him* some credit for.' "It gave me a chance to work with them—and then I would go back and I would work with the governor on the story—and he'd tweak it—or do something to it—and the thing that impressed me from the very beginning was that he was *very* available and *immediately trusting!"*

"And, I thought, 'This is unusual. Now, here's a man who has had an interesting career in the entertainment business; he is now the Governor of the State of California. He doesn't know me from a bale of hay, other than the fact that Lyn said, 'This guy is O.K.'—and, he *accepts it!'*" "I later talked to Lyn about it and he said," 'Well, you've got to understand; it's because he's the product of the industry in which he worked.' "He would go in on a movie set and they would say," 'Ron, here's your director, here's your writer, here's your producer,' "And he accepted them at face value. So, he accepted *me* at face value."

"And then, after a while, when he got used to my writing skills, he asked me to give him a hand on a couple of speeches—and I kinda' moved into *that* a little bit. The way we would do that—the way he and I did it—was—Ron would call me in and say, *"I need to give a speech on such-and-such a subject to this particular group of people and my understanding is they are interested in this—and this—and this—but I need to know more about what their interests are."* "So I would get a hold of the organization to which he was going to speak, and I would say," 'Tell me some of the issues that are of concern to your industry, or your company, or whatever.' "And I was basically doing it like a reporter's job." "Then I came back and wrote those things up and would call in and get an appointment to talk to the governor and I would say," 'O.K., here's what I've found out—these are the things that seem *most* important—and here are my thoughts on this.' And then he'd say, *"O.K. that's good, but I want to emphasize this and this."* I'd say, 'O.K. do you want me to do a draft?' And Ron would say, *"Yeah!" "Please!"*

"I briefed him." "Not only on what the subject matter should be—but on the need for it." And he would say, *"O.K. let's see what it looks like."* "So, I did a draft—and then I would take it in—and he would *'massage'* it—he would change a word here—or takeout a whole paragraph—there—or write in something entirely different. It was really a very cooperative effort."

"Then, after he approved the Final Draft—he would convert it to his 4 X 6 or the 5 X 8 inch cards. With the Ronald Reagan 'shorthand'—with the 'R'—'U' for 'Are you?' and the like—he got *very* comfortable with that."

'Lyn and I had a discussion on: 'How do we better get our message across?' "In light of the fact that the press didn't always feel the need to spotlight an important issue, just because the governor made a statement on the subject. Or, they would leave out *key* information. I think the first big issue was the State Budget." Lyn said,

'You know, it's dull stuff and how are we going to get across why we are doing this or that?' "And I don't remember if that's when the decision was made to *shut down* the state mental hospitals—about how we could save money—which, by the way, was a decision that was a TERRIBLE MISTAKE!" "How do you look at all of the homeless people that are wandering around on the streets now—who really ought to be, probably, locked up in some of those places?"

"They shut down the state mental hospitals, not all of them—some—just for a short time. The idea was to return those people to their *home* communities. Where they would be well-cared for. Well, the communities didn't want them!" "However, it represented significant savings to the State Budget—and that was during the Governor's CUT, SQUEEZE & TRIM era." So I remember saying, "Governor, you've had a little experience in the entertainment business—why don't we produce our own televised REPORTS TO THE PEOPLE?" "And—if the stations won't take them, as PSA's—to hell with it—let's buy the time and run 'em!" "He thought that was a great idea." So, I said, "Let me take a crack at one—on the budget—I think that was the *first* one. So, we called on Cap Weinberger, State Director of Finance, 'cause he was good on-camera—except that when Cap was on—he wore a blue suit and he had all this stuff in his pockets—and he looked like a chipmunk."

I said, 'Cap, let's clear the pockets.' "So then we had Weinberger on-camera explaining a lot of technical aspects, with a blackboard or meatpaper on an easel—I mean this was pretty primitive stuff, when you think, today, of the technology—we were *learning*. It had never been done before."

"So, we got all the Weinberger film, and then I wrote the portion for the governor, which was the majority of it—I forget what elements were in that particular film, but, if RR was talking about college campuses or talking about building roads, or whatever the budget implications were—I would get the cameraman and we would go out and we would film—so that we could *cut away*—and we'd have the Governor's voice-over—and it would show—"*Here's a road being built—*" or—"*Here's a scene on a college campus* —or—"*Here is such and such*"—whatever the issue was that we were describing."

"And then, after we shot that stuff—so that we had a lot of footage to cut-away *to* —then I wrote the basic script for the governor, and we timed it out to twenty-six minutes and thirty seconds."

"I remember the first one we did—in the main conference room of the Governor's Office. We had lots of space, lots of room for the cameras, lights and tripods. We had Teleprompters, when necessary—and Ron would come in and perch on the edge of his desk and the cameras were 'rolling'—and he would do it in *ONE TAKE!"* It was wonderful!" "Yeah!" "Absolutely *incredible!"*

"What we then had was—Ronald Reagan—on-camera—we had his speech—we did the close-ups—we did the pull-backs—we shot it with a couple of cameras—and then the job was to take those elements and edit them down so that we could start with Ron and then when he started talking about some of the major elements"—he would say, *"Now, here's Cap Weinberger to give us the details on how we're going to do this allocation."*

"And then we cut-away to the stuff we had done on Weinberger—and sometimes, we would cut from Weinberger to some of the scenes he was describing—then, we'd go back to the governor—and it ended up being a pretty slick production. And. it *worked*—and it just *PISSED OFF* the media, because they weren't able to edit *any* of this stuff!" Because we bought the time—through GOP #1 or some authorized donation fund—and the stations had to use it!" "We *bought* the time!" "It was a new thing!"

"A couple of things that I remember about Ron, aside from the fact that he was really *very easy* to work with: There was one incident when, for some reason, I had written the speech he was going to give in Bakersfield, CA—and it was a *hot* night in the summer—and Mike Deaver, Art Van Court and I were there—this was an outdoor event in some open-air stadium—Buck Owens & The Buckaroos were performing. The local mayor—and all this stuff—(generally acts, dignitaries and politicians) and of course, everybody wanted to do their own 'thing' on the stage. The governor was sitting in the limo, along with all of us, with the engine running—the air-conditioner on—and he was getting 'antsier' and 'antsier.' the hotter it got. There was *no* end to the speeches that were going on beforehand—at this big, Republican, "red-neck" crowd in Bakersfield."

This town could get real hot and dusty with the smell of freshly-pumped oil mixed with citrus blossoms permeating the heat waves silently wafting up from the freshly-turned soil of the San Joaquin Valley floor. Home of oil field 'rough-necks,' Merle Haggard's country music and summer-time bugs.

"I could sense that RR was getting pretty antsy—so I leaned over to him and said, 'Governor, would you like a drink?' And Deaver looked at me—shot me one of those deadly looks, as though thinking, 'How dare you suggest that!' "And the governor said, in effect," *"Well, Tom, what do you have in mind?"* And I said, 'Well, there's a bar out there—I can get us a couple of drinks—would you like a nice *cold*—Daiquiri?'

He said, *"God, I'd love it!"* "Oh, it just *pissed* Deaver off to a 'fare-thee-well.' So, I went out and got a couple of Daiquiris."

"It should be noted that this man drank—*rarely*—very rarely—but he did, occasionally like a frozen Daiquiri. It was a hot night and the mosquitoes were out—but it did the trick!" "It did the trick!"

"He calmed down and enjoyed it and relaxed—and finally—it was his turn to get up—and he gave his speech and did a very good job." "A *standing ovation*—as usual."

"I remember—one of my jobs was to stand in the back of the room—auditorium—in a stadium—anywhere I could be seen from the podium by Reagan—you kind of had to weigh it or 'test' it—to get his attention."

"This example was set early-on by Lyn Nofziger in his trademark pose holding his watch hand high in the air. And RR'd look over the glasses—if he was reading—or, if he *wasn't* reading—if he had the contact-lenses on and he'd look out there—into the crowd—and then you'd put your arm out—or *up*—and you'd point to the watch—and sometimes you'd get a 'ten' minutes or 'five'—or whatever—with the (RR's) fingers—and then finally I'd respond with the 'cut across the throat'—to say, 'It's time, Governor, it's time to get off.' "And—it worked." "And we developed a very—a *very easy rapport.*

I didn't travel with him an awful lot. When I did—it was to a great extent because we were trying out a new speech—we were trying to do something—special / different—but he was *very easy* to be with. I remember Art Van Court and I would travel, and Art would say, 'We're going down to Southern California—want to go with us?' "I'd say, 'Sure!' "And it gave us a chance to talk."

"I was *never* part of the *Inner-Circle*—I was kind of resented, I think, by Deaver and by Meese—and certainly by Paul Beck. But I was Lyn's guy and Lyn and I had a very good relationship. Lyn, basically, really made it possible for me to be there."

"The *one* event that I remember as being a *turning point* in my relationship with Nancy (N.R.)—was when I wanted to do a television REPORT TO THE PEOPLE on the College Campus issue—on the Governor's stand on Education."

I asked Tom to flesh that out for me and talk a little about the college campuses. We around RR were all pretty keyed-up over the issue of *unrest* on the college campuses. Ellick growled, "UUGGGGHHH!!!" "It was a time—when there was tremendous unrest on the college campuses! Mario Savio and his gang had taken over Sproul Hall at the University of California at Berkeley—The Bank of America building was burned at UCSB Santa Barbara—it was the result of a lot of so-called '*College Unrest*'—there was a *radical* element moving through the University System—a period of lawlessness—a lot of professors were a part of this *"Free Speech Movement"*—(a 'red-herring' for anything goes)—it was really a *very scary* time!"

'There was some danger to the governor on these campuses,' I said. Ellick replied, "Oh, absolutely, Curtis!" "That is what I am going to—on this story. We had a very good story to tell on *education*. The governor was *very* supportive of the California educational system."

"And, if you recall, he had a sign over his door that read—**"OBEY THE RULES OR GET OUT!"**—(Made into bumper-stickers, now in the RR Presidential Library in Simi Valley, CA.) And he said, *"That's the policy in* this *office and that's the policy in every university in this state—and I'm going to crack down on these thugs—but I want people to understand that I support* Higher Education *and I don't support Anarchy!"*

And I said, "Let's do a movie on *that*—let's do a T.V. report."

"And so—we did." "I fleshed it out—I filmed it—I don't remember how much of this material ended up in the final version—but I remember, we were able to get him, RR, in Southern California, to meet with a bunch of college kids in a 'give-and-take' session—he was *terrific* at it! We had him with some younger children in another session—I don't think that made it into the film. And then, I shot a lot of other stuff—on the campus. We showed some scenes of *destruction,* property damage—we showed *picketing* and *rioting*! I'm trying to remember what some of the other elements were—but there was *one* thing that was really critical."

"Bottom line is—I had about 99.9% of the other footage shot—that we would 'cut-in' to the film—and I had the portion written that was Ronald Reagan's narrative, *from* which we would 'cut-away' to these other scenes but, I needed to get RR on a college campus. I had written it so that the scene was of him in a *contemplative* mood, walking through a campus with some students sitting on the lawn—of him walking—*through* them and *by* them—they were studying—they weren't paying attention to him—but he was in a *contemplative* mood—and the idea was that I would have his *voice-over*—his kind of train-of-consciousness type of thing—it was a very *important* part of the production! But I needed to get Reagan on a college campus—to do it. And I remember, it was a *big* deal—Lyn was nervous about it"— he said, 'Well, we've got to round-table this one!' And I thought—'Oh Shit!' "If I hated a word or statement—it was," 'We're going to have to *round-table* it!'

I smiled and was sure Tom knew who was going to have to look at it.

"Oh Yeah, Curtis!" "I knew The Boss—The Man was going to be down at his home in Pacific Palisades over the weekend"—so RR said, *"Are you going to be in Southern California?"* And I said, "Yeah, I can be down in Southern California." "And so—I flew down there and drove out to the house. I had never been out to the governor's house before. I went in and there were Meese and Deaver and Nofziger and—I don't think Bill Clark was there, then—and the governor and Nancy—all in the living room—and I was kind of shown to a seat in the corner." "They were doing all this business and finally—whomever was in charge of the meeting said," 'O.K. Tom, why don't you explain what it is you want us to do here.'

"So, I explained it." 'We've got the film shot.' I said, 'Governor, you've approved the script—we've got nearly everything in the 'can'—but we don't have it *all* 'in the can yet—we're ready to do the editing—but I need this scene.'

And RR said, *"I've worked it out with Art Van court (AVC) and Art can get some plainclothes L.A.P.D. guys, young-looking guys and girls, to appear to be the college students—we can do it at UCLA—just down the street—on a Sunday afternoon."*

I quizzed Tom, 'So *they*, the young cops, were going to be the college students on the Lawn?'

"Right." "Right." "Yeah!"

And, Tom told him, 'Governor, basically, we can block off an area of the campus—it's a Sunday afternoon—it's going to be very quiet, anyway—I've got a great location, where the mood is there and—there are trees—and—it is really perfect for the thing—and we can get *you* down there and back in twenty minutes.'

'But—I need, maybe forty-five—fifty seconds—is all I need—but I need *this* scene—to show your caring, and your concern!'

"Well, there was *SILENCE* in the room—and I kept thinking—'O.K., where are my supporters, here?' "And—there was just—*SILENCE*—and Nancy looked up at me—and then she looked over at the governor and said, *'No Daddy, we can't do it—it's too dangerous!'* "And then, as I remember, Meese and Deaver and someone else said," 'Yes!' 'Yeah!' 'That's true—we're going to have to re-do it, Tom—you're going to have to come up with a better idea—blah—blah—blah…'

I thought, 'Well, O.K., let's see who the decision-maker *is* here.' "And so I just was very quiet—and everybody finally got quiet too—and the governor looked at me and I said," 'Ahhh—Governor—I think this is a *very* important scene—it's **YOUR** call!'

Then Tom described this shocked look of amazement and a stifled murmur by everyone as the—'OH GOD!'—look from the group.

"A throat-clearing, raspy growl—belched from the group, 'OH GOD!' And the Governor of California said, *"Tom's right—we're going to do it!"* "Well, that broke the die as far as Nancy and I were concerned. She was very cool to me afterwards. And Deaver, as I recall, was *very critical,* but didn't say anything because it was the governor's decision."

"But he made it clear to me that," 'This by God better work and there had better not be any glitches!' I said, 'Listen, Mike, I love this guy as much as you do and I'm not going to put him in harm's way—but, you know The Man—let Reagan be Reagan!'

"And he was." "Nancy didn't want Reagan to be Reagan, in that case." "But, we did it!"

"And it was NO big deal." "And afterwards everybody thought and said, 'WOW, this is really great!'

"And we went on with the rest of our lives."

'Why,' I asked, 'was it necessary to 'stage' the event—the shoot?'

Tom said, "I think it's really important to remember the context of this event. This was a time of tremendous *violence* on the campuses. I mean, there were times when the governor's life was *really* in peril when he went on campuses as a member of the Board of Regents; to a Regents meeting. Nancy had a *very legitimate* concern. And that's the reason I made sure—working with Van Court, who was head of security who had worked it out with the L.A.P.D.—that they could, indeed, insure his safety."

"And—could we have some friendly college students? Well—there were certainly a lot more friendly college students than UN-friendly ones." "I believe that the UN-friendlies were so *radical*—if we had approached a group of students, randomly, to say, 'Would you be interested or willing to do—da-da—da-da—da-da?' "The word would have spread, and the concern was—that the *radicals* would have found out about it and they would have created an incident—and we didn't want to do that. We wanted to insure the governor's safety—and we all have to remember that there was *no* Secret Service protection at that time. There was Art Van Court, and that was it, except for the two CHP officers, Dale Rowlee in the north and Barney Barnett in Southern California. You took your life in your hands when you were going with Ronald Reagan to a lot of places, in those days, particularly to a college campus; because of this *radical* element." "You were there, Curtis."

I then told Tom I had been approached by Van Court as early as 1964 while working for the Goldwaters and again during the Reagan campaign to go thru a qualifying procedure for a number of various types of firearms, both in Southern California and at the CHP Academy in Sacramento and was taught to carry them responsibly in all kinds of dangerous situations with Ron , Nancy, Skipper and Patti.

During the campaigns, I had applied for and obtained a Concealed Weapons Permit from Orange County Sheriff's Dept, the Newport Beach Police Department and the City of Sacramento Police Dept., with full C,I. & I. and N.C.I.C. background checks and clearances.

These permits were for "personal protection" but, coupled with some strict rules and training, it gave the others around RR some measure of confidence to know someone would back them up and be there in the 'pinch.' During the previous three years, prior to RR becoming governor, I had received instruction from officers of the Intelligence, Narcotics and Traffic Divisions of L.A.P.D. in a number of phases of law enforcement including convoy-driving, executive protection tactics and the use of higher-powered, vehicle-stopping weapons and ammunitions. We trained constantly, *intensively;* especially during the nine-hundred days of *full-time/ 24-7 / on-call* commitment.

Unknown to most of the staff, except for the security chief, the legal affairs secretary and a few of us in close proximity to the Reagans, our quiet communications colleague, Bob Tarbet also had a Concealed Weapons permit, issued by the L.A.P.D., and carried a weapon when he traveled with us and the Reagans. This was reconfirmed in 2005 by both Lyn Nofziger and Urania Tarbet.

Tom continued, "Do I think he was 'chicken' that we didn't use regular college students?" *"NO!"* "I think it was *prudent.* The L.A.P.D. guys and gals were very young looking—they were plainclothes people—they *looked* like college students. It gave the *effect—IT INSURED HIS SAFETY*—and—it made *certain* that we didn't, in any way, tip off the fact that he was going to be on campus—which could have put his *life* in peril!"

"Now, I have to tell you that *that* event just really 'broke the die' between Nancy Reagan and me—because she knew that I was not trying to go against her wishes—I was trying to go *with* the governor's wishes. He's the guy I worked for. I didn't work for Nancy!" I almost shouted,—"Ooops!" "Wrong!" He didn't get it— but numerous others didn't either. Tom was doing his best to give RR maximum exposure and insure his life was not in danger—and produce a film which showed the world how Reagan really felt about students and education.

"But the relationship was very cool," he continued.

"I remember a number of times I would be going over to the barber shop at the Senator Hotel across from the Capitol and Nancy would come in with Skipper (Ron Jr.) at the time I'd be getting my haircut and she'd be waiting while the barber was cutting my hair—and I would try to be cordial to her. She would always be very *cool—very aloof."* And I thought—he laughs, 'Well, O.K.'

"Well—it *did* bother me—because I certainly didn't want to have a difficult relationship with the wife of the guy I worked for."

"And, I remember—I would have a recurring *nightmare*—which is the thing that made me decide it was *really* time to leave. In this dream I was walking along a riverbank (he then describes the American River east of downtown Sacramento) with Nancy Reagan on my shoulders—(he laughs)—and, over on the other side of the river was a road, and on that road we could see the governor's limousine." Nancy said, 'Go into the water—we have to find Daddy!' "And so, I was wading into this river—and the water was getting higher and higher and *higher*—she was on my shoulders saying, 'Faster—faster—we're going to miss him!' "And then—I would wake up." And I thought, "*This* is *not* going to work!" "Well, at about that time, 1970, the election was being held—the second term was beginning—they were starting a purge of some of the quote 'less desirable' staff people. I got the word that my services weren't going to be necessary very much longer. You could just feel these things."

"I had developed a number of contacts outside of the Governor's Office, 'cause one of the things that I did for the administration was a lot of the outside contact stuff."

"We set up a Program Development Unit." "We came up with some ideas that would show a more *compassionate—caring* side of Ronald Reagan—to counter some of this *'hard line'* imagery."

"We started the Family Visitation Programs, in the state prisons, for example—where convicts who were about to be released spent a couple of nights on conjugal visits with their wives and families—prior to being released—to give them a chance to interface with the family again. I did some of the interfacing with NASA. We brought Neil Armstrong out—and the moon rocks. But, it was time to go. I had developed a relationship with Bob Fluor, who had been very close to the governor—and the Fluor Corporation." (chemical plants, etc. / projects worldwide). "I was given an offer that I couldn't refuse at about the time that Meese and Deaver were saying, 'Well, it's time to move—we're going to make a lot of changes here.' "That was the end of my *official* period."

"I was asked to come on board and put together a public affairs / public relations program for the Fluor Corporation. I became Manager of Public Affairs, then, later director and later, vice-president—and I ultimately ended up running the Fluor Foundation."

"My years in the California Reagan Administration—it was a *wonderful* period in my life! I remember RR *so* well—such a *warm guy!* Years later, when I left Fluor—I went to Sacramento to assume a new position as President of the California Manufacturer's Association. the lobbying organization for California businesses. I made it a point to get around and talk to all of the members of the legislature, including the Democratic Leadership, as well as the Republican Leadership."

"One guy whom I went to talk to was Senator Bill Greene. Bill Green was a liberal, Black senator from Los Angeles."

"Senator Greene was very active in the Black Caucus in the State Legislature—at one time he was their chairman. I went in to his office in the Capitol Building and reintroduced myself."

I said, "Senator, I don't know if you remember me but I'm now president of the Manufacturers Association—I'm looking forward to our being able to work together—and I don't know if you remember this, but we first met when I was working for Ronald Reagan and, for some reason, the Governor's Legislative Liaison to the Senate, former Senator Vern Sturgeon, was out and had asked me to run some interference and go up and see whether the Black Caucus would be willing to meet with the governor."

"The governor really wanted to meet with them. Now why Vern didn't do it—I don't know—but for some reason he asked *me* to do it. I had worked with a lot of Democrats." "Senator Green remembered that very well," and he said, 'You know, Tom, after you made that approach—I got all the guys on the Caucus together and we were really waiting (more like laying-in-wait) for Reagan—and we were going to 'jump' his frame, when he came in there to meet with us—and we were going to be real *tough!*' "And Bill Green kind of glowered." But he said, 'That son-of-a bitch came in there—he came in there and he absolutely *WOWED* us!' 'It didn't mean that we were going to always agree—but it let us realize that *here* was a man we could work with. And, *here* was a man who would trust *us* and we could *trust him!*' He said, 'I'll NEVER forget that!'

He said, 'I remember *you* as the guy who made that possible—sure I'll work with you—and I'm glad you're over at CMA.' "So, that was another residual benefit of my years with the Reagan Administration. But—it's a *tribute* to Ronald Reagan."

"It's a tribute to the man that he was—and the *very approachable, honest, straight-forward* guy that he was. People *loved* him—and you can understand why!"

I asked him if he had any frustrations about RR—where there were some tense moments dealing with him personally?

Tom said, "The most difficult situation, of course, was the one where I basically put it to him and I said, "It's *your* call, Governor." "That was *tense!*" "But, there was no animus between the two of us."

"I think there was only one time when he was *very* angry with me. I had an office outside of the 'Golden Horseshoe' of executive offices. It was kind of neat—because it was private and I didn't have a lot of traffic going through there. I remember one day I was sitting at my desk—and I had my feet up on my desk, and I was working on something." "We had these old wooden call boxes on each desk—they were a kind of antiquated intercom system inherited from Governor Pat Brown—and I didn't realize it, but I had kicked the key to the governor's personal office right across the hall where he was sitting at his desk doing some work." "And this thing kept buzzing and buzzing —and—*buzzing!*" And, finally The Man realized somebody was buzzing *him*. And—I remember being startled—because this voice came out of the old wooden intercom box, which we never used, saying, *"Who the hell is it and what do you want?"* Tom laughed. "It was Governor Ronald Reagan." I said, 'Oooohh—Governor—I'm in trouble!' 'This is Ellick—and I kicked the box and I really apologize!' 'Didn't mean to bother you.' And he said, *"Well, God Damn it, I was trying to get some stuff done, here!"* 'Governor, I'm *REALLY* sorry!' Reagan then said, *"O.K." "O.K."*

"That was it. That was the *only* difficult time we ever had."

"I remember some other interesting times. Curtis, you know these incidents, you were very much involved. It was when we were in Miami in 1968." "Yeah!"

The light bulb went on in his brain.

"I had taken a leave of absence. One of my fondest memories, too. Those were the times! I was working for the Young Americans for Freedom—(YAF grew over thirty years into the Young America's Foundation which purchased Ronald Reagan's

Ranch in Santa Barbara, CA—Rancho Del Cielo—in April of 1998). We had come up with this idea as the governor was going to the various state delegation's caucuses, at the different hotels—of staging these so-called *'spontaneous rallys.'* Balloons, banners and bands—the whole thing! It started out pretty elementary. I remember the first one."

"I don't think the governor really knew what we were planning there—but we made a deal with Van Court that he would be bringing The Man into the auditorium, into the hotel lobby, into wherever it was going to happen—he was going to meet with the delegates of *that* particular state—and I would be standing there with a microphone and portable P.A., and in some cases there would be television cameras or media or whatever—and Art would 'zero-in' on my bald head—and bring the governor over to where I was and RR would say, *"Well, what a surprise* this *is!"* or *"Well—this* IS *a surprise!"* Then I'd say, 'Governor—we just happened to be here'—and—'would you like to say a few words?'

"And, then, he would go into his extemporaneous speech. After we did that a couple of times—we got it down to a system—and then—it really got more formalized."

"I think *you* were behind this thing, Curtis—(actually this type of 'demonstration' was honed into a finely-orchestrated production by our own clandestine activities operative, Sal Russo, with some help from George Young of S-R, (see their chapters in this book—under the overall direction of Tom Reed)—we ended up with balloons, and, sometimes we could get a band and we had some wonderful young female volunteers called The Reaganettes—dressed in bright red and white cheerleader-style outfits—and they would come in with Pom-Pons—and—I mean—towards the end of that convention—we were '***cookin***'—we were in *high gear!"* The Reaganettes would be lining the way—and Art would be bringing or leading the governor in—with a phalanx of U.S. Secret Service—and I'd be down at the other end—huge, eager crowds milling around—with my microphone and portable P.A. system—"

"It just *happened!"* "And, he loved it—he absolutely *loved* it!"

And so did everyone who saw it.

"Oh, it was fun!" "Yeah!" "It was just great—and—after the convention—when obviously, he did *not* get the nomination—and we all came back to Sacramento—tough times." "Tough times!"

"I was not part of the inner-circle group—to which he came—or who were with him in The Governor's Suite when the results came in."

The California Favorite Son Delegation, including members of the Kitchen Cabinet held a large reception for the Reagans at one of the hotels along Miami Beach, probably the Deauville, our "lead" hotel, or the Fontainebleau, and honored Ron and Nancy for about two hours, with music, speeches, cocktails, cheers and tears.

That's where and when the Reagan's Secret Service Special Detail Agent in Charge, Ed Hickey, who had endeared himself to the Reagan family and staff so much, was asked when leaving the SS on his impending retirement to come to Sacramento to take over the position as Security Chief in the Governor's Office, on the retirement and movement of Art Van Court to an appointment as U.S. Marshal over Northern and Eastern California; not bad for an L.A.P.D. Narcotics Division detective who never made sergeant, but who displayed a total dedication to Ronald Reagan and his principles and who was willing to volunteer on *every* day off, whenever called, to the detriment of his own family.

"I remember flying back to California—and the first day we're back in the office—I was over in the Program Development section—I remember looking up and—there he was!" "He came through the offices and he said," *"I just want you to know how much I appreciate all you did!"* *"It was disappointing—the results—it was a long shot!"*

The 1968 California Favorite Son Delegation / Reagan for President boomlet.

"But," Ron said, *"We gave it our BEST!"* *"I just want you to know how much I appreciate the time you took—and for being there—and for having those wonderful 'SPONTANEOUS' rallys!"*

"I've *never* forgotten that. It was a wonderful, *noble* thing that he did!"

I asked Tom how he thought Ronald Reagan may have influenced *his* life—if at all. And, did he think *he,* Tom, added anything to RR's accomplishments as he moved out of the Governor's Office and into the presidency?

"Well, taking the last question—first: I don't know that I contributed much, if anything to his greatness. I think his *greatness* was there—it was latent—he developed it as he went along. And, again, if left to his own instincts; he made the *right decisions.*"

"I guess a case-in-point probably would be to go back to that story about the video production on the UCLA. campus. I think he normally would have deferred to Nancy and his 'handlers,' and *not* done it."

"But, the way I put it to him—and said, 'You know, Governor, it's *your* call,' caused him to realize it was, in fact, *his* call—and let him be himself. And he did. And he made the *right* call! He also became 'General Manager' of *himself*, by doing that. I don't mean that this was the first or the *only* time—but I think it was important."

"The result of the production and airing of the film? Oh, it was *excellent!* It was very well received. And then, I believe, it did help turn, at least enough public opinion that they realized that Ronald Reagan was not out to destroy education in California, and *that* was the objective! I think it taught him and those who followed, in the capacity that I had in the Governor's Office, and on into the White House— the importance of television as the communicating vehicle—and that sounds presumptuous, because he had been in television as well as the motion picture industry. But the use of television film—as a communications or a propaganda device—I think was something that we illustrated—we demonstrated—and we basically started out using during the gubernatorial years."

"Notwithstanding the fact that RR was such an effective communicator during his own 1965/'66 Campaign for Governor using television and on back to 1964 to the legendary, televised "A Time for Choosing" speech on behalf of Goldwater."

"He certainly effected *my* relationships. I mean—my relationship with *him* is something I'll *never* forget!"

"It's nice when people find out that I had worked for Ronald Reagan, they kind of look at me with a little different view and say 'Whoa!' "O.K., they may say, maybe you're *not* such a *klutz* after all."

"I remember him fondly and it's so hard for me to think of him in such a state of decline, today."

I told Tom, 'I like to remember him as we were sitting on an airplane and he would be telling wonderful stories. And pretty soon everyone was in the aisle—and all of the flight attendants—and all of the personnel and staff were crowded around.'

"Absolutely!" "He was a great guy—and I thank whomever coined the phrase, "*Let Reagan be Reagan.*" "I have a feeling it may have been Lou Cannon—I don't know." "But it is so true." "His *instincts* were Right On." "He was a wonderful man and I am honored to have been able to carry a spear for him—it was a *great* experience—and a wonderful opportunity!"

"This was at one of the many backyard staff or legislative garden parties that Ron and Nancy gave during the summer months at the Executive Mansion on 45th Street in Sacramento. As you remember, there was a huge double or triple lot, the big swimming pool in the backyard, lots of flowers and oak trees shading the guests— and I remember, I had my two sons there and we in the Program Development Unit wore, as our kind of 'badge,' our Mickey Mouse watches. And we had given a Mickey Mouse watch to the governor—and he loved it!" "He wore it all the time."

There were many staff members, legislators and neighbors who have recited various accounts of this story: Each person has their own view and understanding of what really happened and how it affected them, personally.

Here is Tom Ellick's version:

"I remember, we were standing by the pool—I was standing on one side of RR—and my two sons were with me and the governor was talking to Mike, my older boy, who was twelve at the time—and all of a sudden the governor said, "*MY GOD!*"—and he dove into the pool with all his clothes on—and he rescued Bob Keyes's little girl—his daughter. Bob was the only black member of our staff—and was responsible for race relations—or Urban Development."

"Wonderful, wonderful guy!" "And Bob and his family were there and his daughter had gotten too far out in the pool and literally, was *going under!*"

"The governor saw it—reverted to his lifeguard days—and dove in with all of his clothes on. It's something that my kids have *never* forgotten!"

"I remember he got out of the water and said," something like, *"Pardon me for interrupting our conversation!"* "I mean—*that's* the way he was!" "Then he went in and changed out of his wet clothes."

"He came into my office the next morning—which he didn't do very often—he didn't roam around—but he liked our group for some reason and he said," *"My watch is ruined—do you think you could get me another one!"* "And we did—another Mickey Mouse watch."

"Maybe six or seven months before President Reagan left office—my wife, Maryellen, had to be in Washington and I hadn't seen him since he left the Governor's Office."

"Anyway, Bill Clark, made it possible for us to go in and have a little chat with the president. We walked into the White House—went in through the East Entrance, came along—down—a long corridor—I was amazed at the degree of security in the White House! The lady who was assigned to us said, 'We've only got a couple of minutes, Mr. and Mrs. Ellick, because he's got some people waiting in the corner office, but he's in a press briefing—and he'll be out—and he'd like to just say "Hello." "He knows you're here but doesn't have a lot of time!'" I said, 'Hey, that's fine.'

"We were waiting over against a wall and suddenly the doors fling open and here's this 'flying-wedge' of Secret Service guys—I mean—I've *never* seen anything like this!.."

"They came out of the room and then veered sharply to the left, over towards the Oval Office—and the President of the United States was with them—looking down at some notes—and he looked up—over the heads of these other people and said, *"I know that face!"* "And the 'V' wedge parted—he walked over—and he gave me the big double-handshake—you know the one—and then he said, *"Excuse me, Mrs. Ellick, forgive my manners—I'm Ronald Reagan."*

"Maryellen,—I remember her look—complete surprise at RR's shy graciousness, especially after some *nine* years!" "It was so gracious of him—instead of continuing to say, *"Hi"* to me." He said, *"I'm forgetting my manners."* "Forgive me, Mrs. Ellick, I'm Ronald Reagan.*" "And we talked for a minute." He said, *"I'm really sorry that we* *don't have more time."* And I said, "I understand that Mr. President, but have you got time for a little story?" He said, *"Yeah."*

And Tom proceeded to tell the president about some American veterans he had met who had just come back from a reunion, in Germany, of soldiers of the WW II Battle of the Remagen Bridge over the Rhine River. There were German, along with American servicemen at this reunion and many had been complimenting President Reagan on his decision to attend the wreath-laying ceremony at the Bitburg cemetery, in the face of blistering attacks and blasts in the press about Jews around the world being furious that RR was doing this, in view of the fact that it had recently become known that some German "SS" officers were buried there.

President Reagan responded, *"If the American people could understand how important it was that I did that." "Helmut—Helmut Kohl was really in trouble and we needed him to be re-elected." "We didn't want Germany to go back to the Willy Brandts—the Socialists." "I knew it was important to Helmut—I knew there was some risk—but, when the trip was planned, we didn't know there were any SS officers buried there!"*

"The majority of German and American veterans who gathered at the reunion seemed to say," "You know—he did the right thing."

"He was magnificent!" "It was, maybe six months before he left office—and that was the last time I saw him." "He remembered me." "He could not have been more *gracious!"*

Chapter Four

THE SCHEDULER: A TOUGH BALANCING ACT

Patricia Gayman

"He was a very private person." "Reagan was not a pretentious person." "Sometimes staff made RR seem *ostentatious*." "He was not!" "Even a number of his Demo enemies had respect for him." "His *humor* had to be the major thing." "He disarmed them." "It was clearly his *own* humor; it wasn't stuff that anybody wrote for him."

Schedule Secretary / Scheduling Director to California Governor Ronald Reagan: Two terms—eight years. 1964—Worked for California U.S. Senator George Murphy in Washington D.C. Later for Sandy Quinn in scheduling during 1966 Reagan for Governor Campaign in L.A. Headquarters. A tall, warm, friendly lady of quiet compassion. Wm. P. Clark, Jr., said, "Make sure to record her low-key chuckle—it was so genuine."

I always felt time spent with Pat was a treat. She was perfect for RR, in a *tough* job.

In the last year of Reagan's administration he appointed Pat Director of Consumer Affairs for California. She still lives in Sacramento.

Pat Gayman remembers Reagan:

"I first heard about Ronald Reagan from my folks. I was teaching school and my father worked for JPL (Jet Propulsion Labs) in Pasadena. He was part of the Cal-Tech Management Club. They had Ronald Reagan there to speak to them in 1963 or '64."

"My father and a neighbor in La Canada / Pasadena, decided that they liked Ronald Reagan's, The Speech—A Time for Choosing"—(for Sen. Barry Goldwater) so much that they wanted to distribute it."

"They obtained a copy of The Speech and then had to get Reagan's approval. This had to be Spring 1964. I remember answering the phone and it was Ronald Reagan. I didn't know enough about what was going on —but I tried to keep him on the phone until my mother got home. I gave her the phone. I was home from teaching that summer and my father, mother, myself and this neighbor's family, starting in June till right before the election, probably distributed a quarter of a million copies of 'The Speech' all over the country. People wrote for them, they would call—we sent them all out by Flying Tigers Cargo. This wasn't done through the organization at Cal-Tech

Management Club; it was just my father, mother, me and the neighbor, Bob Heather, his wife and son. Of course, there was no Internet website with e-mail and downloads and no wealthy 'angel' to help us. Just assemble them, fold 'em, lick 'em and stick 'em."

"At first we had to up-front the money, copy it at ten cents per page and hand-collate the whole thing (eight or nine pages each) for the first thousand or so. We got to be good friends with the callers on the phones. Then, after the election, I left and went to work for Sen. George Murphy (R) California, in Washington D.C. in January 1965."

"I left Washington in August 1966, came to L.A. and worked for Sandy Quinn on the Reagan for Governor Campaign in the old Wilshire Blvd. H.Q. Quinn, fresh out of Sen. Murphy's D.C. office, handled Reagan's scheduling and, right, you were there doing the advance work, Curtis. Sometime in there I met Ronald Reagan—who knows when. It was a whirlwind!"

"After the general election, Sandy went over to run the (complex and elaborate) Reagan Inaugural Committee and I went with him. Part way through that—whomever was doing scheduling for the governor-elect—wasn't working well at all. It was given back to Sandy. I was moved into the Schedule Secretary's position in May 1967." "That function was shifted to be under Lyn Nofziger. With that many people on the gov's staff there were some issues to be resolved—but there didn't seem to be long-standing problems with anyone."

When asked how Reagan responded to the people he worked with, Gayman said, "He threw his glasses a lot. (laughs-chuckles) It was such a *benign* gesture. He'd take these funny little glasses off—throw them down on the desk," and he'd say, *"Damn it!"* (Pat laughs—chuckles again—then we both laugh loudly) "And that seemed to be the extent of it." [The past or present tense of verbs such as 'laughs' or 'laughed' sometimes changes due to the fact that these actions occurred on recent audio-taped interviews]

"Of course, I always took scheduling things to him and I remember Mike Deaver telling me," 'You know, I think Reagan throws his glasses at *you*—more than anybody!'

It was generally the people he was to meet, the tight schedule or the event itself that bugged him, not the messenger.

"As you know, I'd hardly ever go to him and tell him, 'I'm really sorry to tell you this, but that speech is cancelled!' As you recall, he was so terribly popular that everybody wanted him. And, not only that, he was good! He was *popular* and *good!"*

"We received many invitations—stacks of them—stacks! I remember, I used to send out all of the turn-downs, and Ronald Reagan—or the Auto-Pen—would sign the acceptances. But that caused a lot of problems. First of all, probably because I was a woman—and—with the title of Schedule Secretary—you know, a woman sitting in her office someplace, willy-nilly turning things off, at her discretion. So Lyn was getting a lot of flak—and—well—upset, not because the decisions were wrong, because a lot of those decisions were Lyn's; but it was the way it was done that was the problem. So, we changed it around, which worked a lot better for everybody, and that was: The governor signed all of the turn-downs and I signed the acceptances, because when they got a letter from Ronald Reagan saying, *"No,"* they said, "Oh, O.K." "And when they got a letter from me saying, "Yes!" "They were happy. A 'yes' from anybody, works. They didn't care who signed it."

"We took so many things in; letters, well-wishes, requests for personal appearances, speeches, etc. He wrote the *best* letters in the office. He used to get a lot of complaints. Remember, people used to talk about "The Nine-to-Five-Governor."

"And they never saw the size of his briefcase—the stuff that he took home from the office every night—and brought back, *done*, reviewed, checked, edited, corrected, modified—and signed—the *next* day!"

Pat and I reminisced about one of several of us whose job it was to go to the Executive Residence and take the last minute paperwork. Pat recalled how Sandy or Phil and later Bill Clark or Ed Meese would say, "Mrs. Reagan wants you to come by and bring these things—they're going to be in bed at eight." And I'd say, "It's now quarter to eight—don't worry, it's O.K." And I'd knock and politely stand there in the hallway leading to their bedroom—and they'd usher me in. Then I'd bring in more papers to be signed, and, invariably Nancy would say, *"Well, Curtis, when is he scheduled to come home?" "I certainly hope he's here right at 5:00P.M.!"* Telling this to Pat, it sounded like a 'broken record.'

Many times Nancy had dinner plans for the two of them.

Pat and I laughed. I said, That was her constant admonition. Followed by Pat's, "To *all* of us!" "Sometimes she called me, sometimes, she didn't—it depended—on the situation—the types of events." I reminded Pat that Nancy was pretty much in *all* of our lives, checking and questioning. Pat said, "Yeah, I'd say so."

I recalled that Nancy wanted to make sure that Ron was protected—time wise and rest-wise.

"Correct!"

I asked Pat how Reagan treated her when he dealt with her, and she with him, in her job as Schedule Secretary.

"He treated me really well, I thought, but no different than he treated anybody else—which really made me pleased. I was kind of glad that he threw his glasses at me, because if he had just been benign—but he threw his glasses at everybody else."

"There weren't many women in the Governor's Office or on the staff—and I was just pleased that he treated us all the same way. I never heard any complaints, otherwise."

"He was always polite, and very often, funny. Very often, funny!"

"He was very jealous of his time, as you know. We had to schedule, very particularly, around him—to allow him free desk-time, allowing him free speech prep-time to go over his speech cards and re-do his cards—and all of that stuff." Pat said. "He was terribly, (strongly), disciplined! Very disciplined—not to extremes—but he was focused—and he would do what he was supposed to do—and if you could catch him at a time when he was a little relaxed—why, gosh, it was fun—and funny!"

"I used to go in to his office or study—they would have times that I could schedule for things that I thought were appropriate—and they were usually—oh—all different kinds of things; events. I remember, once, the John Deere people wanted to come in, because something was happening and the administration in California was doing something that they didn't like."

Something was happening here in California, it may have been the Agriculture Dept., or Industrial Relations—some state agency—was doing something the John Deere people didn't like and they made this appointment for just fifteen minutes and they were going to the governor about it." So I walked them all in and I said, "Now, you be sure to tell Governor Reagan what it is that's ticking you off."

They said, "Oh boy, we're going to do that!" "So, (she laughs) I walked them in and introduced them all—and the governor stands up and says, *"Hi, I'm Ronald Reagan."*

"That was enough for me, having watched the same scenario unfold dozens of times."

We both roared with laughter and Pat said, "I mean these guys just visually—*Melted!* The governor started to chit-chat with these people, which he never totally, really liked doing—for fifteen minutes—and—when it's over—I'm leaving with them—when he called me back into the office and said, *"**Why** did I have that appointment?"*

"They had never told their story nor asked him for the change or assistance they had insisted on and requested time for in the first place!" "They were completely undone and taken off guard." Pat said she just shrugged and thought—'what could I say?' 'Well, Governor, you did it again!' "He disarmed them—and he wasn't even trying."

We laughed until our sides split. It was similar to vignettes and anecdotes repeated and revisited daily, as the various groups and individuals came to the hallowed halls of the Governor's Office for help or to complain and left, forgetting the reason for their pilgrimage, as they were befriended by and stood in awe of, as well as an equal to, this uncommon man—whom they identified as one of them. Some would say they felt the experience was *unforgettable!*

Pat said, "I thought it was really funny, here were these hard-bitten 'men of industry'—just melting. It was thrilling to watch."

Pat recalled the number of hours we all worked in those first couple of years after RR became governor. "Until June or July, we'd work until ten or eleven o'clock at night—then go out and have a couple of 'belts' and be there, in the office, at six or seven the next morning."

"But, we were young!" "It's not anything that would appeal to me at all, today—but that's just what we did back then."

I mentioned that it just seemed so right, and so exciting.

Pat concurred, "It was *very* exciting!" "But it was a lot of hard work—and a lot of hours."

I asked Pat what it was that made this Reagan administration different from the men and women in the smoke-filled rooms of former Governor Pat Brown, for instance. Did Reagan engender or stimulate this dawn-to-dark team work? Pat surprised me with her reply: "Well, he did—and it was very exciting—but there was a lot of this that happened with Senator George Murphy, when I was with him in Washington. There's something about working for somebody who is already well known—and I'll bet you the Schwarzenegger people are experiencing the same thing."

"Because, when I went back to Washington and was working for Murphy, in the Senate, with all of the staff people working for other senators—people would always ask me, 'What's he really like?' People were just fascinated by celebrities and Hollywood. And, when you start working for one—it's kind of a different milieu—and people were really fascinated with it—and that's kind of exciting, in and of itself!"

One of the more unique events she remembered scheduling and accompanying Reagan to was one of the first Rat Decathlons—that's—R-A-T—as in the rodent.

"Little white rats." "They were experimental rats which he was supposed to hold in his hands. It was put on by Sacramento State College.

Today the PETA people would have gone crazy and organized a mass march on the Capitol. RR did it—but only *once*. He never did that again, but he was always so gracious, even when he didn't want to be somewhere.

The Flight of the 'Turkey Bird.'

Turkeys played a key role in Ronald Reagan's 1965-1966 Campaign for Governor.

In the winter of 1966 it was obvious that travelling by car and train wasn't going to cut it for candidate Reagan, in spite of the fact that he did not like flying!

Several of us were brought into the act to craft a plan whereby some suitable aircraft, preferably one with a stellar safety record, could be arranged to ferry the candidate, travelling staff and press around the rural regions of California.

The craft that made the cut was offered by Mervin Amerine, head of the California Turkey Growers Association.

The plane affectionately known as the "Turkey Bird"—a silver DC-3—a more modern version of the famed C-47 twin-engine, Army Air Corps workhorse, used to fly over "the hump" into Indo-China in WWII. A tail dragging monster with loud, vibrating, radial engines. It's true! Merv offered the airplane he flew *live* turkey chicks in to RR and he accepted! This unusual story is told in a separate chapter in Vol.1, with photos.

"It was a kick, Pat recalled, especially for the press who, along with Reagan, many times set up a raucous applause each time the plane completed a landing!" "An incorrigible bunch!" "It was so funny!"

Pat agreed that *humor* had a lot to do with that campaign and later on—in the Governor's Office. "Oh Yeah!" she said.

Thus, when Nancy Clark Reynolds, T.V. Press Liaison, scheduled a photo-op presentation of a live Thanksgiving turkey with the California Turkey Growers Association in the Governor's Conference Room—how could Pat and the governor turn them down? More Governor's Office levity.

We had so much mail coming into the office, we had to sort and sift through it for possible "kook" mail from bad guys. Then, if a threat to the governor or some sort of unusual letter or package would appear, we would turn it over to our law enforcement unit to investigate, some for possible threats or bombs

During that time, even in my small office, I was given an outside citizen volunteer who had been a Reagan supporter to help us open and route this flood of mail. We were told the volume of mail was eight to ten times that of the previous governor.

Pat said, "Well, I remember we had so much mail, I can't remember if it was June or July, but poor Jean Beaver in the mail room could not keep up with it. So, they loaded it up and carried all of it to the Governor's Council Room, where the staff's wives and kids and everybody were brought in at the same time and started opening up these stacks of mail—trying to get it to wherever and whomever it belonged. Of course, none of us could cope with it, once we got it all in our offices. The good news was: It was out of the Mail Room and on our desks—but there was *no way* to cope with it."

You had to rely on volunteers to handle it since there simply was *no* budget to allow for hiring anyone to do that kind of job. A major problem was that it was beginning to *age*. Events came and went—without attention.

Pat recalled, "There was a lot of 'bad' publicity about the 'mail pileup.'" "There were pictures in the papers and everything—stories about how much mail was coming in and that the system wasn't designed to handle it. Besides Reagan's celebrity, a lot of things were just pent up."

"Every new governor gets a lot of mail, because people who couldn't get anything through with the last governor, tried it with the new one. Pat Brown had eight years of saying 'No' to a lot of people about a lot of things."

"In addition to the *celebrity* factor—everybody said, 'Yay—we've got a *new* guy here, let's send a letter and try again!"

"I had done my Washington D.C. thing and that wasn't a place I felt very much at home in. So, I didn't have an interest in going back to D.C. after RR won the presidency. I felt very fortunate that I'd had that experience with Sen. Murphy, first. I didn't interface with the Reagans much after that, except that he appointed my mother to a commission, and we went to the White House and saw him when he was president."

"People have written huge books about what the *essence* of Ronald Reagan was—what made him tick."

I reminded her that a number of those people didn't work for the man and, also, many of the books have been self-serving.

Pat continued , "He was a very private person, I thought." "He was very genial—and—he was good to work for—but he didn't wear his heart on his sleeve. There were a lot of things that were not apparent to me—he kept to himself—which I thought was kind of nice—a kind of *reserve* about some things. That was refreshing. He, many times, would be deep in thought."

Pat was right, he was a *private* guy. When Security Chief Art Van Court and I handled advance, communications & back-up security, Dale Rowlee, security, logistics, driver and with Bob Tarbet, handling overall communications, were with RR; we thought the best thing we could do was to give him the privacy, the time—the space he needed to gather his thoughts and craft his speeches; so that he could be prepared for the next event, interview or issue-statement. It was something we did almost instinctively, from the beginning.

Pat expressed her thoughts on the Old Governor's Mansion in Downtown Sacramento, which Nancy Reagan was criticized for moving out of after she found it intolerable. "Do you remember how dark it was inside that place? The only room that ever got any sunlight was the breakfast room at the back of the mansion near the kitchen. What a terrible place, especially for someone coming from Southern California with the kind of openness of the ranch-style homes there—a lot of natural light. The Old Mansion, which was built perfectly for its time, when you needed small windows because you didn't want to let the cold in—you didn't want to let the heat in—it was awful—I didn't' like it either; I would have moved too. There wasn't anybody around for Skipper to play with—no one—nothing. There were no other neighbors.

It wasn't good."

Just commercial: liquor stores, gas stations, a hotel, winos; in a word—'seedy!' Nancy was determined to find a home for her family in a real neighborhood and kept "bugging" me about it every day and every night, until I went out and found the right one.

I discovered that Pat had a different insight or feeling than a number of us did about the fact that Skipper, over the years, said he felt that his father never paid any attention to him. In later years, publicly, he expressed resentment.

"I know," Pat said, "I suspect it may be true." "He couldn't have had much time to spend with Skipper, because that briefcase the Gov. took home with him every night was packed with papers—and they were done in the morning."

"The governor did his homework."

I weighed in: Yet, every time I saw the governor with Skipper, he did *not* ignore him—he always made time—in little bits and pieces—today it's called "quality time"—he was always gracious to Skipper, teaching him or spending time talking to him. I always found that to be true—even when we put on the parties at the Executive Residence, like the staff and legislative BBQ's in the backyard by the pool; Skipper was there! Not locked in his bedroom, but, swimming, enjoying the great food, being introduced to the guests and freely mingling and talking with them. It was like we were one big, extended family. He was *involved* because Nancy & Ron wanted the children to have a normal life. (See photo page with Skipper and Patti doing all kinds of activities with Ron and Nancy)

Pat recalled that during one of these famous parties the Reagans held in the backyard of their home, she wore an authentic Victorian bathing costume, the kind ladies wore at the beach, when their bodies couldn't be shown—with that silly cap on their heads, a full bathing dress, high around the neck, down to the knees and long sleeves to the wrists, with pantaloons down to her ankles.

"It was made out of heavy cotton and as I sat on the little scaffold, the board, over the 'dunk tank'—the governor grabbed the baseball away from whomever was next.

He said, *"Give me that ball!"*

*"This is for all the times you sent me to all of those places I **didn't** want to go!"* He pitched the ball once, and—**WHAMMO! SPLASH !** Down I went! I had tennis shoes on and once they filled with water and the outfit got wet—this garment weighed a ton, and as it pulled me under I thought 'Oh My God,' I'm going to drown in the 'dunk tank' in the governor's back yard."

We all helped put these affairs on. The Reagans tried, at some of the events where it would "fit" to have the neighbors and their children attend these backyard BBQ's and parties in order to get Skipper involved, and Patti when she was not away at school.

Pat said the Reagans spent a lot of weekends down in Southern California, "Which made for a bifurcated life for the kids."

I told Pat that from back in the sixties to this day, Ronnie Jr., (Ronald Prescott Reagan) the "Skipper" I knew, has always been quiet, sullen, *cynical* about his parents—and the time they spent (or didn't spend) with him. Recently he has written a couple of articles which have been more *open—understanding*—a little more *gracious* and *accepting* towards them—but, generally, he indicated that his dad never took the time for them that some other kid's dads had with their children.

Pat said, "Well, I think probably, it's *true*—because he didn't have it to give. Look at how much time he spent on the road!"

Even when he wasn't on the road with his bulging briefcases and Banker's Boxes loaded with bills to be signed or worked over; he was gone a lot, campaigning, at speaking engagements, and responding to various man-made and natural disasters.

Pat thought seriously about this and said, "Skipper was young when Reagan went into the governor's office and a teenager when his second term was over. I am sure it was difficult. Even though Reagan was called this—he wasn't a 'nine-to-five' guy; that wasn't his job." "He was *always* available!"

Pat asked me if I recalled Mike the gardener? Indeed I did. I remembered his presence around the office when we'd arrive each morning with the well-placed, decorator's touch of fresh flowers in every office where there was a vacant table or desk.

"Mike Seeboth was his name," Pat said. "There was a flap which developed around him. There was this little closet right near the back door to the governor's office, by the elevator. Mike used to arrange his flowers there. He had a little stool and a little table—he'd pull them out—and he'd greet the governor nearly every morning, whenever the governor would come up in the elevator and go in the back door of his office. And that was Mike's wonderful little place!"

"Well, somebody got the idea that this wasn't appropriate. They were going to move Mike—out—down into the basement, someplace. And Mike was not enchanted. He liked where he was—he thought this was pretty neat. So, one morning, when the governor came up in the elevator, Mike said, 'Governor, they're gonna' move me!'

"He went to the *top*." "No middle-men here." "Mike didn't mess around."

The Governor said, *"What?"*

Mike said, 'Yeah, they want to move me—they say it's inappropriate that I be here.' 'They want to move me into the basement—and I don't want to go!'

The Governor said, *"I'll take care of it."* "And Mike *never* moved." "I thought that was just wonderful."

"Reagan was not a pretentious person. Some people made him seem pretentious, but he wasn't. Sometimes staff made RR seem *ostentatious*. He was not!"

"Future generations of Californians and history buffs have Ronald Reagan to thank for one of his off-handed remarks made in answer to a question asked by the press in the Capitol's underground garage one morning, when he arrived for work." Pat said that in Reagan's second term, Senator Jim Mills, a Democrat leader, who became president pro-tem of the State Senate, told her this story:

'During the hey-day of the hoopla and hubbub surrounding the study of the structural integrity of the Capitol Building and it's proposed restoration vs the construction of a new set of structures; huge twin towers, one for the Assembly and one for the Senate as well as new Legislative Chambers, to be located at the other end of Capitol Mall, a few enterprising members of the Capitol Press Corps met the governor as he arrived in the underground garage and prepared to enter the elevator to take him up to his office, —to ask him his views on the plight of the grand old symbol of California government, whose gold-leafed dome, it had been recently learned, rested precariously on mortarless bricks!"

According to Senator Mills, Governor Reagan said, *"Well, I kinda' think it ought to be restored."* "Nine little words." He added, *"It's a great building and it looks good."*

"That's all it took." "This off-hand comment in the garage." Pat said, "This was without any 'mini-memos' from the cabinet secretary or any staff input—this wasn't anything but the governor's *gut* feeling." Sen. Mills said, 'If it hadn't been for the governor making that statement—we would have had a hard time saving that building.'

"Reagan's comments are one of the main reasons that the Capitol was restored. RR always spoke from the heart, but he also spoke practically and I remember Sen. Mills used to have difficulties with the governor on some things, but he was certainly appreciative of his thinking and his statements on *that* one."

"Even a number of his Demo enemies had respect for him. They enjoyed him. He disarmed them! His humor had to be the major thing. It was clearly his *own* humor, it wasn't stuff that anybody wrote for him." Pat laughed. "These weren't lines that he had memorized."

We laughed at those interesting, scintillating, many times thrilling, fun days and agreed—"It just came right off the top of his head—it was so *easy!*"

Reagan has been compared to Abraham Lincoln, in many of his beliefs and principles.

His sense of humor, however, mirrors that of the twentieth and twenty-first century financial icon, also from the Midwest, Warren Buffett who, it has been said, used humor to *disarm* his opponents and even his friends. So wrote James Detar in Investor's Business Daily from a feature article in Leaders & Success, from IBD dated September 27, 2000.

In my last question to Pat, I asked her if she thought that Reagan's applying himself and his dedication to doing his job well during his years as governor helped him learn the legislative process to make him a better president.

She answered, "I would think—of course—I would think it would have been *essential*—Oh Yeah! I would think he would have had to 'cut his teeth' on this beforehand. I can't imagine becoming President of the United States without some kind of major experience like this. I can't imagine going on to be president without some governmental experience."

"The midnight Budget sessions, all of those legislative bills which went into the night, as we all waited patiently in the Gov's Council Chambers, before word came down that at last they had passed and could be signed by the governor."

Chapter Five
THE CREATIVE SOCIETY

Dr. Jim Gibson

"In the *WORST* of times he had a sense of humor—to help carry him through!"
"He was an *intellectually* bright man." "I thought Reagan did an *excellent* job as governor; first and second terms!"

Jim lives with his wife, Georgina (Gina), high in the foothills overlooking the old town of Claremont, CA, and the renowned Claremont Colleges and Universities between Los Angeles and San Bernardino, along the old highway where dark green citrus groves are now sprouting new subdivisions, on the way to Palm Springs. He has a great view of the original orange groves and some of the earliest, turn of the twentieth century, southwest-flavored architecture on the quaint, tree-canopied streets of the quiet towns serving the academic community described as the 'Ivy League of the West Coast.'

His original field, when he was in college, was Political Science. He was hired right out of Claremont Graduate School, thru the good graces of his professors, by BASICO, Inc., Behavior Science Corp.

Dr. Jim Gibson suffered a horrific accident while celebrating the success of the man he helped along the road to the presidency, which made details more difficult to recall.

During *President* Reagan's Second Inaugural festivities in 1984, the mild-mannered, conservative, intellectual Gibson was stopping by the International Hotel in D.C., doing some "corporate-advance-work," to pick up room keys for various guests who planned to attend the many inaugural activities all over Washington.

Standing with some friends at the 'Grand' hotel entrance, beneath the porte-cochere, Jim was ushered into the back of his waiting limousine (by now he was an executive at Atlantic-Richfield Oil Co.) to continue on to the next event. The chauffeur had just started to drive away when the accelerator somehow 'stuck' in the open position; similar to 'flooring' the gas pedal! The big car took off around the circular drive, apparently completing at least one lap, as it gathered speed. The driver made every attempt to control the situation—with NO success. He was unable to find an escape route or a 'soft' landing. Why he didn't turn off the key or place the gear shifter in neutral Jim did not know. The rapidly accelerating vehicle slammed, head-on, into a brick, stone or concrete wall—that part Jim could not confirm, exactly. On contact, Jim was propelled through the inside of the limousine like a human torpedo and he exited through the front windshield. He nearly died of his numerous injuries. It has taken him nearly all of the ensuing years to attempt to recover and he is still not really feeling up-to-par. He lives with constant *pain* and migraine headaches, which can't be treated.

Jim Gibson was always so serious. Dressed to a store-window perfection, always dark suits with a vest, dark crew cut hair, carrying either a couple of his trademark 'Black Books' or a bulging briefcase. Now, as I sat in Jim's living room, some thirty years later, interviewing my long-lost colleague, he looked a bit more rumpled with wisps of graying hair, looking at six, slightly faded, black and white photos arranged in a frame—that and the clothes on his back were the only material things left after his magnificent dream-home burned to the ground in the massive wildfires of 2003—here he was sitting next to RR in the back of the Gov's limo, Dale at the wheel, Van Court riding 'shotgun' and Nofziger shooting a dozen or so frames with his personal camera (candid shots) from his perch on one of the jump seats at his two laughing, critiquing subjects, fresh from a speech, with standing ovations, delivered with all of the gusto the audience had yearned for.

Reagan had taken Gibson's research material and polished it into another masterpiece; this time for a group of San Joaquin Valley farmers who needed to know that the new administration cared about them.

Gibson had written the 'Black Books' as part of his research assignment for Drs. Stan Plog and Ken Holden at BASICO during the 1966 Reagan for Governor Campaign. Fourteen little loose leaf research books of exactly how each of California's State agencies and departments functioned. Fourteen volumes divided by subject: *Agriculture, Finance, Resources, etc.*, their mission-statements and operations. Jim said when he came aboard the campaign he was asked to do *research*, not necessarily issue —research, it was "more than that." It included some "rough speech writing," as well.

Gibson said, " I found that Reagan was a better wordsmith than I was! So, I didn't mess around with that anymore. BASICO had been hired by Spencer-Roberts to do the research for the campaign and I went to work for them to do *that* research. I had never met the candidate, and I had no idea how long this was going to take."

"I probably had been working for Reagan for six weeks before I met him in person. I had never seen him in a motion picture, but I had seen him on television before. Everybody had *seen* him. I saw him make The Speech for Goldwater; which *"speech,"* by the way, should have gotten Goldwater elected—it didn't—but, it should have."

"I'll tell you an odd incident about those pictures of us which Lyn Nofziger took in the back of the limousine. It may have been June or July 1967—after Ron had taken office—and he'd gone out of Sacramento to talk to the state agricultural people. The San Joaquin Valley Farmer's Association—that sort of group. And he goes down there and he gives a *Knockout Speech!*"

"And I'm saying to him when we are returning to the Capitol, "Where'd you get all of that information, Governor?" "Reagan stopped and thought for a moment and said," *"Jesus, Jim, don't you remember?" "You gave it to me in February!"* " I didn't even remember researching it. He had gotten *ALL* of that out of the *Little Black Books!*" "He already had the facts." "He assimilated them." "He was the *best* speechwriter around!" "He was *incredible!*"

Jim produced the little black book on *Agriculture* in early 1966 and it was continually being updated. I asked Jim if Reagan had any trouble remembering facts.

"No!" "Hell no!"

"A lot of people in the outside world, who weren't close to him, couldn't believe that this man didn't just *memorize* the facts, but he *understood* them—**he was intellectually bright!" "He was an intellectually bright man!"**

"I came into the Campaign for Governor in 1966 after Spencer-Roberts had gone out in 1965 and tested the water and decided they could get RR elected. Right after that they (S-R) were hired by the Kitchen Cabinet and then, they started filling in the holes with the people they needed—one of which was research. So, they went to BASICO, who were primarily doing psychological research for school districts, and met with Dr. Stan Plog."

"BASICO had seventy-five PhD's on their staff—not all housed in their offices or anything like that—but available for various projects. They did psychological evaluations for students and programs—that sort of thing, so I went to work there. They were located in Panorama City—I was living in Pomona and commuted daily—forty miles each way through the L.A. traffic! It was tough. I worked hard hours. I arranged my hours so that I didn't have to go over there in the peak traffic times—and, of course, I came home between ten o'clock and midnight. I worked ten hours per day!"

Gibson, who hadn't formed an opinion about Ronald Reagan during his initial work for him at BASICO, was very analytical about his research task.

He said, "My field was Political Science, so my mind-set was—'Now, what would I need if I were going to run for governor!' What would anybody need to know if they were going to run for that office?'" "So I set up my research program to answer that question. In other words, I didn't sit down with RR and say, 'What do you know about agriculture!' 'What do you know about the State of California Finance Department?' "None of that." "I didn't have those questions in mind. I just decided—*Agriculture*—he needed to know these things—and I went ahead and researched them. I prepared the *basics*—on what made the California agricultural system work. What it was—what the crops were—what it meant to the state in terms of dollars—income—and where it stood in the nation. All of that kind of thing."

Jim meets The Man

"I recall the first time I met him. I was very nervous. I had been to his campaign headquarters many times, but I hadn't been to his house. The first time I met him, I met him at his house. I went to his house because we (the staff) were all meeting there, to leave in one car. And, there is a certain amount of professional curiosity about whether the kind of work you've been doing and turning in is going to be acceptable. So, it makes you a little nervous. Generally, I'm not nervous meeting celebrities—certainly *he* was a celebrity, long before he decided to go into politics. I guess I had that professional curiosity / nervousness about it. I was just *slightly* nervous. I didn't think—I didn't understand Nancy Reagan's relationship—or I would have *really* been nervous! Because, if she had been reading everything that I had been turning out—I might have been *fired* the day after the Primary ended, too, like Dave Tomshany was. Anyway, the meeting turned out well."

"He had an incredibly good sense of humor—and in the *worst* of times, he could find something humorous about it, and—that's a *good* quality."

"I would meet with Reagan daily. I went every day. I traveled with him *every* day. Sometimes I would go with him—but I wouldn't go to attend the event—I would just go to be there in case they needed something—background-information, research, facts. Because I knew where everything was in the black books. Sometimes I would go to see what questions came up—whether he was adequately prepared to respond to the questions he'd receive."

"For a while we'd try to anticipate the questions that might be asked—that would arise from the event—and that didn't work out very well—because what we thought would come up *never* came up. So, I started going to the events, listening to the questions, finding out what those people were gonna' ask him. And that was a good way to do it, because we got on to a different level than we were on before, and that worked."

"I remember his speech-writing method—with the *cards!*" " *Oh Yeah!*" " The now-famous cards were four by six or five by eight inches. He used both sizes, but the larger ones were better—because he could see better—remember—he wore contact lenses—but when he really had to do some reading—then he put on glasses."

"He had glasses that were *that thick*—(forefinger and thumb indicating)—about half an inch."

Jim said he marveled at Reagan's grasp of difficult subjects and his job. When asked how he thought Reagan did when he traveled with him to these events, since RR had never been a congressman, nor even a state senator or assemblyman, Gibson replied, "He'd never been elected to *anything*, except the Screen Actors Guild presidency, which may have been a tougher job than being governor. I thought he was *intellectually bright!*"

Jim repeated this phrase several times.

"I appreciated the fact that he had an *incredibly* good sense of humor—when things really got tough—he could find something humorous in it." "And that—*that* says something about a man. To me it does, anyway. I didn't have any doubts at all that he could be a *good* governor."

"I only stayed two years with him in Sacramento. I had to get my dissertation finished and get my PhD. I decided to write my *first* doctoral dissertation about Reagan. About him in this regard: 'What does a candidate *say* during his campaign?' 'What does he *do*—after he takes office?' "The dissertation was crafted on the premise that what Ronald Reagan *said, spoke, stated,* during his campaign is exactly what he was attempting to achieve and was actually *doing*—as governor!"

"Unfortunately, it was rejected by an outspoken critic of RR, who was one of the liberal professors on the Review Committee. This Pat Brown partisan-professor was adamant and openly challenged me after reading the thesis, stating, 'Brown didn't do this!'

Gibson said he replied to the reviewing panel member, 'Now, wait, it doesn't matter *what* Brown said, What I am getting at here is—what Ronald Reagan *said,* and what Ronald Reagan is *doing*—are the same!' 'It doesn't make any difference *what* Brown said.'

The professor demanded Gibson rewrite the dissertation with the warning and the inference that even if he re-wrote it one-hundred times—if it was on the same subject—'it might not *ever* get by me!'"

Gibson's major-professor suggested that the best thing for Jim to do was to choose another subject. Gibson's frustrated, anguished comment: "Time was a-wastin' and I finally picked another dissertation topic that had something to do with planning—state planning."

A milk-toast subject devoid of acrimony and road-blocks—rather than Gibson's personal, one-on-one analysis of Ronald Reagan's determined, focused follow-thru on his statements and promises made during the campaign, long *before* the election.

The influential professor had 'torpedoed' the thesis on Reagan's veracity and integrity, in effect, rejecting it the day it was presented. The year-in-the-making, 216 page dissertation was 'banished' to more than thirty years of solitary confinement in the dust-bin of the university's library files, like an anti-Communist treatise in the former Soviet Union.

It took many months of coaxing to get Gibson to agree to try to locate and retrieve this historic work.

Entitled: THE NEW POLITICS:
Ronald Reagan and the Creative Society,
By O. James Gibson

A Dissertation submitted in partial fulfillment of the requirements for the
degree of DOCTOR OF PHILOSOPHY in Government.

This thesis includes a detailed playbook of the entire 1966 campaign for
governor.

It will be donated, along with Dr. Gibson's oral history audio-tape, to the
Ronald Reagan Presidential Library & Museum in Simi Valley, CA.

I asked Jim if he thought Reagan had done a good job as governor. He replied,
"I thought Reagan did an *excellent* job as governor—first and second terms!" "He
sought direction, he sought information and he followed the recommendations
of his advisors. Yeah! He also found some capable people. Cap Weinberger, for
example. Cap was a good guy!"

Regarding Reagan's upper staff, like Ed Meese, Bill Clark, Mike Deaver: "There's
an interesting story about Bill Clark. After his second year in law school at Stanford
University, Bill said to himself, 'I can pass that Bar Exam.' And took the Bar and
passed it! He was appointed to the Superior Court bench, later to the California
Court of Appeals and finally, to the Supreme Court—and he *never* graduated from
law school."

"I think RR appointed him because he felt Clark was a very capable man—as
we all knew he was." "I worked often and closely with Lyn Nofziger. I felt there
was a synergism—a working camaraderie with Reagan, Lyn and many of the staff,
including ourselves. Everybody felt that way about Lyn. It was a *team effort!* Yeah!
Lyn was good at that. And RR was good at that."

It was more than a job for these people who worked so closely with Reagan.
Gibson was good at what he did because he looked at Reagan's needs and at the need
to take care of business. I reminded Jim that it was a *commitment.*

"That's right, Curtis." "We *all* had a commitment," Jim exclaimed, suddenly
energized, "Yeah!" "*Yeah!*" "And I often spent more hours in that office than I spent
at home—including sleeping—because I would take a break, have dinner, and go

back to the office—and I'd be leaving there at about midnight. The next morning, I'd try to get in by nine—usually it was ten o'clock. I could easily work a ten to twelve-hour day, including Saturdays—but not Sundays. That was pretty normal."

Why did Gibson do this?

"Because I had a lot of work to do." Jim's answer was insufficient and weak. I told him that even if he worked in a factory he would have a lot of work to do. What was the underlying, fundamental reason *anybody* would be motivated to do this? Without further thought, Gibson shot back, ***"Commitment!" "Commitment to Reagan!"***

"I could have worked only three hours per day or four or even ten extra hours per day—my salary wouldn't have been a dime more; I'd still get the same pay. I knew that."

I reminded Jim that most of us, including himself, worked between ten and twelve hours every day; whether Nofziger thought it was necessary—or not!

"Yeah!" "And that was commitment to Reagan!" My theme was: *"Damn it!"*

'You worked—did all this work to get here—now, let's make sure we do it *right*—once we're here!' *"Yeah!"*

Chapter Six
THE ICONIC RECEPTIONIST

Jackie Habecker

"There is no question, he was a real human being who was interested and cared about others, especially when he went around to say, *"Goodbye and Thank You"* when his second term was over." "That's pretty unusual." "I do not find this a perfunctory act!" "I think of all of those personal notes he wrote, primarily to Mrs. Reagan, but to others, as well." So thoughtful."

"My children have no idea, today, who my favorite governor was." "I wouldn't tell, ever." "I started with Governor Earl Warren." "I worked a good part of his administration, part of Governor Goodwin Knight's and from Governor Brown, senior, (Edmund G. "Pat") on, up through part of Governor Pete Wilson's administration. I worked for a total of seven governors. Not always as receptionist. When I first started working in 1945, I was just a clerk-typist and later became a secretary. Eventually they needed an alternate receptionist at the Governor's Reception Desk, and I became *that* in Governor "Pat" Brown's first term. "Then, in his second term, I became *the* receptionist, and continued in that job through part of Governor Wilson's administration. I didn't do any further, additional, work in the Governor's Office, after finishing my work as Receptionist for Governor Pete Wilson."

"I retired at that time. I could have gone back and worked as an 'annuitant' part-time, but in that sense it would have been very difficult for me. I was so used to being there and knowing everyone as they came in-(all of the players, governor's staff, legislators and their staffs)-if I had to be *only* part-time, there would always be someone new coming in and the next time I was at the desk, I would feel very bad if weren't able to recognize them."

Talk about dedication to one's job, Jackie was the quintessential loyal employee.

"So I chose to end my state career—and I had enjoyed every year of it!"

"I first heard about Ronald Reagan during his campaign for governor. And, of course, I knew who he was from his career."

"My first face-to-face meeting with him was probably the night or early morning of Reagan's first inaugural. Reagan took the oath of office at the stroke of Midnight on January 2, 1967. He came into the Reception Room—and they kind of congregated there afterwards. I was on-duty that night. As a matter of fact, the person who worked with me to relieve me at the desk and I came in early that evening to kind of clean up the office and make sure it was presentable and we were there for the entire proceeding. We did not go to the Inaugural / Oath of Office under the Capitol dome. We stayed right there at the Reception Desk. We were actually vacuuming and cleaning prior to the Inauguration."

The office could best be described as *shabby*. No amount of cleaning could correct it's sad condition. Rundown carpeting with holes in it, faded draperies, chipped paint and scratched, worn and soiled, sometimes shaky furniture. But when those huge double doors, with their gold-leaf lettering announcing **GOVERNOR'S OFFICE** swung open to provide access to the most powerful, sought-after, stimulating, most-photographed and photogenic governor in the history of California, everything turned as bright as a sun-shiny day after a rain shower. Seated across the large, imposing Reception Room at her historic leather-top, 'Partner's Desk,' with the controls and communications which made could make a visitor's quest a reality, was Jackie Habecker, the official greeter known as the Governor's Receptionist. Jackie was tall, attractive, polite, businesslike, and always impeccable in a tailored suit, or dress, and in her elegant red hair—*Stunning!* To many of us youngsters, she looked as if she had just stepped out of a high-fashion magazine.

She presented the picture of decorum and became a real asset to the governor's staff. Jackie had a winning smile, but she was considered 'reserved.' She learned many of the office secrets and *never* told *one* of them! It was written all over her face and showed in her actions—she *loved* her job!

"It was quite a thrill to see him come in—as governor. Skipper was just a little boy. He was very young, then. Today, I find it very hard to say, 'Ron Reagan' I still want to say, 'Skipper'—because, to me, there was only one. I wasn't introduced to Mrs. Reagan, then, and didn't meet her until she started redecorating the office."

That's when I got into trouble with Mrs. Reagan, myself, I told her.

"And, of course she was in the Reception Room a great deal. She replaced the old desk made by prisoners, that I had been using, with a beautiful antique Partners-desk, which, I believe, is still there."

"When the governor had a press conference, which was more or less a weekly thing, I would see him, and then sometimes, never, during the course of a day. The little conference room over to the West side of the office, was used as a press briefing room, and then he, with his entourage, would proceed from there out into the main hallway of the Capitol Building where they had a Press Conference Room—and he never failed to look over toward me, as he was going out of the office—and—say, *"Good Morning!"* "I felt I was in a really privileged spot, just to have that much of his time."

I recalled that He was always like that—with all of us on the staff. Jackie agreed, "Very much so." "And, *you* of course remember the whole staff being in the large Council Room behind my desk. Just for a meeting with him, or maybe it was a birthday celebration."

Indeed, I remembered the birthdays! Later on, to the day President Reagan left office, Nancy always had a chocolate cake aboard Air Force One, whenever the President traveled, in order to celebrate anyone's birthday who was with them at the time.

"The birthday parties for everyone on the staff, and everyone just loved to hear him tell tales and Mrs. Reagan was always there." (along with Skipper and Patti, whenever they were in town) "Yes, there was lot of this *giving*, which was a part of this early staff! Of course, I am sure that *you,* above all, would remember that when he first became governor, Arthur Van Court was there, as well as you—but—there was really no organized, state security for the governor, because one day, as I was returning from lunch—he was headed out the front door—I was in the hall—and this was very early in the administration—and he spoke to me."

He said, *"I'm going over to the Treasurer's Conference Room for a meeting."*

"No one was with him! I stepped inside the door, and it dawned on me, 'I wonder if he knows where the Treasurer's Conference Room is.' "So I opened the door again and went back out, just as the governor was turning to come back in." And he said, *"I don't know where I'm going."* "So I walked him over to the conference room. That was one of those rare moments when I would have had that close contact with him!"

This was one of those unforeseen moments when the governor just realized he was supposed to be at a meeting and took off, with that jaunty, purposeful spring in his step, to attend it. I am sure he gave no thought to the need for a security staffer to accompany him to a meeting inside the Capitol Building and just down the hall a short distance. This had to be about the time that we were requesting Dale Rowlee abandon his CHP uniform and adopt a 'plainclothes' look—to appear less conspicuous. Jackie and I both agreed that it was the strength of character, integrity and above all, *loyalty*, that made Dale so indispensable. "This is the same loyalty we *all* had to have," Jackie said.

"I always felt, you had to be *loyal* or you should *not* be there!" "Yes!"

Yeah, I agreed. Someone, obviously forgot to alert Dale, me or Van Court to the fact: 'The Governor is leaving—*NOW!*'

"As a matter of fact, just another aside: Having worked in the previous administration, which was Democratic, I'm sure that it took them some time to realize that I could be a very loyal person—and that time was when they had the National Governor's Conference in Palm Springs in '68. I was asked to go with them and work on that conference."

"Then I knew that I had been accepted! I did go down to Palm Springs. I was working at the front desk where the governors and their wives came in and handing then their brochures and their identification tags and things of that nature. I have the book on that particular conference and somewhere there is a picture of those of us from Governor Reagan's Office working there. It was a wonderful experience!"

"It was always my pleasure to work in Governor Reagan's office—I thoroughly enjoyed it! I was so privileged. My daughter, who was a teenager at that time remembers the wonderful times we had going out to the house for all of the backyard parties with the big barbecue."

That's why I hate seeing Skipper going on television blasting his folks. He was *always* included! Jackie agreeing said. "I know, I felt that way, too."

He acts like his father and mother never did anything for him or included him. But you and I both know that he was included in all of those events that were held out at the house, the Executive Residence, on 45th Street.

"With that big barbecue where the entire office staff and families and neighbors were invited. I went! My daughter, Debbie went and she remembers it so well! The Reagans included everyone. It is such a fond memory. Plus—I'm jumping ahead now to the second term—I was invited to the little cocktail party at the Sutter Club, prior to the entertainment at the Memorial Auditorium, and I was able to take my daughter, again—so she has some very wonderful, vivid memories."

"I had a couple of security incidents in the Governor's Office. The previous administration had installed a 'trip bar' a button under my desk to alert the State Police (actually buildings & grounds guards—not police-personnel) of such an incident. Also they had installed electric releases or openers on the office door locks, as well."

"Unfortunately, there were the disturbed people who had messages to send or give to the governor—and one lady was just going to barge right into the Council Room—and I literally had to go over and pull her away. Someone had left that little door ajar, which was also controlled from my desk"

"And, of course, we had the demonstrations—they were *scary*—yes! One young man is in one of my vivid memories. He was claiming he had amnesia—and I talked with him for a while—and I asked him if he would allow me to call the State Police to talk with him and they could, perhaps, help him. When they came in—he had a little shaving-kit-like bag—and he had a *loaded* .38 pistol, I believe, so they took him out of the office!"

Whenever we received strange packages we had a procedure to take them immediately across the Main Hall in the Capitol to our additional offices where we had a small team of people running security background checks on prospective appointees; The Special Services unit. Jackie recalled, "When people came into the offices, such as our staff people, sometimes demonstrators would occasionally try to jump up and go into the inner offices, while I was pushing the button to allow access to the doors for our staff people. Unfortunately, times became more and more difficult. I watched it evolve."

The recurring expression of anger on the part of Governor Reagan, which so many of us remember was, when he really got incensed, he would throw his glasses down—or across the Council Table. I recounted this little expression of displeasure on the governor's part to Jackie and asked her if she had ever seen him express dissatisfaction with— *"Never!"*—she shot back. "No, I never observed anything like that." "He was always gregarious in greeting people and—as one might say—kind of a trite expression—he was a *wonder."*

"Ronald Reagan always, to whomever he was speaking, whomever he met, expressed a genuine, sincere interest. I think that was very true! I think he worked very well with the legislature. I saw a lot of legislators standing by in the Reception Room, waiting to be ushered in to meet with the governor. Occasionally, a person didn't want to be held up in the Reception Room. In that case Kathy Davis, the governor's personal secretary or the Executive Secretary would give me a heads-up to press the button and admit that person the minute they arrived. Sometimes things got a little bit 'testy'—if *they* were a little bit 'testy'—it was a little bit hard to calm them down—to make them realize it would just be a short time and the governor would be with them."

Jackie did that with dignity & diplomacy. She said some didn't want to 'cool their heels' as if they were in a dentist's office. But, she added, "Others were wonderful—and very understanding."

Bernice 'Bea' Smith was the Governor's Office Manager. She arrived nearly four years after Jackie had been hired into the Secretarial & Steno Pool. This personnel pool included a number of young ladies who came right out of high school and some individual secretaries who worked for the cabinet officers.

The Governor's Receptionist, Jackie Habecker, began her work as Assistant Receptionist to the Governor in 1959, years before Smith came on the scene. Some of us feared 'Bea' Smith, as if she were a prison warden, because of her stern demeanor. She ran a 'tight ship.' Jackie had a two-fold task: to report to Smith while answering to the highest level of the administration, the executive secretary or chief of staff.

"In December of 1974, at the end of his second term, Bea Smith took the governor around to each unit in the office, so that he could say, *"Goodbye"* to them and thank them—and she brought him to the Reception Desk. I thought that was a very nice thing for him to do. I'm sure it was not *her* suggestion to do that; it was *his*. He wanted to go around to each unit—he was just *thanking* me. But I don't know of any other governor who did that. Of the seven governors I worked for—we may have had a letter from an executive secretary-chief of staff or a letter from a governor."

"I recall having letters from a couple of governors thanking me or the others for their service—but I am almost certain that Governor Reagan was the *only one* who wanted to go around to each individual unit and to every person to say, *"Goodbye* and *Thank You!"*

That's pretty unusual! There is no question—he was a real human being who was interested. I did not find this a perfunctory act at all!" "No!" "You can see a *geniuses* in people like Reagan. I can't remember any time when he met anyone, that he didn't smile."

"I think of all of those little personal notes he wrote, primarily to Mrs. Reagan, but to others, as well." "So thoughtful!"

Governor Reagan's press conferences generally created a lot of interest and a mild hubbub every time he left the office to conduct one. Jackie said, "Other governors would hustle by me and go out the door, and come right back into the office when it was over. With Governor Reagan, it was different. Everyone would be standing in the hallway, some of our own staff lining the walls of the office, inside—waiting to see him when he came out to go to a press conference—or—they'd be trying to follow behind (some of the senior staff, Nofziger, and one or two security people)—just to get near him."

He seemed larger than life. There was a constant crush of press, camera crews, Capitol visitors, school children's classes with their teachers, spectators, tourists and well-wishers, at first—then, later came the 'crazies' and the demonstrators; whenever the governor was going anyplace in view.

There was a menagerie of citizens clamoring to get a glimpse of RR, maybe a handshake, an autograph or a chance to hear that melodious, resonant, signature voice, with the soft rasp offer a few words of wisdom, in the midst of all of this cacophony.

Thru the din, on his return from one of those press conferences, Jackie said, "He just broke away from everyone else—came over to me as I was leaving the side door of his office—said, *"Hello!"*—he reached down and I introduced him to my little grandson."

"He extended his hand."

"I have a picture of the governor with my then-three year old grandson, Greg and me. I was on vacation but I had come into the office to pick up something, and my little grandson, at three years of age, is looking up at him not knowing who this big, tall man is and he wouldn't actually extend his hand to shake hands with the governor. That appeared in the newspaper the next day, and I have the same picture which I had sent in and had the governor autograph; and this is what he said, *"Dear Greg, I'll get that handshake one of these days."* and he signed it Ronald Reagan." "I have it framed and it's on my dresser." "That was so precious." "How many men would take the time to do that?" [That photo appears in this book, Vol. 1.]

This spontaneous meeting in the hallway and, half-open, side-door to the Governor's office was the last thing either of them had planned to do. But it was so like Reagan—to be so gracious, to all of us.

Jackie recalled, "Oh Yes, Curtis!" "As a matter of fact, when you see the photo you'll wonder, 'what in the world is she holding?'

"I was having my kitchen remodeled—I was on vacation—my stove, everything, was disconnected and taken out—my friend and colleague, Joan Benbrook, was going to loan me her electric skillet, since I was using a little Hibachi to cook on."

"So, I'm holding this electric skillet in a big brown grocery bag—and, of course, I'm holding onto my grandson's hand—and in my casual clothes—(unheard of)—and the press moved in to photograph the whole thing."

By this time I am laughing uproariously! These were the times that were so very special.

"But what he wrote on that photograph was precious." "I have such wonderful memories." "I was *inspired* when I worked there."

He respected the *office* of the governor. He never went to work without wearing a suit; neither did we, except when Van Court and I accompanied the governor when he went horseback riding. He set the tone for all of us. And he was the same, years later, in the Oval Office.

"Yes!" Jackie said, "That's why we had a dress code."

Surrounding this entire issue of respect and a dress code, I recalled, I *never* saw Ronald Reagan treat people, who worked for him, like *employees*. "No!" Jackie agreed.

He treated us warmly, like members of his extended family.

"Yes," She agreed. "He did."

Chapter Seven

INSPIRATION FROM THE TOP

Ken Hall

"He was such a wonderful, down-to-earth, kind of a person." "I don't know that I have ever met a person in high-office who ever had *less* of an ego than Ronald Reagan." "That's what made it so much fun to work for him."

Ken Hall reminisced

Ken Hall was raised in Pasadena, CA, graduated from Pasadena Public schools and received both a Bachelor's Degree and a Masters Degree in Political Science in southern California, before joining Governor Reagan's staff in Sacramento in 1967.

Ken was appointed Assistant Legislative Liaison to the Governor, Special Assistant to the Governor for Education, where he interfaced with nearly all members of the governor's staff, and later was appointed Chief Deputy Director of the State Department of Finance, a cabinet position, in which he remained from 1971-1974.

Hall recalled how the governor would get all of these funny letters from the public out at the house, the Governor's Executive Residence. "He would sit there in the evening and write answers to all of these letters, until we figured out how to stop them from going to the house and get his mail (this flood of letters) away from him. And he would bring these hand-written-response letters into Kathy Davis, his personal Secretary, and she would have to type them into formalized responses—so she saved a bunch of those letters and put them in her book. They are hellacious, priceless. He wrote them out by hand—he was such a "down-to-earth" guy—it was just kinda' crazy—he would write 'em out by hand—and then he would come in—and we would have some great policy at the time, that we're going to cut off the welfare stuff or something or other—and then he'd get a letter about this person who had gotten cut off—cut off the welfare list—because of *our* policies, and he'd say, *"Now, I didn't know that we were going to do* THAT!" (Laughter) *"Now, did we really cut her off?"* 'Well, yes Governor, because of our policies. The policy was—*she* didn't qualify!' Reagan would say, *"Can we do something to help her?"* 'Well, let's see if we can get her some charity aid, or something.'

"He was just such a wonderful, "down-to-earth" kind of a person. You talk about a person that *never* really had an ego. I don't know that I have *ever* met a person in high office who ever had *less* of an ego than Ronald Reagan. That's what made it so much fun to work for him!"

"I remember to this day—a funny story—Lynn, my wife, just loves this story—it is so much of his *essence*. We were in a Cabinet Meeting—and—we're talking about something or other and we put a piece of paper in front of him, RR—and he doesn't have his glasses—There's maybe eight of us in the room, something like that, and he *is* the Governor of California—and—if he wants to go to the bathroom—or whatever—we're all going to sit there and wait for him. But, this time, he doesn't have his glasses—he says, *"Oh, excuse me!"* He jumps up from the chair—he goes running into the back study—at full-gallop—to grab his glasses—comes running back to the chair, sits down, and says, *"I'm sorry to interrupt." "I'm sorry!"* I mean—'Wait a second, Governor, *You* are The Governor—if you want to slowly stroll to the other room; why not? Well, we're not going anyplace. You do *not* have to *run* to the other room—and feel like you are interrupting us!'

We all seemed to be working together for the common good—and *he* instilled that in us, didn't he, I asked Hall?

"Yes!" "Uh Huh." Hall said. "Very few people, I think, were pitching for their own agenda. I think they were very much pulling together—under his leadership and under his broad tutelage. But there were a couple of things—a couple of attributes that he had, that made *that* possible—that you wouldn't see, as an example in a Gore administration, today. An example would be—He was very much a person who created a *circumference* for you to stay within, but did not care about the details of what occurred within that circumference. And—he's obviously been faulted on that in the national press."

"I would also identify that as a *wonderful* attribute. His ability to be able to step back from those day-to-day issues, helped enormously, in terms of the accomplishments that we had in the Capitol."

Team Players

"Ed Meese was great, Bill clark was great, Lyn was great; I mean we had very good, strong staff and they all had their own kinds of attributes that they brought to the scene, and that helped enormously. But the governor's ability to be able to release himself from the details was, I felt, part of his leadership *attributes* and not one of his leadership *negatives*. He would never have been able to lead, if he had been the *detail* person. And there would be a kind of check and balance within the office, to make sure that everybody understood that everybody has got to stay within this circumference."

"And if you got out or even started getting close to the circumference—somebody else would 'call' you on it—and then we'd have to go and debate it with the governor—and the governor would be present on those issues where we got close to the *circumference* that he had established for a particular policy. It worked well! What it also did was to make it possible for us to focus on those areas when we were making a change in policy—or where we were going to detour from where we had been. Or where we were going to come close to that circumference—and kind of check that philosophical circumference that we had been working within. And I would work on that on Tax Policy, day in and day out—and—there were *always* the questions on our tax policy that we would work through with the governor. And, because, each of them were highly visible, public policy issues where we wanted him to know: 'Governor, do we want to increase the sales tax because we are going to decrease the property tax, kinds of issues?' "And here's how the balance works. His ability to be able to *release* the details made it possible for us to more sufficiently focus on the broader policy questions. As long as Reagan had the team in place to implement the details; he could concentrate on the broader policy issues. I thought this was one of the characteristics that made his administration strong."

"Let me go through three or four that I think just show why his role as governor was *very* unique. Now, since I have stayed in Sacramento over thirty-five years I have seen four other governors since then, and I look on the Reagan years as really being *very unique.* If somebody ever did do an in-depth analysis of California's governors; I think Ronald Reagan's governorship would come to the top in terms of being one of the *premier* governorships of the century!"

"One of the attributes was his ability to be able to be focused broadly and not on the details. A second capability that he had was his uncanny ability to understand *people*-relationships. I don't think he ever cared about psychology. He would tease us about—*"Don't ever go to a psychologist, I don't trust those guys."* I don't think he was ever a great psychologist. But—boy, in my job, I could bring in politician after politician —I could put them in the back office with the governor, just one-on-

one—then the legislator would leave—we'd come back to him asking, 'Governor, Governor—how did it go?'

And RR would say, *"Oh, he's going to do what we wanted him to do."*

'Well, how in the world did you get him to that?' Kiddingly—'I mean We don't have that many judgeships.' (to dole out) "We'd tease back and forth like that. He had that uncanny ability to take someone like Bob Moretti—a gutsy, Democratic House Speaker—he was Italian by heritage and he had all of the *"Godfather"*-types of characteristics as he ran the State Assembly, with an iron hand—and win him over."

"He was a "dyed-in-the-wool" partisan, hard, gut-fighting politician. But Ronald Reagan and Bob Moretti had the greatest respect and the greatest appreciation for one another. In the early 1970's there was a huge property tax / sales tax / education act change—SB-90 that I managed for three years, and that legislation was the Reagan-Moretti Tax & Property Tax Relief Act, of that era. The *reason* that came together, successfully, was because of the personality of Ronald Reagan. You wouldn't have been able to pull that off if you had had a George Deukmejian or a Pete Wilson kind of personality. You had an ability of a person, in RR, who was able, in some kind of an uncanny manner, to get a Bob Moretti to say, 'You know, I really kind of like that guy!' And I'd go to the speaker and I'd say, 'Bob, aauh, the governor needs to talk to you.' He'd say, 'Oh, hey, that's great!' 'No problem.'

"You saw this as RR was governor. You *saw* it as governor! I was not able to translate it—and predict it before he became president. But, *boy,* you sure saw it in him as governor! I mean politician after politicians, who were our cantankerous adversaries—and he being able to "melt" them into—'*Yeah*' I *really* like that guy!' 'I hate his politics, but, you know, he really *is* a nice guy.'

I asked Ken if that wasn't one of Reagan's leadership qualities.

He said, "Part of that too, I think, was a warmth that he had. Now, one of the faults of the governor, that both of us would know, was that he would never remember your name (others praised him on having such a great recall of people's names).

"The personal issues that you go through were just *not* his thing—you didn't sit there and share with him about how difficult it was to clean out the garage last weekend, or something like that. *We* didn't have the personal relationship. But you always felt a great *warmth* with him!"

"He did have that ability to grasp complicated issues—and synthesize them into appropriate policy-kinds of questions. We would work on all sorts of crazy details—on tax bills—arcane kinds of stuff—they were big policy questions, but, very arcane kinds of discussions. He would have the ability to be able to take those arcane kinds of debates and translate them into the policy issue of the moment! One time, I remember, I was charting-out for the governor and for the leadership of the legislature—we had eight or ten super-politicians of Sacramento in the room—and I'm writing out this chart, and I'm trying to show the competing characteristics of two different policies on a tax act—and—the governor, as soon as I finished the graph—well, I hadn't quite finished the graph—meat paper on the walls, etc.,—and I'm kind'a doing it on the floor and on the fly—and I'm just starting to put it up on the easel—and the governor says, *"That's crazy, that's just more money!"* As he points to the opponent's position. And then he kind'a carries it into detail. While he is faulted for *not* focusing on the details, he had an uncanny ability to be able to take those details and to translate then into appropriate *policy* kinds of debates. It was an attribute that helped enormously when you're moving fast with legislation, and you've got to make fast decisions—his ability to be able to pull out that "core" of that policy question and be able to focus on it." "It helped enormously!"

Reagan's Warmth

Two funny little stories.

In the early 1970's we had a State Budget Act that has *not* been adopted on time.

[Ken Hall shifts from past to present in his excitement to describe the scene]

"It's late—it's eleven o'clock at night—we were coming right down to the end, down-to-the-wire—for the adoption of the State Budget. That same night, my life-long friend from Southern California, had come to visit me. So, I tell my friend and Lynn, my wife, 'You guys go to Frank Fat's (*the* watering hole for legislators and lobbyists) and I'll meet you there for dinner, at 6:30.' I worked it out with Frank—he sent me the bill—but I can't make it. I'm stuck running up and down the legislature's halls. I said, 'When they have finished dinner, tell them to come over to the Governor's Office.' "They came over to the office. It's now about nine o'clock. And, we have the governor kinda' sitting around "shooting the bull" while we're waiting for legislators and I'm running up and down the stairs trying to put the thing together. It is supposed to come out of the legislature so it can get to him, that night, so that we can take action on it in the next two days."

"Well—RR sits down—(Hall laughs)—and there were a couple of other wives and families that were sort of hanging around because all of us were figuring that this thing was going to go a lot easier than it did, so there were about four or five of them sitting around him—and he sits there for an hour and a half to two hours—and he *entertains* the wives and my friends as every once in a while we have to interrupt to go visit with a legislator—and he *regales* them with stories! Oh! Yes! Oh! Such wonderful, wonderful stories!"

"They all just loved the whole evening. You know, they didn't want me, after all, they just loved the chance to meet Reagan. So, my friend gets a phone call at eleven o'clock that night from his wife, that his grandmother has died and the funeral is going to be held the next morning, and can he get home A.S.A.P.? Well, there are no airplanes out of Sacramento at that time. Meanwhile, the governor is planning to fly home to Southern California *that* night—so I said to the governor, 'My friend's grandmother has died, he needs to get back to So-Cal, could he go with *you* on the plane?' RR said, *"Oh, absolutely, of course, love to have him."*

"We go through the evening—finally get whatever our legislative-debate "crisis of the moment" was taken care of—and—Larry has described this story to me with great relish—step-by-step—how you get into the limousine, where you sit in the limo and how the security guys tell him, "No, No, you sit right here and the governor will sit right *here*, no, you don't have to be in the trailer / back-up car—then they got on the airplane, the Jet-Commander. It was described as, "We took off like a firecracker—going straight up!"

"When Larry gets on the plane he goes to the back. And the security guy says, 'No, No!' 'You sit right there and the governor will sit right *here*.' It was just the two of them. So the plane takes off and Larry says, later, 'I don't know what to say, so I don't say a thing.' 'We get up to altitude and level off and the governor says,' *"Well, Larry, we're going to go to work."* And Larry says, 'Yes Sir!' And the governor says, *"Now, here's what we're going to do. We're going to sign a few laws for the State of California."* "These would be all of the non-controversial bills that we've already cleared, as a Cabinet, that are not significant for him to have to look through. So he pulls out this box from underneath the seat, with all of this big stack of bills. And, he says, *"What we're going to do is, we're going to put the box over there—Larry, you're*

going to pull out and open up the file folder—lay it in front of me—I'm going to sign
as fast as I can—I'm going to close it up—and I'm going to put it in this box over here."

Larry said, 'We signed all the way down to L.A. It was priceless. The thought
of it was just hilarious!'

The other *"warm"* story was this:

George Steffes and I are trying to get some bill out of the legislature, in the
middle of the night. It's about two o'clock in the morning, and the governor has
gone home about nine o'clock. We were the team to try to go get this bill out of
the legislature. I forget what the issue was. At about two o'clock in the morning we
said, 'Oh shit!' 'We're aren't going to get this thing out unless the governor talks to
so-and-so "So, George and I look at one another and say to each other," 'Well, who
wants to call him to tell him he has to come back to talk to Senator so-and-so?' Hall
laughs. "We flipped a coin or something like that and I did the calling. So, I call the
security guy—at the guard house—and say, 'Hi, this is Ken Hall at the Governor's
Office—do you see any lights on inside the house?' (No Caller I.D. then.)

Ken Hall could have been a deranged hatchet murderer. The State Police guard
replied. 'Oh no, I don't see any lights on, I haven't seen any lights on in the house for
about the last four hours. They're sound asleep!' I said, 'Oh—O.K.—and thought,
'Oh to hell with it!'

I reminded Ken that that's why I rented a house across the street and down the
block—for this very thing, for the first two years, and I did it because Nancy wanted
somebody to fend off and handle these types of problems.

What did you do, then, I asked?

"I finally called the house, direct, Nancy answered the phone." I said, 'I'm sorry,
Mrs. Reagan, but this is Ken Hall down at the office and I must have the governor.'
She said, *"Uh, O.K."* And the governor comes on and I said, 'Governor, I'm sorry
but, this piece of legislation—we can't get it out without your help.' He says, *"Oh—*
I took a sleeping pill." Then he said, *"But—give me a little bit—I'll be there."* "So, you
know, then you have to go through all the—getting Dale (CHP), Art Van Court,
getting everybody moving—the whole operation."

"Sure enough—forty-five minutes later—he comes in—he's got his brown jersey on—we gave him about ten minutes of briefing, said," 'Governor, here's the deal.'

We said, 'we're bringing down so-and-so' (the key senator / author of this bill). We brought down so-and-so, put him in the study with RR, the two of them talked for ten minutes. The legislator went out the door—we go running in—asking the governor, 'What happened?' 'What happened?'

RR: *"Well, he's with us." "He says it's O.K." "He'll vote for us."*

'Yes!' So we said, 'Stick around for five minutes, Governor, and let's see what happens.' "So, we go running upstairs to the chambers—sure enough we get our vote—we get the bill out—and we go running back downstairs" 'Thank you, Governor, very, very much!' 'Thank you so much!' "I mean, he never steamed—he never stormed at us—he never said anything like, 'Damn or Crud or Crap or Fuck or anything like that.' "He just responded. He was the *same* person, no matter what the conditions."

"Now, if you met him three days later, out of context, he may not remember your name." Ken laughs.

I asked Ken if he'd answer a few questions: When did you first hear about Ronald Reagan? When did you first meet him and when did you go to work for him? Hall gave me this account: "I was the Administrative Assistant for State Assemblyman Newt Russell, in the Burbank area in Southern California."

"My first campaign was in 1964 at the age of 26. During 1966, I was working on Newt's re-election campaign during Reagan's first run for governor. But I was very close to Stu Spencer and Bill Roberts. I had worked for them in the early '60's. It was after the election in December of 1966 and through Bill Roberts, Phil Battaglia and Newt Russell and then on to Bill Clark who hired me to work with Mike Deaver, Win Adams, George Steffes and a few others to begin the transition process to establish the new government. We were the Transition Team for the departmental policy issues, at the time, starting about the 15th of December. While *you* were working on taking care of the governor and Mrs. Reagan, we were out in the departments and agencies finding out how we were going to create a new administration. Bill Clark was our leader during this process. My background really became *administrative governance* and was involved in the "guts" of running the

Executive Branch of government and then the "guts" of running the finances for the Executive Branch. It was during the last three years of my tenure, at the cabinet level where I established a personal relationship with the governor—we would work *every* day on some kind of task relative to legislative and fiscal issues."

"I just feel we can't let this legacy of the Sacramento experience, with the Reagans, be lost. I Hope this helps."

It does, Thanks, Ken.

I, also, remember those midnight runs when my phone would ring with someone looking for Art Van Court, who had, naturally, left Patrick's number at the State Police call-center, the Emergency Operations Center (E.O.C. in the California Disaster Office), so that I could locate him at the home of one of his girlfriends, who wished to remain anonymous; where he'd then scramble to get dressed, into his car and off to guard the governor on his run to the Capitol Building. As he had so ably taught me, we kept our .357 Magnums holstered and close to the bed. Our Ruger .44 Magnum Carbine rifles, with sling and clips, attached to special hardware just a "click" away inside of the electric trunk lids of our *own* radio-equipped Lincoln Town Cars, and above our Military-issue, full-face gas masks, emergency First Aid kits and custom-made Halliburton, high-impact aluminum brief cases with our reduced-size / high-powered, prototype Handi-Talkies, specially made by the Motorola Labs in Illinois, along with a *special* case for the high-tech Armalite, collapsible, Teflon or Nylon based, waterproof, small-caliber rifle and one small case of armor-piercing ammunition for the carbines. No body armor at that time; Kevlar hadn't been perfected, yet.

We tried to prepare for *every* eventuality and went through continuous training to remain "cool" in the face of extreme stress and under fire. I guess we were successful.

Chapter Eight

DEDICATED YOUTH
HELP REAGAN WIN

Sal Russo & Pat Dunnebeck Ingoglia

"We were just children." Pat Dunnebeck Ingoglia said. "I know, we were babies."
Sal Russo added. They reminisced as they spoke of the first time they volunteered
to help Ronald Reagan run for governor.

"I never went to one football game while a student at UCLA. Every morning I was at my table, for a year and a half., setting up tables for both Young Americans for Freedom and the Young Republicans," Pat said.

She had a GOLDWATER sign on her little table and when she carried the sign into the Student Union, her friend from the L.A. Herald Examiner took a photo of her being thrown out of the building.

That photo ended up on the front page of the evening edition, to illustrate the strident, left-leaning, feelings of the administration.

No one in Pat's family had even graduated from High School, however, she said she had achieved a scholarship on graduation from high school and went on to Whittier College in Southern California.

She was twenty years old and still too young to vote; but brimming with a passion for politics and good government. It was after graduation from Whittier that she transferred to UCLA, and was thrown out of the Student Union.

Pat had been involved in every kind of cause like March of Dimes and school political campaigns since elementary school, through high school.

"While I was working in the Governor's Office, it wasn't so much meeting Reagan that was important—it was continuing the Goldwater theme that was important; and Reagan was that person. His philosophy was simple, it was logic, it was not hard to fathom—it was right—it was correct!"

"I was hired by the Reagan For Governor Committee in L.A., in May of 1966, because I was the only member of the Young Republicans who did not belong to the John Birch society."

Pat was secretary of the L.A,. County YR's.

Then Sal Russo jumped in, "Curtis, I showed up on your doorstep at the L.A. Reagan Headquarters in January of 1966. The three of us were like the three youngest members of the campaign staff." (Along with Curtis Mack, whose chapter appears in this book)

I asked Pat when she first met Ronald Reagan.

She replied, "Well, it had to be at the Wilshire Blvd., offices, because that's where I have photographs of meeting him."

Pat applied to be one of the first 'Reagan girls,' was interviewed by Assemblyman Charles "Charlie" Conrad, who was running his own campaign but loved Ronald Reagan, was asked if she took shorthand and before she could explain 'No!'—blurted out—'Yes!' —because she said to herself, 'I can write short words.'

Pat got the job, later was put in charge of the 'Reagan Girls' program (crowd rallyers in red, white and blue outfits, pom-poms, etc.); Charlie never looked at her letters, she just signed them for him and kept copies.

That little 'white lie' changed her life forever. It was like the teenage boys who lied about their ages to get into the U.S. Navy, so they could serve their country in WW II.

"My cause was correct. I wanted to work for this man. It was a teeny, little, 'white lie' and I got my foot in the door. If I had not done that—I wouldn't be sitting here today!" (August 2, 2000, Sacramento, CA)

"When Reagan would come in—it was just so *awesome*—that we hardly said anything to him and we'd just let him have the platform and have him speak. He was always interested in learning what we were doing. When I was working for him on the Speaker's Bureau aspect of it—we took it all so seriously. When Reagan could not go to an event, it was my responsibility to find someone to go in his place."

"So I interviewed these businessmen, these bankers, lawyers and Indian chiefs, to go to these various functions (as surrogate speakers) in his behalf. We took it very, very seriously—and if they were presentable, physically, and if they had the philosophy of Goldwater, or Reagan—and I just prided myself in working very hard in making sure that we sent someone that was just like Reagan. I worked very hard during that period of time—it was *very* exciting!"

I asked her why she did that.

"I think it was an extension of what we started with Goldwater. That we wanted to keep working and—hopefully win an election where our philosophy could be understood." "During those times we really felt the threat of communism and tyranny. I really felt that communism could replace our democracy here in the United States. Reagan spoke—about limited government and individual freedom. We embraced his total philosophy. I didn't do anything, any of this, without the thought that he was going to win! Of course, I believed that he could win—or I would never have gotten involved. It was *our* time. We were always optimistic. They, the other staff people, Reagan, our headquarters staff—it was a wonderful cross-section of people—we were polite to one another—I mean everybody—they would come in off the streets—to do anything for him—to volunteer to speak for him—anything to help! It was a team. It was always a team, right from the beginning!"

Governor's Office Politics

Sal started right off with, "We had that split in the office. At least what we perceived to be a split between the Nofziger faction, if there was a faction which believed that we had to go out and drive to the presidency (add Tom Reed and Cliff White to that faction) versus the Bill Clark and the Ed Meese faction, which was of the belief that, if we are the best and Reagan is the best governor that he can be—then the country will demand or mandate that he is president."

"I seem to remember the *key* incidents. When people left their appointed posts or were asked to resign and all of the Governor's Office doors were re-keyed and the old ones were collected."

Pat recalled, "When Sandy Quinn (and Phil Battaglia) left—they (security) did change the locks and keys."

"I seem to remember getting all the keys back and re-issuing them," Sal said. "Because I remember—the coveted key was the governor's elevator key. The elevator key to the parking garage from the governor's study. There were only about five of them and I had one of them. And it used to irritate the dickens out of some of the senior staff—because they didn't have one—and they'd have to have me get them down there on the elevator. That was the coveted thing!" (we all laughed)

"That's when I saw Neal Armstrong—when he came up that elevator!" Pat recalled.

"I had my front-page newspaper article with his story—and he signed it!"

"I didn't have a key—but I waited by the elevator—for him to arrive."

"Usually the word got around pretty fast when some celebrity or well-known person was about to appear for lunch or a private meeting with Governor Reagan, and many of us just happened to be walking by as they exited from the governor's study or the elevator. You had a sense of pride when RR came up that elevator. I am sure you were just bubbling with pride," Sal said.

I'm sure, I said.

"Um Hm!" "Um Hm!" With broad smiles, they said in unison.

Sal, the deep thinker with the wry sense of humor, a graduate-student of Nofzigerisms, reminisced, "I think the Reagan sense of family and team persisted. It seems to me the bonds that were created during the Reagan governor's days remained. Those were pretty strong bonds. Because they were people that were relatively new to politics—they may have gotten their feet wet in the Goldwater campaign—but this was really virgin activity. Virgin territory. It was the changing of the guard from the old Eisenhower, Dewey, Taft crowd—and it was the new conservative, Western trend. It reflected the change in the country—and they were new people who felt they were a part of something—you know—BIG!"

"At one of the last events we did, we set up, in Orange County before the election in 1966, somebody asked Reagan, 'what shall we do if he lost the election?'" Reagan said that he'd come back to Orange county and *"We'd secede from the Union!"* (laughter)

"And everybody cheered!"

"I think I was probably the only person who thought he was serious." "I thought he was dead serious and I was right with him. That's what we were going to do, all right!"

I asked Sal how old he was at that point.

"I must have been twenty." "I'll never forget that—because I thought, 'Now that's a good idea.' 'Reagan's the man.' "You've got to remember—conservatives were so discouraged." Here was an 'Island of Freedom.' "Goldwater offered some hope—then it got snuffed out so badly—and then Reagan was like the last best hope—this is it! This is the last chance for freedom—in the world."

Pat added, "I think that when we were working there in the early days—we just felt so dedicated. Like those newspaper clippings I read every morning in the Governor's Office—to give to the staff. Every morning I would get there and read all of the state's newspapers of the morning and clip out all of the important issues and—you knew he was going to read these—and you did a good job. You knew he could read a lot and you had to really sift through them—you knew the issues of the day or the week—I mean everyone took their job seriously."

Sal thought back, "Deaver used to have a line which he used to say to me over and over again: 'Ronald Reagan deserves the best that can be done—not the best that *you* can do—but the best that can be done—and if *you* can't get it done—get out of my way and I'll get somebody who can!'

"I was never particularly offended by that, because I believed Ronald Reagan deserved the best. So I'd 'kill' myself to make up for my inadequacies so that nobody could do it better than I could—so that I could do the *best*."

Right, I said.

"Yes!" "We all did!" "And that's how we all felt," Pat said.

Sal added, "We did feel that way." "And we weren't resentful about it."

"No!" "No!" Pat agreed.

"I had lunch with Mike Deaver a couple of years ago," Sal said, and I told him 'Do you know I've quoted you a million times, because I tell people in my office that that's the way they should treat all of our clients, now Reagan was special for me, but they should have that attitude." "And Mike was shocked—that he would say something like that." Sal continued, 'Well most people thought you were kind of an asshole about it—I happen to have bought it.' I thought, 'Boy, Reagan deserves the best—and I'm happy to do the best that can be done!'

Sal went on: "I always thought one of Reagan's great strengths, that surely served him well, but bothered me from time to time, was that he had this great faith in people. It certainly was important in the way he looked at the world—and a key to his success."

"I used to have my 'shots' at him and would complain to him about people I thought were disloyal. He had an expression that he used—it was along the lines of, *"If you hire somebody on to the ranch—they're gonna' be O.K."*

"He just believed that if you went to work for him—that you'd put your personal views aside and you would serve Ronald Reagan. And he believed that! And he did not suspect that somebody had their own agenda."

I asked Sal if he thought that Reagan was suspicious of people.

"No."

In fact, I said, he was so naive in many respects, I felt he trusted, sometimes, the wrong people.

"Right!"

I told them I thought it was just amazing that we sort of gave him that cocoon and that kind of a glass or invisible shield, and yet we tried our best to be absolutely honorable. He could have been surrounded by bad guys—and maybe he would never have made it. I don't know.

Sal opined: "When you get into Washington you have so many people that are operating on their own agenda there. It is inevitable that you end up filling the White House with people that are there for their own purposes, not to serve Ronald Reagan. We didn't have much of that in Sacramento! The second term more of it than the first term. I think it's true of every administration—the resume'-builders show up in the second term. The first term are the believers who want to change the world. The second term are all the resume'-job-seekers, people trying to advance some cause or another."

"My advice, consistently, to Deaver, and to Clark and everybody was: 'The Californians ought to stick together, because we all have a common purpose and we know one another for our faults.' And I remember trying to play a little 'shuttle diplomacy' in 1980 or 1976, whatever it was, when Mike and Lyn were battling away—about—'Look, the things you're saying about the other one—you've got a good point, that's one of their weaknesses—but we know each other's strengths and weaknesses; let's not let any rascals from someplace else get in the middle of us!'

Sal summarized:

"That is a key part of Reagan. He believed in people. They would do the right thing. He believed that if given the opportunity to do the right thing—they would!"

I asked Sal when he first met Ronald Reagan and what was he like—what was his first impression of him?

"One of the guys who was in our Youth for Goldwater political action group was a press intern on the Goldwater plane, during the campaign. In the course of that he became acquainted with Ronald Reagan and kept in contact with him. He wanted Reagan to come to our campus at Cal—Reagan thought and said it probably wasn't a good idea for him to come to the campus."

"So he didn't do that, but he came up and did something else—another event— and he needed to have his car shuttled. So I shuttled his car for him. Boy was I impressed. It was a maroon Lincoln with a black top. He wouldn't fly in those days— so when he came up from L.A.—he drove. He had his name / signature engraved in gold on the glove box. (actually a brass plaque from Ford Motor Co.) I guess Holmes Tuttle had it done for him. Amazing to me was the fact that this car had an air-conditioner. I didn't know that houses had air-conditioners, let alone cars!"

Sal grew up in a family of commercial fishermen on Monterrey's Cannery Row waterfront, with generally cool to mild temperatures year around, where his old-school Italian family worked very hard for everything they received. Certainly Ronald Reagan's shiny air-conditioned Lincoln was unfamiliar territory.

"So, I was really overwhelmed by this car. That was the first time I met Ronald Reagan. I had heard The Speech and he was everything we have come to know about Ronald Reagan. He was charming. He was nice. He was engaging. He was not aloof! You would never have known that he was a Hollywood star. He was "Aw shucks"— as always—he was conversant, and we talked He was interested in what we were doing at Berkeley, he was glad that there was a 'beachhead'—and he went on and on about how glad he was that we were fighting the (conservative) fight there."

And—he was encouraging!" I thought—'Man, I think this guy's the world's greatest!' "I don't think, at that time, there was talk of him running for governor."

"I think he decided that he was really going to run in mid 1965—and I decided that I had to be part of it and I made some foolish assumptions. I had learned in Political Science class that you should 'go where your ducks are.' In this case the most Republicans in the state were in Southern California—in Orange County. So I decided to go *there*. I mean, physically move there—bag and baggage. Yes! And I didn't know one city from another in Orange County—so I just looked at a list of cities and picked the City of Orange in Orange County."

Sal's youth caused him to literally fly by the seat of his pants.

"How's that for dedication?" Pat said. "Unbelievable!"

"I just packed all of my worldly belongings in my car and I drove to Orange.

She asked if he had graduated from college.

"No! I had just finished my freshman year at Cal Berkeley. In order to keep my draft deferment, I looked around to see what colleges were in Orange County and enrolled in Chapman College. My family, the Monterrey Bay fishermen, thought I was crazy. They were all Democrats, to boot! So, I just marched into the Orange County Republican Headquarters and said: 'Here I am!' "And I didn't leave. I was there morning, noon and night. I was lucky in Orange County, because you know how I was, Curtis, I would never leave—you couldn't get rid of me if you wanted to."

I tried to get 'rid' of you—if only to get you to eat, use the restroom, shower and sleep! Russo laughed.

"And I was that way in Orange County, and Denny Carpenter who had become the county chairman, later state senator, and Gus Owen was the executive director and Walter Knott, the patriarch of Knott's Berry Farm, used to be around a lot—and Walter took a liking to me—because I wouldn't leave. Frank White, the general manager at Knott's Berry Farm used to feed me, because I was as poor as a church mouse—and they'd feed me at the Chicken House restaurant at the Berry Farm and give me Boysenberry preserves, which I ate morning, noon and night. I had that three meals a day! I was so poor."

The only other activity Sal did 24 / 7 was *work!* I watched him.

"Later, when I got to the headquarters in L.A., lived on the Reagan fund raisers." "Thank God Reagan went to a lot of fund raisers—because that was the only food I ever had!"

Sal drove dignitaries to the events, he helped set them up and was an all-around 'gopher' both in Orange County and L.A.

After the bad press generated by Reagan's walk-out from the convention of the all-black California Chapter of the National Negro Republican Assembly in Santa Monica; RR decided to step up the number of events he would do, statewide.

"Reagan had an Orange County swing right after that 'downer' time," Sal said. "There were too many events at the time—because *you* were overwhelmed with events, C.P." "So, I got put in charge of three of them. One of them was the rally at Cal State University at Fullerton. The campus was new and they had never had a rally there before. We had no idea whether we were going to get one student or one thousand. But we did have a huge crowd, I remember. That's how I got originally hooked up with you, Curtis. That's when I worked with you, on those events."

They really went beautifully! Especially on the heels of the bad-press event, I had mentioned.

"I felt that I was the beneficiary of the good events—not that I didn't do a good job—but good timing and being in the right place at the right time, helps. It is scary that I had security responsibilities at the time as part of your Advance Man's Checklist. It was tricky having a female escort the candidate or dealing with security agencies at the time."

The Advance Scheduling Handbook referred to 'Advance-men,' at the time.

"When I think about doing a speaker's bureau, Sal, Curtis, and what was I— twenty-two years old? Pat said. "And I'm deciding who is going to speak for Reagan!"

I thought out loud, 'In the Goldwater Campaign in '64—following those conservative ideas—we had this common bond. It was like some *underground* movement.'

"It was! We were not welcomed! No question about it." Sal and Pat agreed.

"I had been very tolerant of people that I think are kind of 'nutty,' in politics, because I remember so vividly in the early '60's, even before Reagan, feeling unwelcome at things / events. That I was some dangerous 'Right Wing' person! And I probably had some kooky ideas, myself," said Sal.

Pat countered, "Well, I think that our kookiness was that we had a lot of *passion*. And people didn't have a lot of passion at our age."

"We were motivated because we thought there needed to be a revolution—and we thought Reagan could be our revolutionary leader," Sal said.

Pat's ideology came out, "I felt, very strongly, that I was probably more Libertarian than conservative (less government) and then, when I saw the books in Reagan's office, being more Libertarian, I was very excited about that. And he kept it *secret* too."

"Right, he was a lot more Libertarian than anybody ever gave him credit for— that's for sure," Sal recalled.

"I don't even think they thought of it," Pat said.

Sal got into the history of Reagan's political views here: "He was *very* Libertarian." "During his governor's years—on the social issues—he was very Libertarian." He became less so, later."

"Yeah, I thought he had changed quite a bit when he became president," Pat said.

Sal added, "He talked more conservative than he actually was. His conservative rhetoric got higher, I thought. But his conservative actions didn't. You have to be careful in the use of terms, here."

"If you talked to him when he was governor, he was definitely much more Libertarian than people thought he was. His sympathy with the students, and free speech, as an example. He felt there was a strong support for law enforcement—but he saw an oppressive police power."

Sal continued: "Reagan used more social-conservative rhetoric as his presidency went on. He kept his conservatism, in terms of public policy, more on the foreign and economic fronts; but not on the social fronts."

RR would go out to the Capitol steps for some gigantic rally, it may have been the one for Caesar Chavez and the grape pickers or the Anti Vietnam War/Anti-Draft Rally with thousands marching, screaming and shouting epithets against Reagan or just in favor of their cause; where at one point RR made an aside to Art Van Court and me as we were scanning the crowd, while he looked up into the elegant three or four-story rotunda and balcony overlooking the West steps of the grand old Capitol building, He said, 'God, if it gets much worse, we're going to have to send somebody up there and dump some hot oil on these guys!' Like the storming of a Medieval castle. He would make those little cracks. Well, I don't know whether he was clowning because he had those wonderful, laughable one-liners and he knew we would laugh too.

Whether he was trying to calm us down and not be too fearful or, maybe he was serious. And, then again, maybe he was just trying to pacify Van Court, who was ready to fire up the burners and get the hot oil up there!

Sal was the first to connect, "Yeah, Yeah, Yeah!" (he laughs) "I think that a lot of you mistook his religious faith and his belief in God—and his view of how he fit into that—and extrapolated from that that he must believe a bunch of things that he didn't believe."

I said, 'Hold it'—please expand on that! This is an important subject that I think needs to be fleshed out. Do you think he had a faith in God? I do.

Sal quickly said, "Oh Yeah!" "Oh Yeah!" "He did, but people assumed that because he did, he then subscribed to what some called 'The Christian Intolerant Agenda.' And he didn't." "I remember, he used to make impolitic comments, all the time. It was kind of in the vein of 'locker-room' talk." "You know—you'd never want it quoted—because it's just things that—not to make his sexist but—*guys* just say. And they don't mean a thing."

The difference was, I told them, that they were not said in public forums.

He continued, "I saw that in the Nixon White House tapes. Reagan certainly did it all the time. Reagan was never short of words. He always had some comment to make about somebody who was walking along with their pants on backwards or something. He always had something to say. And those were just off-handed remarks—and he'd be embarrassed if they ever got printed."

But, we always enjoyed the repartee of these little one-liners.

"Right!" "He was not a quiet type," Sal said.

Pat, who had been deep in thought said, "I think it's sort of a release—a therapeutic thing for people—when they do that. On religion, I can remember one night we were at a cocktail party and Don (her husband) and I got on the subject of religion or the Bible—Reagan really knew his Bible. He was talking to us about certain passages and what was happening. I think we were talking about the gift of the Jews and how important they were—and he was quoting sections of the Bible. He kept going on for a long time. It felt like he had a need to talk about his faith. I know that we were (that night) both impressed with his knowledge of the Bible and how it was important to him; that there were many things in the Bible that helped direct his life."

I told the youngsters who had matured into conscientious, caring, successful adults, that this subject is vital; because this is a side of Ronald Reagan that most people don't know a lot about.

Pat continued, "I think he came with his religion. It is not a religion that he found *after* he became governor, or after he was president—or—after he went into politics. I think his faith and his religion was *with* him—when he was found to be a leader. It was there! It was there all of the time. And that's how we all felt—about him."

Sal added, "When he was shot he has said that that changed his life. That he didn't have any right to be there; that he was there by the grace of God. I think he saw his life more spiritually from that time forward. And that may account for why people saw him as more conservative and less Libertarian than I think he really was."

Pat then added, "But, the Libertarian part was that his faith was his. He had his own definition of his faith and it didn't have to be identified with a group."

Sal said, "He was not much of a proselytizer—but I wonder if that was because his father was Catholic and his mother was a Protestant—because he was in a mixed religious household."

Pat went on, "I can remember that Don and I were very impressed with his sincerity. I think that the passion we all had still continues."

You both contributed more than I did. I listened to him, I took notes and I did what he asked me to do, and I gave him advice on things that we shouldn't be doing (events, logistics, scheduling, traveling and issues with Nancy, the Executive Residence and operations at the ranch where we kept our horses—but you, Sal, talked philosophy with Reagan.

He laughed, "I had to do it on the sly, all the time."

But you did it!

"Whenever I got my 'shot' (chance) at him; I worked him over really good," he laughed again. Sal was one of those who appreciated *every* single moment of his time with RR. He felt they were precious and wanted to learn from this man he admired so totally, at every opportunity. Sal said he did it to learn *all* he could from his mentor. I knew it then, because we were as close as brothers, and treated RR like a father and grandfather combined. Some 'sixth' sense told us that RR would make some sort of material change in the world and that we were destined to be a part of it.

Sal ended our interview by mentioning that whenever he was in the White House, it was a rare occasion when the president had *one* moment to talk with anyone from the old California (Governor's years) Reagan Alumni, unless they were involved in current, immediate action-events. Those thrilling old days of discussing social and political issues and philosophical ideas with RR in the 'Horseshoe' hallway on the way to the Executive elevator or a meeting were gone forever, now that he was president.

"How rare and *sweet* it was, we agreed!"

Chapter Nine

REAGAN SETS CORNERSTONE
ON ENVIRONMENT

Reagan & Laxalt meet to Save Lake Tahoe
Nevada State Senator Lawrence Jacobsen

"I guess our reward for these efforts is being able to view beautiful Lake Tahoe—
still blue, still clear—and say, we had a little bit to do with saving it."

Newly inaugurated California Governor Ronald Reagan agreed to meet with his counterpart, Nevada Governor Paul Laxalt in the Winter of 1967 at one of America's largest ski resorts, Heavenly Valley, where the deep powder snow, and the beauty of the 6,000 foot-high pristine lake, were interspersed with lively gambling casinos and a cry for "Help!" echoed through the 80-100 foot tall Ponderosa Pines from lovers of the breathtaking High Sierras worried about the future health of their crystal-clear alpine lake.

Lake Tahoe has been compared with only one other deep lake in the world; Lake Baikal in Russia.

Reagan's environmental record was negatively distorted by the liberal media from his first days in office and his feelings about Tahoe were no exception.

In the winter of 1967 a number of us traveled with Governor Reagan to Tahoe after helping to set up the advance operation, to make the meeting of the two new governors as smooth as possible. It was my first visit to the nearly 1,600 foot deep alpine lake made famous by summering Indian tribes, early explorers and later by Mark Twain. It was breathtakingly beautiful! No wonder it had become such a bone of contention.

Nevada State Senator, Lawrence "Jake" Jacobsen * Douglas County, was a Nevada assemblyman when he first became involved in the complex Bi-State legislation being crafted by the two states to present to congress in the form of the Tahoe Regional Planning Agency, the T.R.P.A., as it evolved from the Lake Tahoe Area Council. The main issue for Jacobsen and his constituents: That, while the concentration of concern was being directed at the preservation of the alpine lake's beauty, quality and clarity; those in authority didn't lose sight of the rights of Nevada's property owners; some whose timber interests and shipping operations, along with their Grant Deeds dated back to the 1870's.

When Jacobsen was informed that Governor Paul Laxalt, who was later known as President Reagan's 'Best Friend,' in the 1980's, called for a 'closed-door' meeting on the future of Lake Tahoe in his office—and Jake had not received an invitation— he said, "I waited outside the door until all of the participants were inside, then opened the door to the Governor's private office and went in." "I asked Paul if I was 'not welcome' and said that I would leave if he, the governor, requested it." Governor Laxalt said, 'No, Hell, just sit down—have a seat!'

Jake said, "It appeared they wanted to have this meeting to get everyone to commit to some kind of an agreement on Lake Tahoe and I didn't see Reagan there at that time.""Paul had either met with him before or just after that meeting in the Governor's Office."

"I think Paul felt that the plan might infringe on private property owner's rights, therefore he might have been hesitant to invite me. This was a large group of people representing various areas and constituencies at Lake Tahoe, as well as the new governor's State Engineer and the Director of Natural Resources."

Jake told the governor that if the group and Paul didn't want him there, he'd 'go right out that door.' Governor Laxalt told Jake to stay, but after the presentation of the purpose of the intended agreement with California and the fact that it would have to be ratified by the respective states and an Act of Congress—it seemed that it would certainly infringe on private property rights; so Jake voted *against* it, in spite of his being among many Republican friends who were strongly in favor of the Bi-State Compact.

Laxalt had a lot of friends in business in Nevada, not to mention the casino gaming business at Lake Tahoe—but he was steadfast in his commitment to join Reagan in working with their respective state legislatures to craft a palatable measure.

Nearly two decades later in his 1984 address to the Nevada State Legislature, now U.S. Senator, Paul Laxalt told the assembled body, "I intended to keep Lake Tahoe from being *raped*—but I didn't intend for the property owner's to be *raped* in the process."

Jacobsen said that Laxalt told him he and Reagan were in 'complete compatibility' over the need for a plan to protect Lake Tahoe. He said, "This was the last time I heard any more about the T.R.P.A. Compact between the states until it came up on the floor of the Assembly."

"My colleagues in the legislature and I later met with Laxalt at the Governor's Mansion, and after that with our California counterparts, in Placerville to work out the details."

"Now that it's all said and done, more than thirty years later, I have to admit *something* was necessary to protect Lake Tahoe."

"I became chairman of the Lake Tahoe Legislative Oversight Committee for two years, even though I was originally opposed to the Bi-State Compact. Today, I think that it was probably the best type of arrangement that could have been crafted for Lake Tahoe, under the circumstances whereby there were *tremendous* differences between the two states. At least it removed the (land use and environment) problems from the courts! It left it up to local control," the senator said.

One of Ronald Reagan's key arguments for this or any government program.

"I think the *best* was realized, anyway, and the people got some representation," Jacobsen said. "It was a topic, now that we can look back on it, that had some *merit*, there's no doubt about that!"

I thanked Jake for his candor.

During the mid 1980's, when Reagan was president, the people of both states were in turmoil over Lake Tahoe, again when the T.R.P.A. restrictions became so onerous that even to install an extra bathroom, construct a concrete sidewalk or pathway of stones to your single-family residence or pave a driveway for an extra car—all on your own private lot or residence—took nearly an Act of Congress. In that period I was elected president of the Tahoe Sierra Preservation Council representing over three thousand five hundred Lake Tahoe property and business owners, who presented their grievances against the T.R.P.A. to their respective state legislatures, various state and federal courts, Congressional committees, some all the way to the U.S. Supreme Court.

It was an arduous uphill fight for those property owners to realize equity but many were successful and fairer rules and regulations were promulgated in the process.

The facts became clearer that this early entry into the field of *environmental protection* by Ronald Reagan, with the help and assistance of his friend and colleague, Paul Laxalt, through lots of hard work and consensus-building, was the only viable solution to accomplish the two key, fundamental objectives: Preserve the Lake and protect private property rights.

Former Senator Laxalt, in his memoir entitled: Nevada's Paul Laxalt: A Memoir, 2000, and through the kind permission of his Administrative Assistant, Tom Loranger, said of his and Ron Reagan's first major environmental effort together, 'I guess our reward for these efforts is being able to view beautiful Lake Tahoe—still blue, still clear—and say,' "We had a little bit to do with saving it.'

Senator Laxalt and I later became closer friends when I became chairman of the Nevada Republican Party and I found I could count on him to support property rights issues as well as confirming Ronald Reagan's early commitment to Environmental causes.

The results were summed up best by Rex Hime:

Rex Hime, whose chapter appears in Vol. 2. of this book, was appointed by President Reagan as his representative to the Governing Board of the T.R.P.A., according to the Bi-State Compact, in which he was not a voting member. Hime served from 1983 until 1990.

"My mandate from the president, was to be his eyes and ears, as well as his voice. It was a dual mission. One, to work to save the pristine quality and nature of the Lake—this treasure—to protect it. Two, to protect the little people, those who were not 'fat cats;' people who had saved their money all of their lives and planned to build a cabin or retire on the property they had been paying for all those years."

"After all of this pulling and tugging, it has now become a real live, quality, destination resort with many positive changes and a strong economy!"

"Individual liberties were protected simultaneously with the protection of the Lake and it's environment," Hime declared.

Reagan Was Way Ahead of His Time

Governor Reagan was instrumental in achieving many notable, positive, environmental accomplishments. I was privileged to be a part of one of those in 1970: The Governor's Conference on California's Changing Environment at the Ambassador Hotel in Los Angeles. It allowed for and encouraged the presentation of a plethora of 'white papers' and scientific, breakthrough, cutting edge documentation and seminars. It included the exhibition of working / functioning experimental electric and alternative-fuel vehicles by manufacturers, including Westinghouse from the U.S. and Enfield from Great Britain; along with others from around the world.

Governor Reagan, in the February 1970 edition of Nation's Business Magazine, published by the U.S. Chamber of Commerce and no longer in publication, in an article entitled: OUR ENVIRONMENT CRISIS, made a number of key statements which he used in speeches, 'white papers' and reports originally generated in the Governor's Office, the agencies and departments of his administration or in the mind of Ronald Reagan, himself. In deference to Nation's Business, and finding no source from which to obtain permission for even these excerpts (which have already been used in other works and press releases) due credit is hereby given to Nation's Business for the following three paragraphs attributable to Governor Reagan:

1. *"There is no conflict between business and government on the necessity for antipollution action. In fact, some industry leaders are far ahead of their government counterparts in actually doing something about pollution."*
2. *"Government can help stimulate the necessary technology in all these areas of environmental protection through wise regulations. But government must make certain the laws make pollution unprofitable for everyone. Whatever regulations we adopt must be uniformly applied."*

"We have enacted the strictest water and air pollution controls in the nation. Last year we adopted a pioneering program to control pollution from jet aircraft. We are putting into effect noise controls." "We have an Environmental Quality Control Council looking into every aspect of environmental control—it will recommend policies for the state to follow."

And he meant it.

Chapter Ten

"GO-FER" MAKES GOOD

Curtis Mack

"I wasn't one that was on the 'inside'—I was the 'gopher' on the staff—and that was fine with me." "I didn't have to be next to him." "I felt comfortable with who he was and what he was doing." "I wanted to help him!"

Curtis Mack was as even-tempered as anyone I had ever met. He was calm, cool under pressure, polite quiet, a business-like dresser and a good representative for candidate Reagan. His essential key ingredients; character and integrity. I don't think I ever heard him complain about anything.

His only political history, he recalled, was on the part of his paternal grandfather who in 1912, a couple of years after arriving in the U.S.A. from Europe, became President of the Teddy Roosevelt "Bull Moose" club in New York City. That was the sum total of his background in politics, until he watched Barry Goldwater on T.V. at the 1960 G.O.P. Convention remove his name from nomination in favor of Richard Nixon, and at the same time send a message that 'the time for conservatives was coming,' and they should 'get off their butts and go out and work and come back in four years, 'if Nixon didn't make it.

"I was impressed more by that speech than anything else Barry Goldwater ever said. I was also fascinated and struck by Reagan's 'The Speech' in 1964, on behalf of the senator, and that whetted my appetite even more. I was an undergraduate student at USC in March of 1966 when it was announced that Reagan was going to come to the campus in early April. I volunteered to be the student contact. And the staff person I was to meet from the Reagan Campaign was some guy named Curtis Patrick. The event was held at Bovard auditorium, the stately, Ivy League-style structure which held 1,600 and there were about 600 students, estimated, standing outside in front of the statue of Tommy Trojan, listening to P.A. speakers. And there was a standing ovation inside and outside for candidate Reagan at that event."

"I walked away saying to myself," 'Ooooh!'" "Gee, I've never done this before, but this is kind of fun! I was twenty-one and this would be the first election I could vote in. Eventually we had all five candidates for governor on campus to speak, but the most students we could round up were a couple of hundred for the other ones, including George Christopher, who supposedly was the front-runner."

"I also worked as a stock boy at Bullock's Wilshire and depended on L.A.'s 'rapid' transit to get me to school, to Bullock's, my parent's apartment and back to USC."

"In May, I quit my job at Bullock's and went to the Reagan for Governor Headquarters on Wilshire Blvd., so I could spend time volunteering, to help the campaign. I was a 'go-fer,' and worked for free."

Curtis Mack could least afford to be a volunteer for anything or anyone—but he said that he felt he was driven and compelled to work for Ronald Reagan, and would do anything to get a permanent job with the campaign.

"When school was out in June, George Young of Spencer-Roberts & Associates, offered me a paid job as the 'Office Gopher' at $100.00 a week. I would do driving, go get lunches for staff or run a piece of correspondence up to San Onofre Drive, Pacific Palisades, to the Reagan home. As I remember, the Reagan's driveway was parallel to the front of the house, and heavily landscaped, so I parked in the drive, walked a few feet to the front door, handed the envelope to some staffer and turned around to see Nancy Reagan tapping her toe on the driveway because she was trying to get *her* car out of the garage which, of course, I had blocked—and drive down the driveway, herself.""She didn't say anything. My first thought—I was in awe! I was in awe, totally!"

"Sometime later that summer I moved from working as the 'office boy/'go-fer' there to working for Ed Mills, the banker in the Finance Office, helping to count the cash and do the bank receipts, besides going to every event I could possibly go to. If somebody would let me go to an event—I would try to get an 'O.K.' to go to it because I wanted to learn everything I possibly could about what was going on in the campaign and fortunately, everybody was very nice to me and allowed me to do that."

"Sharing ground-floor offices across the hall from my office, was the Youth for Reagan operation with Arnie Steinberg and Lou Barnett, whom I became great friends with later on."

"At this point I became somewhat disappointed with what I saw coming out of this 'youth' bunch, so I proposed a plan which I created called First Time Voters for Reagan. I had this plan because I wanted to do something more constructive. Here is where I had a very strong and very *hard* political lesson I learned, as a result of this!"

"I had put the plan together with a budget and one of the people in the office said, 'Why don't you show it to Henry Salvatori,' Whom we all knew was one of Reagan's *key* financial backers and advisors in the Kitchen Cabinet. Here's where I interrupted Curtis Mack with, 'Oh My!' 'That's going over a lot of heads!'

He shot back with, "*That's* the lesson I learned!" Then he laughed and said, "And—Henry liked it. I think the budget was all of—in 1966 dollars—$2,500. And Henry said, 'I'll write you a check.' "A day or two later—Bill Roberts came down the stairs from his offices in the headquarters and said," 'Oh, Curtis, I understand you had a conversation with Mr. Salvatori?' And I said, 'Yeah, Bill, I haven't had a chance to—'He said, 'FORGET IT!' "It was a lesson that stayed with me. That was the end of it; right there. Bill and I became good friends over the years, but that was the end of First Time voters for Reagan. I was just hoping it would be something positive and creative."

"I spent the rest of the campaign working in Finance and put my nose into as many staff meetings as I could."

I asked him when he first actually saw Ronald Reagan, in person. I acknowledged that we had just skipped over a huge area and I wanted to get back to the basic fundamental reason for Curtis Mack's strong identification with RR, which caused his life to take the direction it had taken.

"In person? The first time was at the USC event in April of 1966. I was obviously—affected. Oh, darned right!" "Yes!" "That went extremely well. I became much more attuned to what he was saying and how he was saying it. And, I liked the message—for a more conservative government. That's what I was interested in. I didn't see him very often. I didn't see him that often. I wasn't really *ever* alone with him. I would see him at events that I was working, but I wasn't one that was on the 'inside.' I was the 'go-fer' I was the young 'whippersnapper' on the staff—and that was fine with me. I didn't have to be *next* to him. I felt comfortable with who he was and what he was doing, and I wanted to be a part of *that* and help him."

I asked Mack why he had worked a minimum of twelve hours that I knew that he had worked per day, up to eighteen, sometimes, and a few twenties.

He said, "Because I *loved* it!" "I loved working for *him,* RR, even though he didn't know me from a 'hill-of-beans.'

I probed further, 'How did he treat you when he saw you?'

Mack answered, "When he saw me he treated me just fine!" "But as everybody knows, Ronald Reagan never had a great memory for names."

Some felt he did—others felt he didn't, I said.

"He had a great retention of *facts*—he remembered faces, but he didn't necessarily remember names, unless you were there with him all of the time. He would see me and it was like—*"I know you—you're on my side and on my staff—but—who is this, again?"*

"So, after the election, Ed Mills came to me and said," 'Do you want to go to Sacramento, to be a part of the new administration?'

Mack had one year left to get his degree from USC, plus an obligation to complete his military training through the R.O.T.C. and declined to go to Sacramento, however, he visited Lyn Nofziger periodically at the Interim Government H.Q. at the L.A. Ambassador Hotel cottages, out back where some forty years prior, right there on Wilshire Boulevard, near downtown, according to my Uncle Richard Colyear, Sr., the citizens of L.A. could shoot ducks on a natural pond, surrounded by cattails. The layout, while not an impressive high-rise, provided easy access for all of us. Mack met with Lyn to gather material for papers he was writing for his class on Politics & Propaganda. He kept in touch with Lyn over the years but didn't go to the GOP Convention in Miami Beach in 1968—he was still in grad school.

Then, when school was finished and his Air Force duties were completed, on to the California H.Q. of the Nixon for President Campaign to work for Nofziger, who was Co-Chair of the campaign. Mack got involved in many unique, inside situations, because of his quiet demeanor, his concern for details, his quest for more and more knowledge and his total devotion to Ronald Reagan.

He said he got involved in "A crazy State GOP Executive Committee meeting at the Airport Marina Hotel near LAX the day the infamous Watergate scandal broke wide open." As always, Mack was the 'mouse-in-the-corner,' because he was trusted. This time he watched a contingent of Nixon White House people, including then Attorney General John Mitchell, Jeb Magruder, Bart Porter and a whole lot of Nixon staffers running all over the hotel as if all hell had broken loose. Reagan was there, as well. That cemented more of a relationship with Lyn. Mack now wanted to really get involved in a Reagan presidential campaign. He finally got his chance and attended the GOP National Convention in 1976 in Kansas City, with no key position. Later, in 1979, he was asked to head up Reagan's Political Action Committee known as, Citizens for The Republic—CFTR—with the job of managing $1 million left over from that short-lived campaign. He told Lyn he wanted, 'to be involved in the upcoming campaign' which was gelling in late 1979. Lyn said, 'We need you *here!*' Lyn told him, 'Meese, Deaver and I have been talking:' 'We're going to run Reagan for president and we want you to come over and run the fund-raising PAC.' Mack stayed at the helm of the PAC for *six* years! He said, "It was great!"

"Reagan was our chairman, until he formally announced for president. He and I met a couple of times—but mostly, I ran my own show—called the shots—cut down on expenses and tested the fund-raising techniques. For six years I felt the obligation as the *custodian—the fiduciary of the Ronald Reagan* name. We stayed 'squeaky clean' and away from the campaign."

"I was appointed to the White House Commission on Fellowships, after RR was elected president in 1980, and in 1985 the president appointed me to the National Oceanic & Atmospheric Administration—NOAA, as its director. Everything from the National Weather Service to Fisheries. I had twenty-three ships and thirteen aircraft—I was ready for anything."

He laughed—mostly at how far he had come—and—at the *awesome* responsibility.

"I was back there in Washington for two and one half years before returning to L.A."

February 1981: We were in the first month of the Reagan Administration in Washington. I had been back there a couple of times and was invited to the White House to a briefing and had the privilege of attending this meeting in the Cabinet Room. It was the unveiling of the President's First Economic Package. I was one of the last one's to walk into the room, and there were name cards out for everybody, in front of each seat, and I was walking around trying to find *my* name—and I suddenly *saw* my name—and I said, 'Oooh!'

"And I looked to my left and I saw the name there and I looked to my right and I saw the name there. The fellow on my right was a fellow by the name of Meese— the fellow on my left was a fellow by the name of Reagan—*President Ronald Reagan!* I was sitting in what would normally have been the Secretary of State's chair, in the Cabinet Room." "I was stunned! "I thought, 'WOW!' 'Not Bad!'"

'Not bad at all for a stock boy and 'go-fer' from Southern California!'

"When I was head of NOAA and went out and talked with staffers, deputies and attorneys, I thought, 'What would President Reagan want and what would *he* do under the same circumstances?' "The thing a lot of us tried to remember, above all else, was we were representing *him!*"

The thing a lot of those staffers remembered about Curtis Mack was that he practiced this theme: 'I know it's my decision; But what would Reagan want and what would *he* do?'

Not 'what's best for Curtis or anybody else'—but what does the *president* want to do?' "Those were the things that were the *fun* parts of being back there in D.C.!"

Today, Mack is the President of the Los Angeles World Affairs Council, a position he has held since he retired from NOAA; and George Herbert Walker Bush's administration took over in 1988.

Mack said, "Today we host the Defense Minister of Columbia. Last week were the wives of the Nobel Peace Prize Laureates of Northern Ireland, and Monday night will be the Foreign Minister from Egypt." "Heads of state, heads of governments, ministerial opposition—people from all around the world, all of the time—trying to get people to think about international affairs—then they can make up their own minds."

Mack, unselfish, dedicated and determined, took everything he had learned while working for Ronald Reagan and turned it into success and a benefit for the people of his community, his state and, in the process, *himself* and *his family!*"

THE FORUM ON CURRENT EVENTS
presents

Ronald

Reagan

19 January 1963

8:00 p.m.

topic

'**A Time For Choosing**'

SPEAKING AT

SACRAMENTO SENIOR HIGH SCHOOL

AUDITORIUM

34th and W Streets   *Sacramento, California*

Program / brochure announcing Ronald Reagan's public appearance at Sacramento High School to give an early rendition of THE SPEECH, A Time For Choosing." 1963.   (Dennis Warren collection)

Reagans with Texas Sen. John Tower at 1964 GOP National Convention in San Francisco. (Curtis Patrick collection)

FRIENDS OF RONALD REAGAN
1300 WEST OLYMPIC BOULEVARD, SUITE 300
LOS ANGELES, CALIFORNIA 90015

DAVID H. TOMSHANY
SO. CALIF. COORDINATOR   389-3129

PHONE 381-5771

Reagan for Governor Committee

3257 WILSHIRE BOULEVARD   *David Tomshany*
LOS ANGELES, CALIF. 90005   ASSISTANT CAMPAIGN DIRECTOR

Dave Tomshany's earliest Friends of Reagan business cards for 1965 / '66 Reagan "Brown-Bag" statewide tour to take "pulse" of voters.

Later first RR for Gov. Committee / Assistant Campaign Director.

(Dave Tomshany collection)

EXPENSE STATEMENT   REAGAN ACCT.

SPENCER - ROBERTS & ASSOCIATES

For period **15 OCTOBER '65** to **31 OCTOBER '65** inclusive

DATE	ITEM	AMOUNT	CHARGE TO	DATE BILLED
15 OCT	PARKING	1.75		
16 OCT	TELEPHONE	1.40		
18 OCT	BOURAGES TR A VEL???	3.00		
19 OCT	BAGGAGES ON TRAIN	5.00		
20 OCT	FOOD & TIPS (R&W)	5.40		
20 OCT	BUS TO AIRPORT	1.10		
20 OCT	AIR FARE TO LA (WAL)	14.18		
21 OCT	TELEPHONE	.40		
26 OCT	TELEPHONE	1.25		
27 OCT	PARKING - ????	2.50		
28 OCT	TELEPHONE	.60		
31 OCT	PARKING	1.00		
31 OCT	TELEPHONE	1.10		
	MILEAGE 1466 @ 8¢/mi	117.23		

TOTAL 155.96   SIGNED _____

Typical Dave Tomshany & Reagan's 1965 "Brown Bag" state-wide Tour Expense Sheet.   (Dave Tomshany collection)

Dave Tomshany's powder blue 1965 Mustang convertible on display at the RR Presidential Library in Simi Valley, CA. Dave & Reagan both drove the little car over 15,000 miles throughout the state to speeches & public events to test the public's acceptance of RR as a viable candidate. (Curtis Patrick collection)

NOTE - TIMES AS SHOWN ARE TENTATIVE. IF CHANGES ARE PLANNED — YOU will be NOTIFIED

RONALD REAGAN'S SCHEDULE FOR JUNE 6 (from Hank McCullough)

ELECTION DAY 6 JUNE '66

leave	Burbank	8:45 a.m.
arrive	Sacramento	10:45 a.m.
leave	Sacramento	11:20 a.m.
arrive	~~San Francisco~~ OAKLAND	11:55 a.m.
leave	~~San Francisco~~ OAKLAND	12:30 p.m.
arrive	San Jose	12:45 p.m.
leave	San Jose	1:20 p.m.
arrive	Fresno	1:55 p.m.
leave	Fresno	2:30 p.m.
arrive	Bakersfield	3:00 p.m.
leave	Bakersfield	3:40 p.m.
arrive	San Diego	5:00 p.m.
Leave	San Diego	5:45 p.m.
arrive	Los Angeles International	6:15 p.m.

NOTE — MR. REAGAN will be ABOARD A DC-3✳ CHARTER AIRPLANE. SUGGEST AS LARGE A GROUP AS POSSIBLE FOR EACH AIRPORT RALLY, INCLUDING YOUTH FOR REAGAN. REQUIREMENTS FOR EACH AIRPORT INCLUDE, SPEAKERS PLATFORM, P.A. SYSTEM, REAGAN GIRLS, LITERATURE FOR DISTRIBUTION & IF POSSIBLE A BAND. PRESS & TV MEDIA WILL BE NOTIFIED FROM So. Calif. Hdg.   Dave Tomshany

✳ THE TURKEY BIRD

Reagan & Press / Media official schedule aboard DC-3 "Turkey-Bird." The Final Statewide Swing to "touch" the voters on Primary Election Day June 6, 1966. (Dave Tomshany collection)

Reagan & Dave Tomshany at Port of San Diego Press Conference fielding & answering some serious questions. (Dave Tomshany collection)

Nita Wentner Ashcraft N. Cal Vice-Chairman. Finance 1966 RR for Governor Campaign., with Ron & Nancy Reagan. Credited with making the arrangements with Mervin & Nancy Amerine to use one of their DC-3 live-turkey transports to carry "the man who wouldn't fly," Ronald Reagan, to every little 'boondock' town in the state of CA; helping him beat his opponent, Pat Brown.
(Nita Ashcraft collection)

The Friends of Ronald Reagan Committee
cordially invite you to an informal reception
to meet
Mr. and Mrs. Ronald Reagan
San Francisco Hilton Hotel
Continental Ballroom
Saturday, September 25, 1965
7:00 to 9:00 P.M.

The enclosed is the invitation to which 5000 people responded.

Nita

Nita Ashcraft
2700 Pike Dr
Napa CA 94558

One of over 20,000 invitations sent throughout the San Francisco Bay Area in September 1965, for the public to meet Ron & Nancy Reagan. 5,000 people responded & spent hours waiting in a line to greet them.
(Nita Wentner Ashcraft collection)

Inaugural Message of

RONALD REAGAN
Governor

Delivered during Inaugural Ceremonies
at the State Capitol

January 5, 1967

Nita Wentner Ashcraft's personal copy of Governor Reagan's Inaugural Speech delivered at the State Capitol in Sacramento, CA, four days after taking office. (Nita Wentner Ashcraft collection)

Dear Nita
    And we didn't wake
up at midnight & discover
we were "pumpkins".
    On the other hand I've
known some pretty care free
pumpkins.
            My Best Regards
                Ron
        Ronald Reagan

Personal note to Nita Wentner Ashcraft, inside RR's Inaugural Address, referring to his officially taking the Oath of Office as governor at slightly after Midnight, Jan. 2nd 1967.   (Nita Wentner Ashcraft collection)

THE CITIZENS COMMITTEE TO ELECT RONALD REAGAN GOVERNOR

Wishes to Announce an...

OPEN HOUSE and DEDICATION

of

RONALD REAGAN's

SOUTHERN CALIFORNIA DRIVE-IN CENTER
(Wilshire & Hoover)

CALIFORNIA'S FIRST DRIVE-IN CAMPAIGN CENTER

**All Friends and Supporters
Are Invited to Attend**

TIME: 3:00 P.M. to 4:00 P.M. Tuesday, May 3

PLACE: Southern California REAGAN DRIVE-IN-CENTER. Phone 381-5771.

PROGRAM: Mr. Reagan will be present and will speak at 3:30 P.M. Entertainment personalities will make guest appearances! Calypso band & folk singing group will provide entertainment.

Refreshments will be served.

PARKING: There is available parking at the Center.

★ ★ ★ ★ ★ ★

COME — AND BRING YOUR FRIENDS!

Poster announcing Opening & Dedication of California's First Drive-in Campaign Headquarters, RR to speak, refreshments, entertainment. Public Welcome.
(Bob Tarbet collection)

RONALD REAGAN FOR GOVERNOR COMMITTEE
3257 WILSHIRE BLVD., LOS ANGELES, CALIF. 90005 • DU. 1-5771

IMPORTANT ANNOUNCEMENT!

RONALD REAGAN

WILL GIVE AN ADDRESS
OF MAJOR CONCERN
TO ALL CALIFORNIANS

FRIDAY
February 25th, 9:30 p.m.

ON

KTLA Channel 5
LOS ANGELES

AND

KOGO Channel 10
SAN DIEGO

MR. REAGAN WILL SPEAK LIVE FROM SAN DIEGO.
WE URGE YOU TO VIEW HIM AND ALSO NOTIFY YOUR
FRIENDS AND NEIGHBORS.

A WINNER—RONALD REAGAN!

A CITIZEN POLITICIAN

Poster announcing early RR for Governor Campaign Major Televised Address From San Diego, CA, February 1966. (Bob Tarbet collection)

Author, Sandy Quinn, Art Van Court; security & advance with Bill Friedman & Buck Ware part of the team, out there somewhere in the pressing crowd of happy well-wishers, clearing path for candidate Reagan to meet & greet the huge crowds of citizens who came out to see & touch "The Man," 1966. (Buck Ware collection)

A happy candidate Reagan smiles. Actor Chuck Connors follows, as L.A. County Sheriff's Deputies & CHP help the advance team move Reagan through the closely-packed crowds.   (Buck Ware collection)

Reagan greets RR Girls in bright colored outfits while actor Chuck Connors towers over him watching the crowd with RR personal security, L.A.P.D. officer Bill Friedman on right.   (Buck Ware collection)

Security Chief Art Van Court & author confer on next RR move on typical day of many rallies. 1966 Reagan for Gov. Campaign. (Buck Ware collection)

Reagan introduced by his proud bus driver to friends in friendly, squeezing crowd. Author, Art Van Court, Sandy Quinn help clear path at local, grass roots 1966 RR for Gov., rally. (Buck Ware collection)

Security Chief Art Van Court, author & Ret. L.A.P.D. Lt. Niel Nielsen, RR
security & advance team discuss details of coming events.
(Buck Ware collection)

Nancy Reagan shares a rare quiet, lighter moment with1966 RR for Governor
Campaign bus driver as the tour moves into "high gear." As rallies, speeches,
public events & reception requests pour in from all over California; the candidate
becomes more popular every time he speaks or is seen in public—& the tour
becomes a rolling "juggernaut!" (Buck Ware collection)

RR addresses families around huge pool at Soledad Sands Park.
(Buck Ware collection)

Candidate Reagan speaks to families at Soledad Sands Park, North L.A. County.
Candidate hits wasteful state government spending, high taxes & campus unrest,
over & over again.   (Buck Ware collection)

Buck Ware in tuxedo standing watch while advancing the Reagans, actor /
comedian Danny Thomas, comedian Jack Benny & security from every agency
& department within one hundred miles of Sacramento, during whirlwind early
January, 1967 Inaugural celebration festivities.   (Buck Ware collection)

Reagan's 1966 Campaign Transport PlaneDC-3 N63440 Owned & piloted
by Mervin Amerine-Amerine Turkey Farms-Amerine Air-with his wife, Nancy
Amerine, as flight attendant / hostess.   (Amerine family collection)

A-12   Thursday, Sept. 22, 1966   THE MODESTO BEE

Bee Photo

California gubernatorial candidate Ronald Reagan, center, has an unusual supporter in Oakdale turkey grower Mervin W. Amerine, left, who has refurbished a DC3—which he uses most of the year for carrying turkey poults—to help the Republican candidate fly to speaking engagements. At right is Harold Bayley, co-pilot. Amerine flys the twin-engine plane himself.

Grower Flies High For Reagan

Oakdale turkey grower Mervin W. Amerine is literally flying high for Republican gubernatorial candidate Ronald Reagan.

Amerine, a long-time GOP supporter, has refurbished one of his three twin-engine DC3 aircraft — which he normally uses to haul turkey poults—in time to use it in Reagan's political campaign.

For the campaign the Reagan DC3 got a new interior and complete mechanical refurbishing.

Amerine, along with co-pilot Harold Bayley, flies the twin-engine aircraft up and down the state, donating his time to Reagan's campaign.

Besides running the airport and Amerine Turkey Breeding Farms, with his brothers Raegan and Richard, Amerine is a director of the Oakdale Irrigation District — currently in the throes of budget planning —and is active in other Oakdale civic affairs.

So far the Oakdale Municipal Airport manager has donated four or five hours of "air time," and has given Reagan a standing offer for air transportation.

Modesto Bee article 9/22/66 with photo showing Mervin Amerine, pilot & Harold Bayley, co-pilot, going over maps & schedule of next campaign stops with an interested candidate Reagan. (Credit: Polaris Images nyc)

RR is flanked by smiling Reagan Girls wearing red-berets & crisp, bright red & white outfits, in preparation for telephone-bank surveys by RR Girls, showing Reagan ahead in 1966; his first Campaign for Governor. (Buck Ware collection)

Nancy Reagan signs autographs for eager Reagan Girls & thanks them for their support & hours of work. These sharp, well-dressed girls spent hours & days out in front of the candidate & the advance team helping to make each event a success. (Buck Ware collection)

Election Day elation as Nancy greets an ecstatic Governor-elect, Ron, at airplane with smiles & hugs. A smiling Lt. Governor-elect, Bob Finch as Security Chuck Ward, in dark trench coat, keeps a quiet, vigilant look-out.
(Bob Tarbet collection)

Lyn Nofziger at his best, briefing reporters & media people at L.A.'s Biltmore Hotel prior to RR making his post election / Victory statement, after his huge win over Governor Edmund G. "Pat" Brown.   (Buck Ware collection)

A serious moment in the Post-election Press Conference as Governor-elect
Ronald Reagan tells reporters of his future plans for the new administration.
(Buck Ware collection)

Lt. Governor-elect Bob Finch & Governor-elect Reagan stand at podium
answering reporter's questions after making their Victory speeches at the Los
Angeles Biltmore Hotel, November, 1966.   (Buck Ware collection)

State Supreme Court Justice Marshall F. McComb, Nancy Reagan, Ronald Reagan, Pastor, Bob Finch stand in front of statuary in Capitol Rotunda preparing to take the Oaths of Office. (Buck Ware collection)

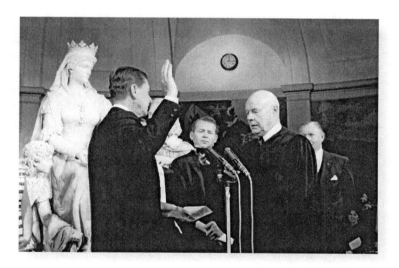

Ronald Reagan takes oath of office as Governor of California with Lt. Governor Bob Finch visible over the mics in Capitol Rotunda. U.S. Sen. George Murphy looks on behind Justice McComb administering the oaths; moments after the stroke of midnight (see clock), Monday, January 2, 1967.
(Buck Ware collection)

Photo taken from balcony in Capitol dome overlooking Governor Reagan & Lt. Governor Bob Finch & the Official Party as they took their Oaths of Office. (Buck Ware collection)

Ronald Reagan takes official Oath of Office from Justice McComb & is officially sworn-in as Governor after Capitol Rotunda midnight ceremony. Son, Ron "Skipper" Reagan (Ronald Prescott) leans on his dad's desk as Nancy Reagan chats with Maureen, RR's daughter behind them.   (Buck Ware collection)

Communications / security advance-man, Bob Tarbet stands watch over California's First Lady, Nancy Reagan & friends in ball gowns, during 1970 Inaugural activities. (Photo credit Don Dornan-Los Angeles, CA)

The Inaugural Committee

cordially invites you to attend

the 1967 Inaugural Ceremonies

of

Ronald Reagan

Governor of the State of California

January fourth and fifth

City of Sacramento

To Bob—With Thanks I can never Express
Ronald Reagan
Nancy Reagan

1967 Inaugural Committee   *Invitation does not*
400 Capitol Mall   *constitute admission*
Sacramento, California   *R. S. V. P. card enclosed*

Invitation to Governor Ronald Reagan's 1967 Inauguration ceremonies, parties & receptions for Bob & Urania Tarbet, at which both of them worked on advance during most of the events. A personal note across the bottom reads "*To Bob—With thanks I can never express.*" Signed, Ronald Reagan / Nancy Reagan. (Bob Tarbet collection)

OFFICE OF NANCY REAGAN

October 29, 1999

Dear Eurania,

Ronnie and I were so sorry to learn about Bob's death. Although there are
no words to ease the pain at this difficult time, we want you to know that
you are in our thoughts and prayers.

Losing a spouse is certainly difficult, but we know that Bob lived a very
full and rewarding life. He was a wonderful and great friend to both of us
and he made a tremendous contribution to our staff in Sacramento. Bob
served the State of California and our country with great dignity and loyalty
and we will all miss him. We hope the warm memories of him will bring
you strength in the days and years to come.

Eurania, please know that we are praying for you and your family at this
time. God bless you.

Sincerely,

Nancy

I'm so sorry - we had a lot of good times together

Mrs. Robert Tarbet
P.O. Box 1032
Diamond Springs, California 95619

Nancy Reagan's eulogy sent to author to read at October 1999 funeral of Bob
Tarbet, along with many other eulogies from top Reagan staffers & colleagues
from around the world, who could not attend. See these poignant tributes in the
Tarbet's chapter in this book, Vol. 1. (Curtis Patrick collection)

Bob & Urania Tarbet & Curtis & Joan Patrick continued to enjoy a friendship for life, after more than thirty years.   (Bob Tarbet collection)

One of many gatherings, BBQ's & get-togethers held at the Executive Residence in Sacramento during 1967 & '68. Upper photo, l. to r. Bonnie Rowlee smiling as hostess & host Nancy & Ron Reagan join in the festivities. Russ (18yrs.) & Steve (16yrs.) Rowlee enjoy the fun with the First Family. Lower photo, mild-mannered George Young, from the S-R offices in L.A., wearing bright white golf shirt, hopes volley ball comes his way, See George's chapter, this book, Vol. 1. (Dale Rowlee collection)

Security Chief Art Van Court, l. center, drinks from white cup. Ron & Nancy's daughter, Patti Davis, hands clasped, smiling; talks with her parents. Governor Reagan has arm around Nancy, in center of photo, while everyone seems to be having a good time. (BobTarbet collection)

A smiling, golf-shirt clad Governor Reagan informally poses while entertaining picnicking guests at his Executive Residence, tree-canopied backyard & pool, 1967. (Bob Tarbet collection)

Chuck Tyson , Pat Gayman, author, Maryann Urban & Van Court enjoy rare
moment relaxing at Executive Residence BBQ, 1967. (Pat Ingoglia collection)

Author, Dale Rowlee, Jack Kemp & Sandy Quinn pose for group-shot as
Governor Reagan & staff say "Good-Bye" to Kemp as he finishes his internship
& returns to the Buffalo Bills football team. (Pat Ingoglia collection)

Jack Kemp cuts his Going-Away-Party cake with Governor Reagan & staff in Gov's Council Room-1967. Maryann Urban, Jim Gibson, Jackie Habecker, Lyn Nofziger, & author bid the popular Kemp, "Farewell!" (Pat Ingoglia collection)

Governor Reagan greets, listens, sings & joins in the rally with exuberant youth from "Up With People" in the Governor's Office Council Room—while the staff stand in awe & amazement! (Pat Ingoglia collection)

Governor Reagan & research expert Jim Gibson, creator of the famous Black Books, at their creative & critiquing best. CHP officer Dale Rowlee was at the wheel of Gov. RR's limo & Lyn Nofziger was riding "shotgun" & peppering the discussion with a plethora of one-liners; on their way back to the Capitol after Ron gave a speech to the San Joaquin Valley Farmers Association, 1967. Photos by Lyn Nofziger. (Dr. Jim Gibson collection)

Pleased with success, RR exits meeting into crush of press flanked by Art Van Court (left), Lyn Nofziger (right) & lead thru the crowd by Bob Winzeler, in dark glasses, a friendly Republican businessman / volunteer from Vermont. (Buck Ware collection)

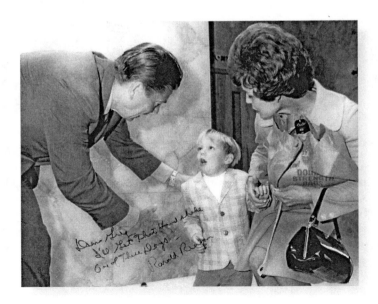

Reagan returns from Capitol News Conference & leans down to shake hands with the grandson of The Iconic Receptionist, Jackie Habecker, who sneaked in to do some extra work on her vacation & got caught.   (Credit: APWirephoto)

Governor Reagan helps Assistant Communications Director, Nancy Clark Reynolds, while she attempts to cut her Snoopy birthday cake; a present from Gov. Reagan. Both were big fans & friends of Charles Schulz's "PEANUTS" comic strip & the cake came as a huge surprise to Reynolds, as you can see by her laughter! (Pat Ingoglia collection) PEANUTS © United Feature Syndicate, Inc.

An RR press conference Communications Director Lyn Nofziger, in his usual manner of keeping things moving, checks his watch one more time & glares at the gathered media & press. (Buck Ware collection)

Apollo 10 Astronauts, Gene Cernan , John Young & Cmdr. Tom Stafford The dress rehearsal for the first moon landing, Command module: Charlie Brown. Lunar module: "Snoopy" Date Taken/Released: November 13, 1968. Credits: KSC-NASA. NASA photo available from SpaceImages.com. PEANUTS © United Feature Syndicate, Inc.

Gov. Reagan hosts Apollo 10 Astronauts, Cmdr. Tom Stafford, Gene Cernan & John Young & "PEANUTS" Creator, Charles Schulz in State Capitol Press Conference & gift exchange in Governor's Office, Sacramento, CA, 1969. (Dennis Warren collection) PEANUTS © United Feature Syndicate, Inc.

California Gov.Reagan & Nevada Gov. Paul Laxalt meet at Lake Tahoe's Heavenly Valley in Winter of 1967 to discuss environmental issues facing the fragile Tahoe Basin. RR made it a family affair with Nancy & Skipper learning to ski on the slopes behind the two governors. (Pat Ingoglia collection)

Gov. Reagan & Communications Director Lyn Nofziger trudge through snow at Heavenly Valley / Lake Tahoe discussing Tahoe's beauty & media issues, 1967.   (Pat Ingoglia collection)

1950's era Deauville Hotel , the Reagan HQ in Miami Beach, with "Welcome Gov. Reagan" & "California Delegation" on marquee sign. U.S. Secret Service (rental) vehicles—Ford / Mercury convertibles & Lincoln sedans are lined up under the canopy—No black Suburbans here for RR's first time traveling with the Presidential Candidate Personal Protection Detail.
(Dennis Warren collection)

Governor Reagan addresses packed hall of delegates at 1968 GOP National Convention in Miami Beach. (Dennis Warren collection)

Glare of lights, waving of thousands of Reagan signs, flashes & bustle of cameras, crazy hats & decorated outfits of dedicated, zealous Reagan Delegates, not to mention the anti-dirty-tricks campaign of our Special Services Team, give Nixon, Romney & Rockefeller a surprising run for their money in the race for the 1968 presidential nomination. (Dennis Warren collection)

The Favorite Son of the California Delegation to the 1968 GOP Convention in Miami Beach, CA Gov. Ronald Reagan eats ice cream during a brief respite while seated with his delegation on the floor of the Miami Convention Center. (Dennis Warren collection)

Gov. Reagan visits key state delegations in several hotels along the Miami Beach "strand," followed or preceded by "spontaneous" bands, celebrities, well-wishers & followers, to churn-up support for his bid as a serious presidential candidate. He is followed by press & media from around the world. (Dennis Warren collection)

Reagan listens to delegates' concerns on the floor of 1968 GOP National Convention.   (Dennis Warren collection)

CA Favorite Son, RR, thanks his 1968 GOP Convention behind-the-scenes team , floor leaders & delegates who fought for the presidential nomination in Miami Beach against Richard Nixon, Nelson Rockefeller & George Romney. RR is flanked by Nancy Reagan & William French Smith, RR's long-time friend & vice chairman of the CA Favorite Son Delegation, who was later (after the 1980 elections) appointed U.S. Attorney General by President Reagan. (Buck Ware collection)

A smiling, armed CHP officer Dale Rowlee, very much at ease on horseback as he provides personal security to Governor Reagan & family on back-country fishing expedition into High Sierra above Yosemite National Park, 1970. (Nancy Clark Reynolds / Dale Rowlee collections)

Governor Reagan & son, The Skipper, hold string of trout while Nancy in background tends camp stove & utensils preparing to cook the freshly caught fish, 1970. (Dale Rowlee collection)

Nancy, son Skipper (Ronald Prescott) & Governor Reagan enjoy rare opportunity
for some High Sierra fresh, pine-scented mountain air & the crashing sounds of
the cool river behind them, with the sun warming their backs.
(Dale Rowlee collection)

Ron & Nancy Reagan pose on High Sierra trip, near Yosemite National Park,
with blue skies above towering granite mountains, sheer cliffs & tall pine trees
as icy-cold, clattering, rushing rivers cascade over rocky falls into the canyons
below. 1970.   (Dale Rowlee collection)

This shiny, new Mayflower moving van traveled all the way from California to Florida with its precious cargo to help Ronald Reagan attempt to win the 1968 presidential nomination. (Bob Tarbet collection)

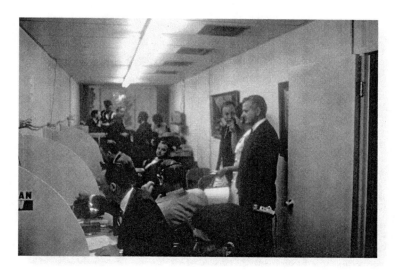

Mystery van's high-tech contents & secret staffing will be revealed in Vol. 2. (Bob Tarbet collection)

Typical demonstration in the 1960's of picket-carrying, marching, chanting, screaming protesters, generally disrupting peace & state business activities along Capitol Mall, through Capitol Park & onto the steps of the Capitol Building housing the State Legislature & offices of the governor & other constitutional officers.   (Dennis Warren collection)

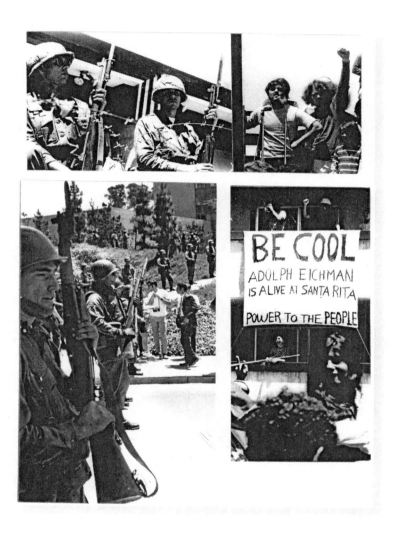

Governor Reagan calls in National Guard troops to protect University of California student's & City of Berkeley citizen's lives & property during days of student uprisings & anti-war protests in 1960's, see Vol. 2. for details.
(Dennis Warren collection)

Chapter Eleven

RUMPLED REPORTER WAS KEY INSIDER

Lyn Nofziger

"*Honesty* , the one word that sums up the essence of Ronald Reagan." "There's one thing that people seem to forget about him and that is, he was a *brave* man." He instilled confidence in people because he had confidence in himself—he wasn't a fearful man or a fearful politician."

Lyn came to us a little bit balding in his rim-of-the-dome, Friar Tuck hair-do, where deep scars must have been slightly visible on the pate from thousands of head-scratchings as he pondered Reagan's next answer to his last question from the working-press and media, through hundreds of press conferences and interviews. This loveable, chunky, 'teddy-bear' of a rumpled raconteur, with his top collar-button undone and Mickey Mouse tie askew, was the quintessential wordsmith who kept all of us, including the candidate and later, Governor Reagan, laughing, feeling upbeat and eager, as the quips rolled forth like "Jelly-Bellys'" from RR's big desktop jar.

Lyn arrived with a strong portfolio of press accomplishments, but his key to surviving and succeeding in RR's inner-sanctum team of advisors was his uncanny ability to connect with the mind of Ronald Reagan.

"Curtis, my mind's picture of you is driving with you down some damned street in L.A. with you talking on two f—'ing car phones at the same time!"

These were big, cumbersome Mobile Phones with the huge transmitters in the trunk. "And me wondering if we were going to have a wreck—steering with your damned elbows!"

This was serious business then. We weren't scheduling our next golf game. We wanted to be ahead of the proverbial 'power curve' with our opposition and this was another high-tech device in our arsenal, which only a few people had access to.

In answer to my question of exactly when Lyn thought RR might be presidential material, he said: "I had been out with Reagan maybe two or three times, on the 1966 campaign trail, and I came back and saw Bill Roberts." (Lyn's first boss & partner in the campaign consulting firm of Spencer-Roberts & Assoc.) I said, 'There's something out there, Bill, and I don't know what it is, but there is a *connect* between Reagan and the people.' 'Bill, he's going to be elected governor and maybe someday, he might even be president.' "And Bill Roberts, with those big bulgy eyes of his, looked at me and he said, 'Oh, Lyn, what will the poor soul do if he is ever elected president?'

The apparent universal theme and indicator of Reagan's displeasure or disdain for someone, some thing, or with the direction some issue was heading, was the throwing of his eye-glasses across his desk or the council table. I asked Lyn if that was his understanding and how he perceived RR when he got mad. After hearing Lyn's answer to how Reagan expressed anger; maybe those of us who had witnessed that little gesture over the years, were wrong. He had a little different 'take' on it.

"Ron would throw his glasses when he wanted people to *think* he was mad! When he was really mad—he *never* threw his glasses. I don't know whether he stewed inside (he laughs) but usually, when he got mad at somebody, he would take them aside and very quietly talk to them—which he has done to me on occasion. When he got mad about issues, then, he would *let loose* sometimes, but he was not a shouter, as you know, or a screamer—or a hollerer. He would say what he thought of the issues and of the people who would be Democrats. He never talked badly about his own people." *"Never!"* "But he would say negative things about people who were not his own people. He would, perhaps, be low-key critical."

Lyn reminded me of some of the other crucial issues we had to present to Reagan, over the years, one, in particular, and we both agreed—RR never raised his voice on hearing the bad news. He was, to use a time-worn cliché, 'calm, cool & collected.' I asked Lyn what kind of a temper Ron had exhibited, which he could verify. I did bore-in on Lyn because I wanted the unvarnished truth and knew I could get it from Lyn.

"Once again, if it was the 'enemy,' why then—I've heard him swear—but I've never heard him shout. He'd raise his voice—a little—and, once again, if he was dealing with our own people, his attitude was: *"Well, what can we do about this now?"* It was *never* RR saying, *"Why that dumb son-of-a-bitch!"* It was always, *"How do we fix it?"* "What did I dislike about Ronald Reagan? What grated on me the most? What bugged me?" ***"Nothing!"*** "He was a *reasonable* man—even when he had a strong opinion—he never tried to shove it down your throat. There was nothing about him that I found objectionable. I wish I could tell you one."

"He didn't lie, he didn't curse, he didn't *demean* you because you worked for him." "He had *no* 'second' agenda."

I asked Lyn what qualities led him to believe that RR was more than just gubernatorial material; that he might be better than other presidents.

He said, "I've never really sat down and looked at it that way. I've always said that there was *something* between him and the people he was dealing with—whom, he was talking to—and it was hard to put a finger on it—but there was clearly a *connect* between them, that's true. Why was there a *connect?* "Maybe it was because he was not shouting at them—he was a low-key speaker—he was not a typical political orator; so people didn't get the feeling that he was trying to shove something down their throats, or anything like that. Secondly, he had learned the theme that if you say the same thing time after time, it has a certain *sincerity* to it—whereas, if you're trying to change what you're saying every day—people never get a hold of what it is you really stand for."

"He *did* that!" One of the things RR said was, *"It is easier to change audiences than it is to change speeches."* "But he was consistent. He was not afraid to say what he believed—even when it went against the popular feeling of the day. But, mainly, it was that he talked to people, whether it was one person, a small group or an audience in the thousands; he talked to them, as if he were one of them. You never had the feeling that he was talking *down* to you—that he was superior—or that he was trying to shove his own feelings or his own beliefs on you. He was (simply) enumerating them and saying what he thought it meant to him. Basically, he was a very *untypical* politician."

"There was one other (important) thing. There was *personal appearance."* I mean, there was the appearance of *confidence* that kind of emanated from him—he would walk in there—and he's six foot one or two—and he was an impressive figure of a man, he spoke with confidence and you had no doubt that he believed what he was saying. That what he was saying was not meant, particularly, to *impress* you, right or wrong. It was because he was speaking from the heart. You *always* had the feeling he was speaking from the heart."

Some of us on the staff compared RR, as he entered an event, especially a large convention hall, to a combination of John Wayne, Abraham Lincoln and Billy Graham, all wrapped into one, larger-than-life man—and the applause was long and deafening! Lyn called Reagan's selflessness, "Obviously a kind of *charisma."* "You put all of these things that we have talked about together—and there is an appeal there that is really hard to define, except that he comes through as somebody who instills *confidence* in you—who makes you want to believe in him and—well, that's *it!"*

'It made us want to work for him, tirelessly,' I said.

"Yeah!" "That's right—it never bothered us."

I reminded Lyn that in his book, NOFZIGER, Regnery-Gateway,1992, that he mentioned, as so many of our colleagues did, the fact that Reagan would leave the office at 5 P.M. sharp—but that many of us felt we needed to be there to catch up on unfinished business; even though RR would encourage those he saw at their desks to, *"Wrap it up and head on home to your families." "There'll be time to go at it again tomorrow."* Always ending with his and Nancy's personal thanks. However, Lyn said with his warm, infectious chuckle, the following line in his own book: that 'the work would have been there the next day, if we'd all left at 5 P.M.'

Two areas where I disagreed with that premise were that of security, the personal protection aspect, which was an on-going 24 / 7 operation and, of course, activities of the Legislative Unit when the Legislature was in session and bills are being passed and must be signed by the governor in a timely manner, under the law. Some interesting examples of each will be found in other chapters of this book.

Lyn, however, added, "Ronald Reagan instinctively knew that most of the damned work that we were doing didn't need to be done until the next day. It's true, a lot of the times people get into high levels in government and they hang around, and they work because they want people to *think* they are working."

Lyn would close up the Press Unit, except for someone on duty to pick up radio actualities from some remote speech venue where RR was appearing, but Lyn would be off to one of the local watering holes, like the Senator Hotel bar, Frank Fat's or The Fire House Restaurant in 'Old Sac,' to schmooze with the Capitol Press Corps and media people to either spread a little of the Reagan P.R., on or off the record, or to see what he could pick up on how some of them were going to slant their next RR stories. He was confident, low-key and one of the earliest 'spin-doctors,' with a pervasive sense of humor. Lyn "tickled" words and ideas like a concert pianist "tickled the ivories." He never shut-off.

Most of them had great respect for Lyn, much of it due to the fact that he, indeed, had started as a beat-reporter, like most of them had.

I asked Lyn to sum up his thoughts and feelings about RR which, in his opinion, can best describe the elusive *essence* of The Man.

These words will accompany the single, overriding word which Lyn continued to use throughout our interview and in his own book: ***"Honesty"***.

"There's one thing that most people seem to forget about him and that is, he was a *brave* man." "That's a part of it—I mean, he instilled confidence in people because he had confidence in himself—he wasn't a fearful man or a fearful politician."

"This was not only when he got shot, but you can go clear back to when he was the Governor of California—the mob was gathering outside the Capitol, the teachers and others, 'cause they were mad that we weren't going to give them the increase in money they wanted—in march after march on the Capitol—and we were there on that Saturday and were gettin' ready to go up to Oregon to see Governor Tom McCall. Those of us with RR said, 'Let's ignore those people and get outa' here!' And Ron said, *"Aw, Art, Lyn, these people aren't going to run me off!"* After which he went out and stood there on the top step of the Capitol," Lyn recalled. "Right in the line-of-fire—facing the shouting, agitated throng." That's the time he said, *"Ladies and gentlemen—that is—if there are any."* "And he faced them down!" "The thing I always remember, which is also in my book, about the time Art (Van Court) came to see me and said that there was a bunch of Caesar Chavez's (grape pickers and farm workers union) people right outside the West door of the Capitol. We tried to take Ron out the back way, and he refused to go." And he said, *"They're not going to tell me where I can walk in my Capitol!"* "And he walked out that door and right through'em! And they parted; just like the Red Sea. And he was kind of chuckling as we went on back to his office."

RR was not only speaking of the unruly visitors on their ranting mission out on the Capitol Mall and at the West door, but also those of us on his security team, when it came to telling him where and when he should or shouldn't go somewhere. What Reagan did wasn't *bravado*—it was simple, inherent *bravery!*

One of the main reasons our security, communications, travel and logistics operations functioned so well for RR was that there was little or no bickering among ourselves or with other staff members. This tone of decorum was born out of respect, loyalty and integrity. The example set by the key leaders, Meese, Clark, Reed and Nofziger. As busy, focused and involved as Lyn was, under almost any conditions: He always had time to answer our questions and listen to our concerns, when it came to RR. He treated us as equals. Lyn helped imbue everyone else on the staff with *respect* and he earned it ten-fold, himself.

Lyn continued, "You know—he walked through those mobs at the university campuses—and he just refused to be intimidated. I was thinking, nobody is perfect and Ronald Reagan, every now and then said dumb things—as does every politician—or things that were not politic—things that, politically, he would have been better off not saying, such as 'trees creating smog' and that great one, that I'll always remember, when we were having our 'scandal' and he and I were flying down to L.A. on the Jet Commander and were landing at Santa Monica airport and there were going to be press there, and we knew it." So I said to him, 'What are you going to say about Drew Pearson?' (the columnist who hounded RR over the 'scandal' which now had grown into a national story) Ron said, *"I'm going to say—if that son-of-a-bitch ever comes to California—he better not spit on the sidewalk!"* (or Pearson could be arrested for breaking some archaic law) Lyn told Ron, as the little jet was about to touch down, 'Ha, Ha, Ha—very funny—now, what are we (really) going to say?"

He knew what Lyn meant.

"So we decided what we were going to say and we got out of the plane onto the tarmac, and the first question from the waiting press was," 'What about Drew Pearson's story, Governor?' And Ron says, *"If he ever comes to California, he better not spit on the sidewalk!"* Lyn said, "So much for preparing—he could just drive you right up the wall!"

He could, I agreed, but recalled that he would make jokes about himself, as much as about other people.

"You're right, Curtis, if somebody had said something funny, somewhere, he'd use it—he didn't care." Lyn said. "Obviously, there were times when he remembered things out of movies, that he translated into *real* life, and there's one particular one—where the bomber's wing had been crippled and everybody's jumping out of the plane, except for the kid in the gunner's turret—and he can't get out—and the captain goes back and he says, 'Don't worry son, we'll ride it down together!' Now, we don't know that this really happened or that the captain really said that—(Lyn laughs heartily)—how could we?"

There were times when he would embellish stories, but it suited the moment and the purpose or point; whatever Ron was attempting to get across.

"Sure!" "Sure!" Lyn agreed. "But that's all right."

Chapter Twelve

NEVER INTIMIDATED

Nancy Clark Reynolds

"RR was absolutely *Numero Uno* in Nancy's life." "All the time." "And *she* was with *him*!" "They were totally *wound* into each other, to the exclusion of everybody else." "This was a totally *interdependent* relationship."

"Reagan was *gracious*—and—FUNNY!" "He had people in 'stitches' all the time—and he was a *total* gentleman." "You always knew where Reagan stood." "He never equated *disagreement* with *disloyalty.*" "Even after working fourteen and eighteen hour days, I could hardly wait to get to work the next morning!"

Nancy Clark Reynolds, she's 73, now, (2001) was still as vivacious as ever, and as compassionate, as thoughtful and focused as Lady Margaret Thatcher, as elegant and attractive as Nancy Reagan, and as warm and genuine as Laura Bush. She illuminated an intense and stressful office! Today she's doing archeological digs all over the world.

NCR, as her initials appeared on Governor Reagan's closely controlled "Blue" traveling schedule, was one of the first people to introduce controversial author Edmund Morris and wife, Silvia, to the Reagans in Washington, during the White House years.

"Long before he got the contract to do the biography, DUTCH, We became fast friends. His 'shtick' was to be intellectual," Reynolds said, as we began opening long-locked doors containing stories from those 'thrilling days of yesteryear.'

In tempering my disdain for the book, I allowed, 'But—Ronald Reagan may have just stumped him.' 'He has—others.'

Nancy said, "Well, but, Ronald Reagan wasn't going to open up—the way a biographer wants him to—he never would—and he always kept a distance from everybody. I don't know—I never tried to probe—I would *never* have asked him those questions about his father and the alcoholism—that's not something I would even think of asking him, because that was *personal.* But when RR offered something—I was always fascinated—but I never *did* anything with the information."

"I know one time we were sitting in the back of the car and, I can't remember how it came up—about custody of children—and he said that one of his great regrets was that in the days when Jane Wyman divorced him—that the husbands— the fathers—never got *"rights."* They always went to the mother—and—he said he regretted that he had never stood up for *his rights* as the father. I never questioned him or followed up on it."

"It was just a comment. And he seemed rather subdued—he seemed quite sad about that. I guess he saw the children once a month, on the weekend—or whatever those arrangements were. I think he felt that one of the reasons he's had trouble over the years was that he didn't have the time to bond and to be—I'm just guessing— *"always there for them."*

"Regarding these interviews with people who worked for the Reagans in so many different capacities: I would be surprised if anybody who worked for him had a really negative word. Now there probably have been and maybe there will be very, very few who don't like him, personally—or—who felt they were cheated and never got close to him."

Nancy was right. 'Yes' In this book there are a few—but very few.

It is almost universal and without coaching, they almost always say the same things, using the same words and nuances about what a *genuine* person he is.

"Well—even House Speaker Tip O'Neill, who had such awful things to say about Reagan—he said such terrible things publicly—and when I attended my son's graduation ceremony at Stanford University, he had the worst things to say about him in the main graduation speech before thousands of people—I was so angry—I was so outraged—that he would use the occasion for a political *"SLAM!"* It's something Reagan would *never* do. But Tip couldn't *resist* Reagan, *personally*, as many people can't."

I asked Nancy to tell me how she first heard about Ronald Reagan and then how *that* evolved into a position in the Governor's Office in Sacramento—when I first met her.

"I was anchoring the Six O'Clock News at KPIX-TV in San Francisco. That was CBS. Westinghouse owned the station—I was also a reporter. In those days, anchors were also reporters. That was probably 1965—but I had heard about him—because, of course, he was a movie star, I mean, after all—I was a big movie fan. I knew of Ronald Reagan and I'd seen him in movies and I knew he was married to Jane Wyman—but I never followed his career in any great detail. I always thought he was a very charming, likeable, good-looking man. And then when he announced that he was running against *Pat Brown* for governor, I thought, 'Oh No!'—'Pardon me'—'George Christopher—a Republican.'" (S.F. Mayor George Christopher was his first hurdle).

Actually, S-R and Ronald Reagan set up the '66 Campaign operations to run, from the get-go against the sitting Governor Pat Brown—the office-holder—NOT the other GOP primary election contenders, in an attempt to curtail or eliminate Republican-bashing—so everyone got in the habit of saying that. Easy to forget.

"I had been a registered Democrat because my father was the Democratic Congressman and Senator from Idaho. My uncles were all governors. Three uncles were governors."

"Two were Democrats, one was a Republican. And I switched parties—in those days, in order to vote in the California Primary, you had to switch parties."

"I voted for George Christopher, Mayor of San Francisco, because—nothing against Ronald Reagan, but George Christopher was my *personal* friend, he was the Mayor of San Francisco, I had known him for years—I'd been to his home—he was my friend! I had nothing against Ronald Reagan, at all."

"Anyhow, I was assigned to do an interview with Reagan when he came to San Francisco—and he went to the St. Francis Yacht Club—and sat on a wall, a stone wall, outside, with the Golden Gate Bridge in the background. That's where I *first* met him. I don't know the exact order of things, Curtis, but he had, like, a tear that was coming out of one eye and I thought it was the wind (big wind at that location, blowing through the Golden Gate, across from Alcatraz Island) and he said he had been in a movie, where the edge or end of a fencing foil, used in a sword-fighting scene, had caught him in the eye—and that he had this tearing problem."

"It's one of those odd things you remember. He was very gracious—we did a great interview—very good—and then I did an interview with Governor Brown. And, of course, Reagan won the Primary—and I told him I had voted for George Christopher—and Reagan just laughed—he said it didn't matter to him!"

"After that, I went to the station and I said, 'I have a great idea.' This was revolutionary, in those days. 'Why don't you let me go for a week with the two candidates?' 'A week with Reagan—a week with Brown—and do different interviews?'"

"And, of course, that would cost the station money—and nobody had ever done that before—anyplace, to my knowledge. So, I did it. And one of the interviews I did was the first time an interview like that had ever been done on *horseback*. Yeah, we had wireless microphones—and in those days, that was an amazing piece of technology."

"We were at the ranch—not the new one in Santa Barbara, Rancho Del Cielo."

I asked if it was the one down in the Malibu Mountains

"Yeah!" "Yeah!"

I told Nancy I remembered it well. My grandparents had pioneered a ranch in Malibu Canyon in the 1930's just a few miles away from Reagan's on the winding two-laner to Malibu Lake in the brushy, oak tree dotted, rye-grass covered rolling hills concealing some of the most famous western movie ranches to brighten a young buckaroos' Saturday Matinee. 'Yearling Row'—I believe he called it—'Yearling Row.'

"Yeah!" "Exactly!" "Exactly!" Nancy fairly shouted.

She always was the vivacious one.

"Out of the movie by the same name." "Reagan was wonderful and relaxed—he loved horses—and I was *passionate* for horses! *Passionate.* I loved to ride, more than anything. So we ran *that*—and we ran an interview I did with Governor Brown—and it won an award. Like a "Golden Globe" of San Francisco. I've forgotten the name of the award—but it was a statue—it was a big microphone. I won it for the series. I followed one man for a week and then I followed another one for a week. That meant I was *off* the air—*live*—for two weeks—and that was something—the studio was very upset about it—but the stuff I sent back was great—and they ran that as a 'Special Series'—and then I won this award. My husband, at that time, was Frank Reynolds, and he and Lyn Nofziger had been friends for many, many years, because Frank worked for the National Republican Congressional Caucus. He was like me—he was an advance-person, he worked for a congressman—he ran his office. Frank's good friend was Lyn Nofziger, and when I went on the campaign—I was the only woman T.V. reporter. I think there were two or three others (in the press only) the San Francisco Chronicle—*you* know—the L.A. Times—and I felt like—I mean—I was always ostracized—and I had to have a cameraman—and Reagan was, of course, charming to me, but Lyn felt very sorry for me and, knowing Frank, he went out of his way to help me get interviews, and do something different than just sit there and say, 'How do you feel today, Mr. Reagan?'"

"Anyhow, as things developed, Reagan, of course, *won*—and Frank got a job offer in Sacramento to run the office of State Senator Jack McCarthy. He was the Minority Leader. So, in those days, a woman went where her husband's job was—and I ended up having to move to Sacramento. I thought surely the CBS T.V. station in Sacramento would want to hire me. And during one of the last interviews I did with RR, I asked Lyn, 'Do you have any connections with this T.V. station?'"

He said, 'Why'? And I told him. He said, 'Reagan is going to *win* the election—I'll need somebody in the press office to handle just television—and you're the only one I know for this job; we need to have a woman, anyway.' 'You're the only one I know—who knows enough about television and radio.' "And that's how it started."

"And that's how I got there and saw *you*—in the Governor's Office hallway—the very *first day*, remember, I was bringing Bob Simmons in to interview Reagan—so that's how it all happened, in a nutshell."

"I did not know Nancy Reagan—until running into her—*Raking you over the coals, Curtis!*"

Nancy R. was in the hall inside the Governor's inner-office complex, the 'Horseshoe,' suggesting I was *not* giving proper care and consideration to the placement of historic pictures, art work and photographs on those most hallowed walls along the corridors leading from the Reception Room, past the Governor's Conference / Council Room to his personal office and study. To this day, I really don't know *who* suggested I attempt this task of being the *Office Decorator*—but I was clearly stepping into uncharted waters of the First Lady's purview—*ONLY*—and muddying-up our excellent, two year and three month-long, relationship; in just about three minutes flat!

"As I followed them around the state—I met her—but I never knew her, never talked to her, *never* interviewed her—I just sort of *saw* her—and thought, 'Gee, she's a knockout'"

"I didn't have any association with her—until the incident in the hallway, just after RR took office, when I ran into her in the hallway—berating *you*, Curtis. I didn't know *him* very well, but I felt comfortable walking in and out of the inner office, since Lyn had told me to go in and out of RR's office as the need arose. So when I brought Bob Simmons in for the interview and someone on the staff asked what all of the commotion was out in the hallway, I told RR and the staffer that it was Mrs. Reagan chastising someone named Curtis Patrick, over the hanging of some pictures or art work." Ronald Reagan simply said, *"There must be some mistake!"*

"Lyn sat me down one day and said, listen, the Reagans don't travel together." I said, 'What do you mean, they don't travel together?' He said, 'Well, some couples don't.' 'If something should happen and a plane would go down—who would raise the children?' I said, 'Well—that's *their* problem.' He said, 'No—that's YOUR problem.' I said, 'What are you talking about?' He said, 'You're going to have to travel with Nancy Reagan.' I said, *'NO WAY, BUDDY!'* 'I didn't sign-on for that, I don't know her, she doesn't know me—and I don't do stories like that!' 'Women stories.' So he, Lyn, said, 'I'll make a deal with you—you can travel with the governor and me and you can do stuff here in the office—but, when *she* travels—you've got to travel with her.' "And I was furious—as furious as I could get after having accepted this job. Anyhow—it all worked out—as you know."

"One day I was supposed to be on a plane with her, going to L.A. Her driver in Sacramento—(usually a State Police officer—could have been a new person on duty—her permanently-assigned officer, Ron Azevedo, was ultimately considerate, attentive and would have stayed until N.R. was aboard) —just *dropped* her off at the airport terminal building and drove away." "Lyn heard about it." "He put me in a car and said," 'Get right out there!' "I arrived and found her 'huddled' in a corner—not crying, exactly—just totally devastated Because she never had to travel by herself."

Thus began, immediately, a new program where either Patrick (myself), Bob Tarbet or NCR would travel with Nancy Reagan on *every* run—if for no other reason than to help communicate with home and RR and handle the logistics of traveling, not to mention the numerous interruptions, autograph seekers and occasional *flaps* that developed.

"These State Police drivers don't know that she had trepidations. That's when Bob Tarbet came into the picture, traveling, along with a Colonel Rowe or Temple—I think it was Herb Temple from the National Guard."

"Finally, I was assigned to travel with Nancy more often. I remember getting on the airplane one time and having somebody behind us start *ripping* into the Governor—I think—about the budget, and she pushed the button on her seat back (NCR laughs) and back it went—and she turns around to this guy in the back and says, 'That's my husband you're talking about—and YOU don't have *ANY* of the *facts* straight!' "This poor guy turned blue, purple and red—and just *shrank* in his seat."

"That's when I knew she wasn't going to put up with any nonsense! I thought it was very brave of her. But, you see, I hardly knew her and all of a sudden—she flips this seat back—and starts—not yelling—but raising her voice—boy could she— and let him have it. And that guy was praying to be dissolved into his seat. He was mortified—and then she flips the seat back up and looks at me and goes, 'See!' I mean something like—'Well, I told him off.' "I thought that was terrific! I thought, I would never have had the nerve. I would have probably just suffered in silence—or 'stewed' in my own juice."

"I thought that was terrific! And that gave me the first clue that he, RR, was absolutely Numero Uno in *her* life. All the time! And *she* was with him!"

"They were *totally wound* into each other!"

"To the exclusion of everybody else. I am sure that's why a lot of people didn't want to be around her—because they all wanted to be close and intimate with him—and they wanted to find out something nobody else knew—"

I said, 'And people were resentful—in a way—that they were so close.'

"Yeah!" "Well, sure they were—because everybody wants a piece of the candidate or the governor or the president—everybody wants a little piece of his time and attention—it's human nature—and he was *lovely* to everyone!"

"Oh!" "He, Reagan, was *gracious*—and FUNNY! He had people in 'stitches' all the time—and—he was a *total* gentleman."

"You know, I disagreed with some of his positions. I was one of the few women around RR. There was Pat Gayman, scheduling, Kathy Davis, personal secretary and Helene Von Damm, Clark's personal secretary who were close to RR but they wouldn't have disagreed with him—much. Kathy Davis was very nice."

"I remember—just to show you how embarrassed I was—I mean—how *stupid* and *naive* I was—one day RR called me into the office—he had this magnificent camera—it looked like a $5,000.00 Canon—one of those things you see in big photo ads, today, with all the attachments and he said, *"Nancy, I want you to wrap this as a gift—because I'm going to give it to Kathy."* "And my jaw fell." I said, 'Governor, you're going to give this to Kathy?' He said, *"Yes, I don't take pictures and this was a gift."* "And he was running on"—I said this to him, Curtis, 'But Sir, don't you think that's a bad precedent to start?' And he said to me, *"Of course not, she's my secretary, and I want her to have it as a gift from me!"*

"I was mortified, because I thought, it sounds like I am saying, 'Don't give her anything!' 'After all, she doesn't deserve it.' I acknowledged, 'Of course—but you were thinking of the long-range possible problems, right?.'

"Yeah!" But I said, 'Giving your staff these kinds of gifts sets a (bad) precedent!'"Oh, I was so mad. He looked *wounded*—when he looked at me."

He said, *"But, she's my secretary, I want to give it to her."*

Like, "Are you going to take this fun thing away from me?" And I thought—'Well, you jerk, Reynolds, and she laughs—you *are* a pain in the ass—it's *none* of your damn business! But I learned immediately, like when I went in and said, 'Oh shit,' to him about what Nancy was saying to *you* in the hallway. I learned instantly that: It's *none* of my business."

'I just smiled when these things happened—or looked serious,' I told her."But you're a man—and I was the *only* woman around who ever talked to him that way, except for Pat Gayman. It was my nature—to speak out" To say, 'This is DUMB, don't do it!' "But I was wrong. But the *best* thing about Reagan—I disagreed with him on a lot of issues—abortion for one, although I was a Catholic—I wasn't a raging feminist or anything—but there were times when I'd go in and say," 'Governor!' 'Governor!' 'I think you're wrong on this.' And he'd say, *"Well, Nancy, sit down and tell me why you think I'm wrong."* "And he never equated *disagreement* with *disloyalty.* It's true! And, I'm sure that's how Mike Deaver did it. Everybody had a different way of saying, 'Governor, I disagree with you.' But, I would just go in and plop myself down and say, 'How could you DO this?' 'This is terrible!'"

Then she gave a hearty, good-natured laugh.

And he would say, *"Now Nancy, this is how I feel and this is why."* "And, I would listen to his argument—and *he* listened to everything I had to say. I don't think he discounted it. I think he took in under advisement, into consideration."

"I think so—I think his mind was pretty well made up. But he *always* was willing to listen. And he would always kinda' just smile tolerantly—like," "*Oh, Oh, here she comes again.*" "And I would do this—on the road."

"One night he gave a *not so good* speech, if you can imagine, and it went on and on and on—and when he got into the car, I said, 'My—what were you thinking of?' (she laughs) And when I look back on it, I didn't say it in a mean way—but I *never* hesitated to speak out—and—nobody else on the Team did either. It's just that I was the *only* woman around on the traveling team; which, at that time in history—was very unusual." But there's something else here. This is the same intrinsic *essence* that I've tried to capture in these special moments we're recalling

And Nancy was quick to say, "Sure!" "Oh Yeah!"

And Lyn just permeated this sort of thing—he generated this kind of thinking where those who were the 'critiquers,' like himself and Jim Gibson, would forthrightly say to RR, 'Holy Cow, Ron what was that all about?'

"Oh Yeah!" "And Reagan was *crazy* about Lyn." "Once, while coming back from giving what was supposed to be a 'short talk,' Lyn said to Reagan, 'Governor, what were you *doing* talking for forty-five minutes?" Reagan would look at Lyn and say, " *Well, Lyn, I guess I just got carried away."* "And there were no hard feelings."

I know, and Nancy wasn't enamored with anyone, I reminded her.

She said, "Well—she wasn't crazy about anybody".

It's true. I understand. She was simply crazy about one person *only,* Ronald Reagan.

"She and I were forced to travel together."

According to Reynolds, there *were* a few people N.R. actually *was* crazy about including Chuck Tyson, one of our key advance-men during the campaign and later Special Assistant to Cabinet Secretary, William P. Clark, Jr., Pat Gayman and the Deavers.

"Nancy was devoted to Mike Deaver and his wife. She loved Mike and Carolyn. She got mad at him once in a while—but Mike and Carolyn were extremely close to her. Now, the Meeses were *not.* She was *never crazy* about Helene Von Damm—but on the other hand—she never tried to get them *fired!* Not until many years later—did things like that happen—and—after all; it was the presidency."

"When I was in New York City with the Reagans, about 1971, or maybe '72, we were at the Waldorf Astoria and I got word that three of my horses had burned to death in a fire at our family ranch. I was devastated! And the Reagans were very sympathetic. Nancy Reagan was really wonderful to me—as we got to know each other. We are totally different kinds of people, but she settled in to realize that she was 'stuck' with me and I kinda' felt that way—that I was 'stuck' with her. But she was really wonderful to me—over all those years! "She *really was!* "She has been to you, too, Curtis."

"I just don't think that her personality is one that generates—warmth—there is a *mystique!* It never will. 'But, on the other hand, we traveled together for *ten* years—then I traveled with RR and the both of them together during another *ten* year period. Mike Deaver and I were the only ones from staff who went on those foreign trips with them. It was just Mike and I or Mike and Carolyn and I."

"Anyhow, back to the barn fire story and the horses dying—RR being very sympathetic."

"We got to L.A., were met at the airport by CHP driver / security man, Barney Barnett, who became Ron's wood-cutting 'buddy,' friend and confidant, years later at Rancho Del Cielo, and in his arms he carried Ron's favorite Italian jumping-saddle. Reagan, who had quietly called Barney from New York, took it from him—put it into my arms," and said, " *This is a small consolation for your loss, but I hope you'll keep it.*" "And that is *so* typical of Ronald Reagan!" "It is so typical." "And all I could think of was, 'And you were *criticizing*—well—you were *questioning* him about giving a camera to Kathy.' "I was just overwhelmed." (The memory of her chastising session with RR had suddenly appeared to bedevil her once again)

"Well—he *was* giving her the camera because she was *leaving.* I remember what I said then," 'Isn't this terribly expensive for a going-away present?' "And that's why Nancy Reagan and I got along. I would 'chirp' at him—all the time. Calling through the hotel door while security stared in disbelief, 'Have you got your slippers on?' 'Now, are you in bed?' 'Now, put the light out.'"

We did this to give a comfort level to Nancy Reagan, when she wasn't on the road with us; simple as *that.* With NR at home and all of us still having an hour or two of more work to do, advance & security prep., work, or trying to get a bite of dinner, prior to turning in ourselves—we recited nightly to RR, 'Rest and relax—don't worry about a thing—don't be concerned about details or tomorrow's schedule—we'll take care of everything—hit the sack for a good night's sleep, Governor—call if you need anything!'

He could be a 'workaholic' on his research and his speeches on the road. 'Exactly.' 'Same situation,' I told NCR. I was privileged to be in that inner-most-space of their lives. Stopping by the Executive Residence, checking in during breakfast in the morning to make sure the new security systems were operating, the cars were running, the children were getting off to school O.K. and if there were any broken pipes or other home-front problems that may have cropped up in the night; and again returning during the hot chocolate and T.V. news at about 8 o'clock at night. Since the main reason I moved my family to Sacramento was to accept the appointment to a position on the governor's staff—I thought it would give the Reagans a comfort-level by living as close as possible, just a few houses across and down the same street; since they basically knew *no one* in the immediate area when we moved them into the newly-leased residence on 45th street.

It was agreed at the top level of the Governor's Staff that this would put somebody on the staff they felt they could count on, close by; other than the State Police who were simply guarding the residence. We understood the Reagan's needs and could respond quicker during off-hours, weekends and holidays. That's why Art Van Court and myself were privileged to be able to go in—and out—and 'tuck them into bed,' so to speak, at night—*he* in his slippers and robe—*she* in her nightie—in their master bedroom—in bed!

It was a *trust* we didn't take lightly. They treated us like members of the family. And RR would say, *"Yes, Curtis. Please come in!"*

'No—No Sir.' 'You're in your—pajamas—you're trying to go to sleep.' And he'd say, *"I know—but let me turn the news down, come on in."* And he would say, *"I know you have some papers there for me to sign—do you have any for me to re-read, to review?"* *"And—what's my schedule in the morning?"*

Nancy Reynolds chimed in, "Yeah!"

And then Nancy Reagan would look directly at me and say, *"What does his schedule say when it's time to quit, Curtis?"* For the uninitiated—Time-to-Quit means: *5 P.M SHARP!*

"That's the role of a political wife," Reynolds responded.

Mrs. Reagan. would then ask, *"Where's he going to be at 5:00 o'clock?"*

"Well—that was the role of a political wife—who loved Ronald Reagan to pieces and didn't want him overworked, and frankly, didn't like sharing him with others. She was the *only* one—we ALL over-scheduled him! And he himself was part of the problem."

"At events RR would say," *"Oh, I want to stop and talk to so and so—."* etc. *"Oh, gosh, let's do this*—(little impromptu events and drop-bys) I would say, "Well Governor, you're thirty minutes behind schedule, now." RR would say, *"Yeah, I know, but—but—I want to see that man over there."* "And then, when we were late, *she* would blame US," NCR continued.

'Oh, of course,' I said. And we had to take the blame, it went with the territory.

"I can hardly think of anything negative—in the ten years I worked for them. It was a *joy* to come to work! He had me laughing and laughing—or—he had me thinking."

I asked Reynolds how many hours she worked every day.

"Oh, well, too many! Listen, my problem was—I had to go out at night with them—after a full day's work."

I was pushing her—I asked her if it was an eight-hour-day. 'Eight?' 'Ten?' It wasn't eight—it was *never* eight, was it?

"Well, no, of course not—but we agreed—we all signed on for that and I had to go out a lot at night—to the cocktail parties, receptions, speaking engagements, etc.—and my own family was neglected. No question about it." "But—I wouldn't have traded it for anything! These are just recollections, but the overall picture is: How could I have been so lucky?" *"SO LUCKY!"!* "To be in the right place at the right time—my husband knowing Lyn—all these things—these *serendipitous* events led to ten of the most *glorious, delightful, fun, fascinating, interesting, incredible* years of my life!" "And I wouldn't trade it for *ANYTHING!" "ANYTHING!"*

"I just felt like I was lucky to be there. I saw him, RR, *every single day*—and—in many of the evenings—and I was with NR a lot—and I got to know her better— and I realized how *vulnerable* she was. How *insecure,* in many ways. We all are. What about her childhood? Why—why was she this way—so insecure? She had a kind of different childhood, too. And was raised by an aunt or something."

"I think Hollywood people are—*suspicious*—because we are considered the *handlers*. You know—the staff—we're like—their *press agents.* "So, she paraphrases from a celebrity who said, "I hire you and—*you* work for *me."* "So—you do what I tell you."

But there's a difference *here,* with Reagan. There is a principled thread of deeper connection, in my opinion, I told her. *You* may have been a Democrat because uncle Harry was—or *you* went for Mayor George Christopher in the Primary because he was a good friend, but once you connected with Ronald Reagan—that was *it!* You, then, started to connect with his principles.

"Oh, yeah!" "Yes!" "I think we all shared an ideology and principles. I am just saying that Nancy came from a world—and he did too—where, if you wanted to fade into the background—your *press agent* took over. It's a different kind of world—*politics*—and, yet it's very similar—and I think she always felt that way. That you were *never* on intimate terms with the staff."

I told her I was aware of that, but the problem that Nancy Reagan faced was— she didn't realize that we loved Ronald Reagan and by that fact or issue—we ended up—loving *her* and her family—and we would have done anything for them.

"I think she knew that, Curtis. Yeah, I think she did! I think she was so over-whelmed with being First Lady. I think that Hollywood is such a *capricious* place— where people come and go, you get dropped. "It's all about—." "Well, there's NO loyalty. There really isn't—and I think that was the first time—I think she *did* appreciate people who were loyal—but I just think it wasn't in her nature to say it ('thanks') all the time. She was almost *paranoid*—no, not paranoid—but she was *fixated* on *him*—Ron—his schedule—everything about him—and I had never in my life met a couple who were completely *into* one another, as they were. Never—in my life! I mean—I know a lot of good marriages and relationships—but they're very independent of one another."

"This was a totally *interdependent* relationship."

"I must say—I was treated so well by everybody. I really did like everybody!

"They were the BEST years of my life, really—although I've always had fantastic—fantastic jobs—and wonderful experiences. I had ten years in television—anchoring the news—so *that* was fabulous, too. That's how I met Ronald Reagan—all these years are connected to one another—but *those RR years*—were sort of the *GLORY YEARS!* And I'm sure for *you*—nothing could ever replace them."

'No!' Was my enthusiastic reply.

"I think we were privileged. It was like the early Kennedy years. People were so enamored of the Kennedys. Well, I think that was true of all of us. I think we were so—*enamored* with the Reagans. But in a good way. "We were willing to do anything—not break laws—but work our tails off, sacrifice anyone or anything and make any kind of offer that we could to be of help, because we *believed* in him and *loved* him."Even when we disagreed with him! He was the man of the future and we all thought he would be president—at least many of us did. But we forgot it all. As the years went on—we all left to go on with our lives—and *he* kept writing and giving speeches. And when he called me and told me and he was going to run for president, again—I had already moved to Washington D.C." I said, 'But, Governor,—'cause I never called him anything else but—I said, **'Governor, You're too *old* to run for president.'** I said, 'Governor, but you're sixty-six—or seven' —or whatever—and Reagan said, *"I know, Nancy, I know how old I am!"*

"Well, it was all I could think of. We had gone through two years of a presidential campaign and he had lost to Gerald Ford. And it just sprung out of my mouth. I didn't say it in an accusatory way." I just said, 'Oh My!' 'But Governor, you're sixty-six years old.' "Which seemed kind of old to me, then. Now I'm seventy three."

"I really considered the Reagans a part of my *extended* family—and because I do, and did then, they treated me like that. I feel so entwined in their lives because they made me feel like I was a *part.* They were just *wonderful* to me."

Nancy Reynolds' sense of humor complimented Reagan's.

"I was like the relative who—they roll their eyes and say," *'Well, she's baack!'* 'I guess we should be nice to her.'

This "Mutual Admiration Society" theme was spawned in the earliest days of the 1965-1966 California campaign—one good thing generated another—from staff members and volunteers to the Reagans—and right back again, from *them* to *us*.

Nancy proclaimed she had made a lot of mistakes.

I said, 'Me too!' The Reagans were forgiving. Reagan was always forgiving.

Nancy vociferously agreed, "Yeah I know." "Oh, listen—he hasn't got a mean bone in his body. Not a *mean* bone! There's *nothing* mean."

"And when I read mean things about him, I think, Ronald Reagan would have turned around and said," *"Gee, I always admired you."* or *"I always thought you were swell."*

Nancy asked, "You remember, don't you, in 1967—'68, I can't even recall the exact year when we went to Berkeley on that bus?"

'Ah, Yes'—I recalled.

"And then they started rocking the bus!"

'Yes!' The bus—surrounded by screaming, long-haired, tie-dyed, stick-swinging Hippies—was being rocked side-to-side. Scary! All we in advance and security could do was to envision the soon-to-be-inverted bus—*burning!*

"And then *he* gets off—and this really gorgeous girl and these professors—all 'Hippied'-up—were the first to greet RR—and were screaming filthy language at him."

"He stopped cold in his tracks and turned to that girl and said," *"Does your mother know you use that kind of language?"* "He was astounded that anybody, particularly a woman, would use that language. And I remember—it just stopped everything—*cold!* That was so typical of him. It was a *shock* to him, too! I don't think he had ever heard a woman talk that way. Language was another thing with RR. Ronald Reagan *never* used bad language—*ever!*"

"If he was telling a joke, he'd say," *"Now, Nancy, I'm telling a joke I don't think is for your ears, so will you please leave the room—or—I will leave the room."* And I'd say, 'Governor, I can listen to anything!' He'd say, *"No!"* *"I don't want to tell this joke in front of you."* "So, I would probably slink out of the room—feeling very left out. But he would *not* do it! And, the other thing he would *not* do—ever—ever. We had a fight about this! I *always* opened the door for him—when I was advancing some event."

"We were coming into this huge auditorium and I opened the door." He said, *"I'm not going through—you go through first!"* And I said, 'No, no. no, Governor—it doesn't work that way—*you* go through there—*in* there—they're standing on their feet, waiting—GO THROUGH!' He said, *"I will NOT go through!"* *"My mother told me that a woman goes through the door, first."* I said, 'Listen—it's going to look terrible.' 'People will mistake me for Nancy, it looks terrible to have a woman going in first.' —'I'm just working for you—I'm just your Advance-man.' He said, *"I'm NOT going through that door!"*

Then Reagan said, *"Now you can decide whether you want to do that or not—but I am not going through that door!"*

"I was mad! Everybody else was waiting for him—and here we were—arguing—and finally, I just stomped in front of him, went through the door, turned right, got out of the scene—and anybody seeing me knew I wasn't with *him.*" "But, he would *not* budge! He was always the gentleman. He put the coats on the ladies—he helped anyone in need—he would help the person across the street, before he ever got to his speech—to his lectern."

I agreed. He was always the Boy Scout.

Nancy recalled, "One day it was one hundred and three degrees in Sacramento; he called me into his office. It can get so hot in the Central Valley of California around the Capitol that the acorns and nuts on the trees seem to cook in their shells, in spite of the cooling, fan-like leaves of the tall, deciduous trees arranged across the green lawns in Capitol Park.

Nancy continued, "There was some 'poor' little girl—with a placard—her husband was in prison. She was all by herself, marching in protest, demonstrating—out front—right outside RR's little office, the study with the thick, ceiling-high, bullet-proof windows in the corner of the State Capitol building." He called me in and said, *"Go get that girl!"* I said, 'Governor, look, I can't go get that girl!' 'The Security Chief, Art Van Court, would kill me!' He said, *"I want you to bring her in here."* Nancy thought, "She might have been pregnant, I don't know." Again, he said, *"Bring her to my office!"* *"I am not going to have this woman walking out there in the sun—it's one hundred and four degrees!"* "It was a big, record hot, day in Sacramento." And I said, 'But Governor, I can't *do* that.' And he said, *"I'm telling you, Nancy, please go get that young lady."* "So—I did. I brought her in, the governor sat her down in his air-conditioned office, gave her some water and said, *"Now, what's the problem, young lady?"* "But he could not bear to see her in that terrible heat—and—called Legal Affairs Secretary, Ed Meese (later Chief of Staff) in to say, *"Now, this is the problem for this young lady, see if we can help her."*

"I believe her husband was in jail or prison. She was all by herself—she had this large card."

I reminded Nancy that I was asked to get involved in many similar incidents. The governor got me involved in this kind of thing all the time. He was to a fault—the quintessential *honest gentleman.*

Nancy said, "Well, he was! He was so un-movie-starish. And, I think that was part of his appeal. That was his *mystique.* It was like the man I met in Illinois. One day RR was there and there was a mob of friendly people—I think it was Tampico or could have been Dixon, where RR went to college—there was this huge crowd. I'm always the one. I loved to get people to come up and meet him, because they usually hung back."

"There was this guy who was way in the back, and I was back there too." I turned to him and said, 'Do you want to meet Ronald Reagan?' And he said, 'That's all right, I don't have to meet him; I know if I did, I would like him *so* much!' "And I could see Reagan exuding this genuine charm and interest in *other* people. I was so taken with what the man had said, that I grabbed him (she laughs at her brashness) and said, 'I don't care if you want to meet him or not—you come with me!' "The man in the crowd kind of summed it up—'I know just *seeing him* and being around him—that he is someone who would like *me.*' He said, "I know I would like *him*—and he would like *me!*'

Nancy and I concurred—when RR was out meeting and touching people—It wasn't a perfunctory act. We both said at almost the same moment: "Well—he wasn't a *glad-hander.*"

"In fact, he was kind of *shy*—I mean—he didn't go running down seeking handshakes and all that. That's why we had to kind of coax someone to come over and meet him. He wasn't going to just plunge out into the crowd. But once you introduced him and they found a common ground—on anything—I remember taking a fellow over to RR and saying, 'This gentleman lives in *your* hometown.'—or—'He lives here—he remembers this or that.' "And Reagan's face lit up." He says, *"Oh, how nice to meet you!" "Gosh, how long have you lived here?"* "And then he starts telling stories of his younger days—to this fellow. But, I just thought—that guy who said," 'No, I don't need to meet him—I know I'd like *him*—and I know he'd like me.'

"And I thought—'that's the thing, I think one of the reasons why Reagan was so *loved* by people—that they knew that he was really a super guy—who would be interested in *them!*' "And, who would *like* them."

"It's always so many of those politicians who ask," 'Are they going to love me?' 'Are they going to fawn all over me?' "Reagan never lost his *human* quality. He was exactly the same behind the scenes as he was in front—and *that* was another incredible discovery for all of us!"

"Because I grew up around politics all of my life—but when the door closed— Reagan NEVER said," 'Well, I hope that satisfies those—unwashed people out there—those slobs.' "He was *always* the same. He *never* changed."

"And people, even those who disagreed with him, or didn't even like him— always would say," 'Well, what you see—is what you get.' "And that's true. You *always* knew where Reagan stood!" She spoke from a position of unequivocal, irrefutable, knowledge.

"*You* had your own experiences with him, Curtis," she said seriously. "Everybody on the staff did."

It took the people who did their specific tasks with him, to understand his inner self, because they really loved him. They wanted to do their best. They wanted to make him look good, even though he always made *us* look good.

Nancy continued, "Many times I would say to the staff," 'You guys don't need me.' 'You know what you're doing—your instincts are correct.'

'You've been around the public long enough—why do you need me?' And, it was like—'Well, you're doing the dirty advance work.' "And when it came to the working-press wanting answers from me about Reagan, I'd say," 'O.K.—but don't talk to *me*.' I would say, 'Well, ask him yourself—don't ask *me!*'

Our discussion turned to advance work. During the 1965 / '66 Reagan for Governor campaign in that old L.A. headquarters building—even before they moved out of the S-R offices—when I was working for Spencer-Roberts as a *volunteer*, for Dave Tomshany and George Young. Those two worked for Bill & Stu and we would go out and meet people and do the advance-work—connecting with the tour, even if RR was just being driven around in Dave's Mustang convertible on the 'Brown Bag' lunch program, and later, as the number of events grew and each one grew in size, meeting the press entourage along the way—phasing in and out of the scene— it was the Advance-Team, those people who got to know the true individual, Ronald Reagan, and we worked fourteen—eighteen hours a day and were ready to *bound* out of bed the next morning. It was exhilarating!

"Yeah!" "Oh, I know—I could hardly wait to get to work!"

"I got involved with the P.O.W. / M.I.A. Vietnam War homecoming thing; they assigned me." The Reagans said, *"O.K., You're in charge of the whole thing."* You *go ahead and plan the 'Welcome Home' parties in L.A., Sacramento, San Francisco— and you go meet these guys—and tell us what we should be doing for them." "What would be appropriate?"*

"And I went over to San Francisco to try to meet the P.O.W. whose bracelet my husband wore. And, it was *John McCain!*" "I walked up and introduced myself to him and said, 'I work for Ronald Reagan.' And he said, 'You what?' And I said, 'Yes!' Then I said, 'I'm here to kind of advance this thing and meet you guys.'

"You see, my guy, whose bracelet I wore, Hansen was his last name, was killed in action. So, I became close to the McCains—we became fast friends—and my son, Michael thirty-four years later, works for McCain, *today.* Michael is the General Counsel for the Senate sub-Committee on Aviation. It was *serendipity!*"

"Anyhow, I met the wife of Hansen—the Hansen girl and her little boy—I told the Reagans that I was wearing the father's bracelet." Reagan said, *"Well, invite her up here—!"* (to the Governor's Office in Sacramento)

I said to him, "Why don't you have a lunch—we'll have a picnic lunch—in the office with ALL of the P.O.W. wives in California—and their children." RR said, *"Great—let's do it out on the lawn!"*

"I went ahead and planned it and set this thing up."

"So we walk out, the governor and all of us,—head down the Capitol steps—towards Capitol Park—but we walk out with ALL these kids, and ALL of these P.O.W. and M.I.A. wives—and the *Black Panthers are there*—demonstrating against Reagan—on the *Lawn!*" "I think it was Art Van Court, his security chief, who took one look and said, "Turn around!" "We're going back into the building!"

That was Art, I remember the whole affair. There were several of us there at the time: Van Court, myself, Rowlee, State Police guys, CHP people and one or two national Guard officers (advisors to the Legal Affairs Sec'y., Ed Meese) and Ed may have been there himself."

"Yeah!" "So we go back inside and have our picnic lunch on the carpeted floor of the Governor's Conference Room. And then the press came in with us and they took pictures. Mrs. Hansen had a little five year old boy and he was just overwhelmed by all of this—and here is a photograph—during the picnic—or just after—of the little boy grabbing RR by the hand, while he is standing talking, and then Reagan is bending down—and Todd whispers something to him—and Reagan throws his head back and laughs, saying, *"He said, Could you take me to the bathroom?"* "Anyway, it was just one of those wonderful moments where Reagan takes him into his little private 'john,' and it was a *GREAT* day! I know there was a picture in the Sacramento Bee newspaper—of him sitting there eating his picnic lunch with those people."

"Ron and Nancy were involved in several things like that. Nancy was genuinely interested in the Foster Grandparents program—and I saw her in hospitals with wounded guys—and I had to leave the ward. It was too *terrible*. I could *not* stand it." Reynolds said that it was, "too emotionally draining."

"She *WAS* Florence Nightingale! One of her *most* shining moments—as she sat and held the hands of guys who were blind—who were mutilated—*BURNED!* It was *too much* for ME—I would just *FLEE!* And she would be in there for hours with them. And I always thought—'whatever reservations I had about Nancy Reagan, were *erased* in that moment.' She never just flipped from bed to bed—she'd spend hours. She got phone numbers of their sweethearts and their mothers and would go home and call them. She *DID!*"

"The Foster Grandparents Program—she *adored* it! When we went to a lot of institutions, with children who were in very bad shape, physically and mentally and emotionally—she would spend the day with them. With the children—and then the grandparents—and then the children again—she'd get on the floor and play with them—and *NEVER* allowed the press to come with her! I saw what I really feel was the *real* Nancy Reagan. She was the doctor's daughter." She told me to, *"Forget the Schedule!"* She wanted to— *"Spend time with those boys, and those children and those grandparents."* "Those were her *SHINING MOMENTS*—and—then—the other thing was the P.O.W. program—she became totally immersed in it."

"We Planned these fabulous parties, which were a huge success. Nancy became great friends with many of them. She wept as she met them. Some of them brought her cups that they had had in prison and she broke down—and Reagan *too*—and then—I had Reagan invite John McCain to be the speaker at the Easter Prayer Breakfast—remember the Prayer Breakfasts? John McCain came and there were *two thousand* men—well, maybe a few women—and John McCain got up, without notes, and talked about his being in solitary confinement—*underground*—North Vietnam—a hot, hot, *hot*—terrible day—he was thrown into this box—and he wanted to die—and he thought about suicide—of course, he was in a tiny box—buried in the middle of a field—and there was *no* shade!"

McCain spoke, 'And then I saw the words of another prisoner—that were scratched in the wood, that said,' 'I believe in God, the Father Almighty!'—and then the rest of the prayer. "There was not a dry eye in the house. Reagan wept. The whole audience went *nuts* (tears)! And since that time, Reagan has always been crazy about the McCains—and so has Nancy. They had a very, very close, intimate relationship."

Reynolds continued to work hard, raising four boys and putting them through college, as a single-mom, after the death of her husband, Frank. She had left the West Coast, moved to Washington D.C., and took a job with the Bendix Corporation in the late '70's—when she got Reagan's call.

"I was in Washington being a big-time lobbyist, and I got this call—and thought—'He's got to be kidding!' "And I meant that in an affectionate way. Reagan said, *"I think I'm going to run for president!"* *"I want to know if you'll help me."* "People kept saying—that some people were too old to run for president. I mean—remember, the press was full of it—the rumors of his candidacy—*not* just about Reagan—but about the age of anybody."

Reynolds' response to this man who called her all the way from California with his *decision*, his thrilling piece of news, his 'life's ambition' finally being realized and coming to fruition—was— **'Governor, You're too *old* to run for president!'** "So it popped into my mouth and out again. And he was so funny—and he said, "*Well, I really would appreciate it—I'd love to have you on the campaign team.*"

And, I said, 'Governor—I would too. I will do anything for you in my spare time—but I have four sons in college—and I'm working for a corporation.' 'I can't afford to work for *you* anymore.' RR said, "*I understand—but you're my only contact.*" "*You're the only one of our gang who lives in Washington, now.*"

"That's true!" Nancy agreed.

He went on, "*We're delighted to know you're there—and the press would work with you—and, if I do get elected—maybe you'll come and visit me at the White House.*"

A typical Reagan remark.

I said, 'Well, ask me to do something—I will do anything—*ANYTHING.*'

'On a weekend—I will give up my vacations—I will do *anything*—but I cannot leave my job!' I said, 'Financially, I can't do it!' "Because my children, who were in college, needed the medical benefits that a corporate affiliation provided. Not possible in the campaign." And I'm saying, 'But, Governor—don't be *crazy!*" "But, he was just as calm and sweet and funny as he always was—and he said, "*Well, Nancy and I would really like to have you aboard.*" And I said, 'Well, thank you very much.' I said, 'Let me *volunteer.*'

"So, as soon as he announced, all the press people I knew in Washington began to call me. These are all, long-time old friends of mine. They all began to call and say, 'You're the only one in town who knows anything about Ronald Reagan.' "So I am happy to say,—I said all the right things." "And *they* did." "The press interviews worked out fine and I never said anything that was wrong—and—I got to know the press again.""I knew them socially—I socialized with them all the time. Then, I joined Ann Wexler, and we had this terrific lobbying firm—and we dealt with the press all the time, there. But that was *afterwards.*"

"It was just that I was always in the right place at the right time." "Always!" "And, when Reagan began to gain and gain and gain—I was amazed, excited and surprised. I really wasn't—except—when you live in Washington—you live in your own world. You've gotta' understand—when he calls and says, *"Gee, I think I'm going to run for president."* I thought, 'What?'

"It was just that my mental state at the time was—'What?' I said, 'But Governor, you're—you're sixty-six.' That's when RR said *those* words, *"I know, Nancy, I know how old I am."*

After President Reagan's inauguration ceremonies and after the galas, Reynolds was asked to move into Blair House and help the new First Lady set up her office operations, secretary and assistants. She stayed six months there—then back to business.

When the Reagans moved into the White House—they would say, *"Come on over—what do you think about this—or that?"* "Mike Deaver would call and say,' 'They want to know what you think of this.' "And I would call—and they would always take my calls—even the president! I tried never to abuse the privilege of old friendships—and then they invited my youngest son and me to the Private Christmas Dinner at the White House, every year—for *EIGHT YEARS!* I was just always *astounded!* Because I didn't expect it. It was just Mike and Carolyn, the Wicks, Charles and Mary Jane, and whoever was in town, including a family member or two and the President's children, if they were in town. It was really wonderful!" "A privilege!"

"I used to fight with Mike Deaver—(she laughs)—I mean—"

We ALL fought with Mike, at one time or another, I told her.

"Mike and Carolyn treated me beautifully—yes they did!' "Listen, Mike could be very *uppity*—if you will. But—in the end—he was *always* supportive of me!"

"One day John Sears wanted me to be fired—because I had made some terrible boo-boo—it *was* terrible—even terrible to me. I didn't know it at the time—it was an accident—and Ronald Reagan heard Sears say something negative, berating *me*, and RR told John Sears, *"It wasn't her fault, I won't have that!"* "Reagan and Mike, too."

"We were a family—just like an ordinary family—that scrapped—except that none of us would *ever* be mean."

"The White House was different for Nancy Reagan. Nancy was *always* 'under siege'—with and by the press—she was like a finely-tuned violin."

My first thought on hearing this from Reynolds, A Stradivarius: High quality, high strung—delicate!

Reynolds continued, "She could be set off in the slightest way—yet her *instincts* were terrific, many times, My God—you know what? The *Presidency,* the *Power,* the *living in Washington*—does that to people!"

"And I do think that Reagan became more distant and disinterested—and—he *never* liked getting involved with personal bickering."

We plumbed the depths and agreed. Especially when people used their power and position to go behind his back.

'No. No!' He was above it and his mind did not want to wallow around in it.

"Of course not—but it certainly hurt him a lot by *NOT TAKING COMMAND!*"

She referred to the Don Regan affair and power plays by Cap Weinberger and George Schultz.

"I'm not blaming anybody—you just wished that once in a while he'd stand up and say," ***"NO, NO!"***

"The first time I noticed something was wrong, I sat on the other side of the President and Nancy's Christmas Dinner table from Mary Jane Wick (W.H. Director of Protocol) and talked to the president—I always did. It was our last Christmas in the White House. It was the first time I had ever seen him *totally distracted and withdrawn.* It was in the middle of the Iran-Contra scandal. I mean, he wasn't his usual self. You knew it was weighing heavily on him—I *knew* it—I could tell by the flick of an eyebrow or—just as *you* could. Anybody as close as we were knows what mood you're in. It was the ONLY time I haven't seen him relaxed and funny."

"Now, he made every attempt—and maybe nobody else noticed it—probably the Wicks did, because they know him very well—but he was a *distracted man—very withdrawn—obviously, something was wrong!*"

"And I don't know if it had anything to do with Alzheimer's."

Chapter Thirteen
CHP OFFICER & GENTLEMAN

Dale Rowlee

"From my viewpoint—there wasn't much about Ronald Reagan *not* to like— there may have been idiosyncrasies, but nothing you would dislike!" "But he sure functioned on his own—his *own* philosophies, his *own* attitudes—he was very *genuine* about that." "He was a very *forthright* individual."

Dale was a California Highway Patrol motor-officer, who began his service to Ronald Reagan during the interim-government / transition period and stayed eight years as the governor's driver and confidant in Northern CA. He earned a special place in the hearts of Ron and Nancy Reagan. He was thirty-eight years old when he started.

Dale was a no-nonsense family-man who was steady-as-a-rock. He was unflappable. He was an honest, quiet, polite, positive straight-shooter. He had a discernible faith in God. Dressed to a military shine in his CHP uniform, Dale, already honored by the CHP, was not only an inspiration to other staff members, but also a fine example of compassionate law enforcement. Frankly, he was a real good example of the kind of quality person whom RR had tried to surround himself with and the kind of person RR was himself.

Dale, I recognized, as did the Reagan family and the staff, as an uncommon man and I was proud to share my small office with him. Otherwise, he would have been stationed outside of the inner-sanctum "Horseshoe" of offices and farther away from Governor Reagan.

Comments from Dale—before the interview began:

"A person on the staff, or a 'wannabe', who couldn't pull their own weight— they were *gone!* Allegiance was paramount—to The Man, his wife, Nancy, and his family—and, to the honor of the Office of the Governor of California. The actual actions of a person, a leader, tell much more than anyone's notes and books. Good examples were set! We had good examples at the top and nobody minded working hard or doing whatever it took to get the job done. Slugs didn't last!"

Dale first met Ronald Reagan in a face-to-face interview for the job of Governor's (Northern California & State Capital) Driver at the old IBM Building on Capital Mall at the offices of the governor-elect's Transition Team, in the first month after the November election.

"Naturally, I was working that day. I was on my motorcycle. I got a radio call from Deputy Zone Commander Stokes asking me to call A.S.A.P on a telephone." 'How long will it take you to get home, change into civilian clothes, and get downtown?'

'Thirty minutes, Sir.'

'O.K., I need you at 555 Capital Mall as quick as you can change and get down there!'

"In thirty minutes I walked into the building in a suit and tie and met Art Van Court, Chief of Security, and another fellow from L.A.P.D. inside the Transition Team offices. (probably Chuck Ward, whose interview appears in this book) I was ushered into the governor-elect's personal office and was introduced to Ronald Reagan."

It must be said, here, that Dale had his name on the 'short list' of applicants who had asked Commander Stokes to be considered for *that* specific job, and who had already passed all of the background investigation checks.

I had previously worked with the officer that was the permanent driver for Pat Brown, a lot, so that I knew what went on at the Governor's Office in terms of the job—and what the responsibilities were. I was then introduced to Mr. Reagan and we talked, and spent about fifteen or twenty minutes together. He asked questions and really, it was not a severe interview. It was just more of a get-acquainted interview than anything else."

"Why it was that I wanted the job? Things of that nature. I couldn't have been more excited. I mean, it was a *great time* for me. It was a very good *first* meeting. He wasn't *standoffish* at all; he was very easy to meet."

"My perception of Ronald Reagan is that he wasn't an extremely outgoing man. He was quite reserved. He was very, *very* personable. But still, in all, he was quiet, too, in his mannerism. It was a good conversation—there wasn't anything that was abrupt about it or—*"I don't have time for this"*—or anything of that nature."

"It was just another part of getting ready for the job he had to do. One of the things he needed to go through."

"So he handled it very nicely and gave me considerable time and attention, for what was going on at the time. A sea-change from the way California government used to be.""Preparing to replace most of the existing government top staff in all of the agencies plus tremendous upheaval on college & university campuses over the Vietnam War." As I left the office he said, *"We'll talk to you." or "We'll be seeing you."* "Something like that. I didn't know at that point who all was being considered for the job or what was going on, but later found out that it was an assignment that *I* was going to receive. I forget really, how many times we met after that, but it was very little. I had contact with Security Chief Art Van Court a couple of times, and then just got things prepared for when the Reagan Family flew into the (only commercial airport) Sacramento Municipal, south of downtown, the day before the Inauguration. We picked him up there and just started the "tour"—and—began our relationship at that time—with the setup of the original governor-elect's first, albeit compact, motorcade into Sacramento. It consisted of the governor's limousine, a lead car, a plainclothes "wire" car / back-up car and a couple of black & white Sacramento P.D. units and a CHP unit or two."

"In those days, there was only one police officer assigned to the Governor's Office. And historically, the Highway patrol had always had *that* position, in there, for a long time before this; for many governors before Governor Reagan."

"And the State Police was / were always in charge of the officers assigned as guards at the Governor's Residence. They, also, were around the Capitol Building— but they were not—*inside*—the Governor's Office or anything of that nature. There was just *one* person and that was a CHP officer."

"That's how we started out. I began my service in uniform, but after a few months it quickly changed to wearing a suit and tie. This was a designated *uniformed* position, but because of the nature of things that took place, all the time, in those days—threats, out-of-control demonstrations, riots, etc. The feeling of the staff around the governor was that, really, this should *not* be a uniformed position. The driver / officer ought to be in civilian clothes, which we immediately went to in a very short period of time. Not more than a month."

On the one hand, it didn't call attention to a public official traveling with an armed force around him or her. On the other, the 'bad guys,' who were interested in stopping that official from conducting his or her duties, wouldn't know who was armed and who wasn't; and with *what*.

"It's called the Executive Protection Unit, now. Then, you were the governor's driver and as such *you* had the responsibility of his security and the family's security, wherever they went, when they were around you or you were around them—'cause you were the *ONLY* person there, many times. Not to belabor this point, but every time we went on campus, there was—*trouble!* The uniform was too much attention-getting—it just garnered attention to the wrong place—the often-times—*hated*—police."

"The campuses had a lot to do with that playing down of the spotlight—the *whole thing!* And, of course, in the early days, prior to the E. P. State Police Unit—we were on our own. There was *never* another person around, other than Art, who phased in and out primarily for public events."

"While I was still in uniform, in the very first days of the administration, I would go pick up the governor in the morning and we had the old Cadillac limousine that had been Governor Brown's car. It was an older, well-used Cadillac, (old, tired and poorly maintained being the operative words) and driving into the office, we came down Capitol Avenue, right towards the Capitol Building—and the car *died* at 16th and Capitol Avenue!" "In the intersection—I mean it just DIED!"

"Now—the Cad limo had quit and I'm sitting in the middle of the intersection—just me and the popular new Governor of California—I got out of the car and started to push it out of the intersection—and the governor got out the other side—and we're *both* pushing it. We pushed the car out of the intersection, over to the curb, locked it up and The Man and I walked down Capitol Avenue—right down through the park—up the steps and into the Governor's Office! I mean *this* was the Security! I was *embarrassed* and *worried!* It's very laughable, *now!*"

It wasn't laughable, then, I told Dale.

"*I* wasn't laughing," Dale shot back.

No, it was embarrassing!

"Well, it *was* embarrassing, and, it was just—it was *ridiculous*—because the car should have been a better piece of transportation than that! But, Yeah! He helped me push it—off to the side of the road—and—*we left it*—and walked right down the middle of The Capitol Park and into the office! About two city blocks.

"We went from that, if you recall, to a 1965 Lincoln Limousine," Dale said.

I reminded Dale that it was Art, Ed Meese, other concerned staffers, as well as RR's *very* concerned First Lady, Nancy Reagan, who asked me to find another vehicle; A.S.A.P. We found a *used* limo in a motion picture studio garage in Hollywood, ready to be auctioned off.

It was a 1965 'stretch' Lincoln that we got through the Ford Motor Company. The Ford people wanted us in a Lincoln and thought it was 'strange' that we wouldn't want a new one. However, the staff and the governor himself felt this purchase was a prudent one under the Boss's now famous, "Cut, Squeeze & Trim" edict to all state agencies and departments.

"It wasn't but a couple of years later when we took trips on behalf of President Nixon and on behalf of Ron's own run for the office (1968 Miami GOP Convention) when we developed a relationship with the U.S. Secret Service and we had a Secret Service Detail assigned to the Reagans, periodically. It was through those contacts and when Ed Hickey came over from them to become Security Chief, after Miami, that we then got another vehicle that was *very* well-equipped to handle our needs. That was the beginning of it—the replacement of the 'junk' cars in the Executive Fleet. The problem was—the governor did not want to appear to be a wasteful spender on fancy cars, while at the same time asking others in state service to *"Cut, Squeeze & Trim."*

I asked Dale if his law enforcement background helped him in dealing with the problems he encountered when moving the governor into various venues and situations and then getting out of them—and—if so—'how?'

"I don't think there's any doubt about it—that it did! There were a lot of things developing at that time. The CHP was active on university campuses around the state, predominantly Berkeley; there was so much unrest going on there *all* the time. And so there became considerable CHP involvement in the things that were going on, on campuses, on the scene (where Reagan went) and in those types of uprisings."

"This immediately became a serious involvement and concern to us; where the governor would need to move from place to place—because of his beliefs—and his *public* statements—the different feelings (vitriolic & antagonistic) that were going on and being said in that element of society." *"Yeah!"* "There was new stuff coming out constantly from C. I. & I.—Criminal Identification & Investigation, the F.B.I., the A.G's Office & the National Guard Intelligence Briefing Reports and it was certainly an advantage to have available timely information that came through the Department (CHP) and the Department of Justice, in those days."

"But the security precautions were *NEVER* the same, as things started to develop in the sixties." Dale continued, "I became the traveling 'First Responder.'"

Well—The Man was receiving death threats!

"And which *you*, Curtis, knew all about and worked on—."

Periodically. Sometimes *daily*, I told him!

"Yeah!" "There was a tremendous amount of information that was just new, and somewhat *hot* & *critical*, that was coming in from sources all over the U.S. Various hate groups were moving about planning demonstrations, etc. The manner of dealing with a public figure that way—which had not been addressed—previously."

I asked, 'You mean it may not have happened during Governor Brown's tenure?'

"No." "No!" "We did a lot of that—but only when dignitaries would be in the state. We were always a part of maneuvering those people around and arranging for motorcades or whatever was required. But the security precautions were *never* the same as before!" **"Far greater!"** "More complex with Reagan."

Dale became the *primary*, day-to-day, on-the-scene travel-ops contact with the CHP—by virtue of the constant security updates coming his way, the constant schedule changes made by the Governor's Office and Nancy Reagan and the constant travel modifications to accommodate the safety of the governor, while still allowing RR to meet, greet and speak to the people; which he insisted on doing. Plunging into crowds!

"I became the primary contact with the Department. (CHP) I mean, (normally) you don't want to exclude the fact that the Chief of Staff and the Legal Affairs Secretary had immediate contact with the Commissioner's Office of the CHP—through the chain-of-command. It was not difficult for Legal Affairs Secretary, Ed Meese, to pick up the phone and call the commissioner and say, 'This is what we'd like to do.' But—as it evolved and the implementation took place—it usually happened that I was involved in some way and when we needed help for something—it didn't go through the Chief of Staff's Office or Legal Affairs—they'd just turn to me and say—'We're going someplace'—and I was told what it was we needed (additional security) when we were planning to get there—and *I'd get it!*" "I prearranged it."

"It developed that this wasn't going to work, to go from the office of the Chief of Staff to the Commissioner—I mean, why would you function that way? That's how it was in the beginning—but it only lasted a very short time."

So you had the authority to call your colleagues and set it up?

"Yeah!" "Absolutely." "When he, The Man, left here and went to Los Angeles, it was through the arrangements from within the Governor's Office and my desk that—'This is what we need—that's what we need, whatever.'

"I could call CHP Officers Barney Barnett, or Wayne Waddell, who came to work with us soon after Barney did."

"Los Angeles was a busy place. It was hard for one guy to accomplish things: meetings, public events, speeches, personal appearances by the governor that were complicated and spread out. Those officers worked out of the Zone Headquarters in L.A."

"They had other responsibilities there during the week when the governor or Nancy were not down there—but their time was fairly much absorbed because the Reagans were in and out of Southern California so much. *You* know, down and back. Overnight and come back in the morning—even during the week. Frequently I would go to Los Angeles with them for some reason or another, especially, if the CHP needed to augment what they had in the way of security. We traveled together a lot of times. We got on the PSA, the Electra, and we'd get the back table—clear in the back end—the tail."

I knew it was unusual for Dale or any career officer to share their insider experiences with *anybody* and I valued our friendship and Dale's trust in me. I asked him what some of the more difficult situations he encountered were, especially at Berkeley, UCLA, Santa Cruz —surrounding the car, the threats that were made in advance?

"Threats usually were not all that difficult. There weren't that many in the early days. They became *greater* as *notoriety* became greater—which didn't take long. But the biggest problem was just *crowd control*, because they would be adverse crowds."

"The *worst* places were the campuses. I don't think there's any doubt about that.

"And that's why, if you go back over history—that's why the Board of Regents meetings got to the place where they *weren't* being held on campus. They were held in the downtown offices of the CA State buildings."

"We had to quit going on campuses because it was too much of a problem. But we would run into the same types of problems, even at fundraisers. I know one time we were in Chico (Chico State College / University) and had a really tough crowd to get out of. It was hard for a very small group, ours, to deal with a pressing, large group of unruly bodies and in those days—they were *vocal and oppressive!* In those days we were a small group surrounding the governor—The Man—and when you finally got pressed and squeezed—when you got pressed by a large number of bodies chanting and pushing—we being the small group of bodies—the only thing you could do was to get yourselves together—and -*MOVE*—*out of there!*"

"And the governor didn't take *kindly* to this, many times." "It took a long time to *educate* him. Not the word I want to use," Dale admitted. (certainly not in a demeaning sense).

Well, I said, you can use that word. He was learning to be governor. He was stubborn and tenacious. He wanted to *engage* with these people.

"But—it wasn't *learning* how to be governor—there were other things that were difficulties in that area for him, I'm sure, but this was learning what he was being *confronted* with—the society in that day. And RR was *NOT* a *naive* man; except Ronald Reagan, in my estimation, always saw the good in people. And he just couldn't believe that somebody had it *in* for him."

I can remember that these people were belligerent—they were jeering!

"*Oh, to say the least! Very belligerent people* They were shouting obscenities. These were the people of concern! Other people—"*The popularity people,*" as RR called them—were just crowds to do with Governor Reagan's popularity—that was not a problem; except that you always had to be concerned with who was intermixed with that crowd."

"But we had a tremendous number of gatherings where it was just—they were just—people who needed to *touch* The Man. And they weren't bad people, I mean, they just needed to touch The Man. And you had to be very cognizant of that, because—why would you want to hurt somebody like that? Why would you want to disappoint them?" Reagan would say, *"Why would you want to be crude or rude or abusive to them—in their eyes—which you would be, if you just pushed past them?"* "So, it was always pretty delicate."

"He was *always* trying to be polite. And, by the same token—here was a guy who didn't back down to *anybody*. And to try and move him out of an antagonistic group or crowd, a lot of times, that was a problem. He didn't want to do *that*. He wanted to stay there and just converse or argue it out on its merits. He didn't want to tell them that they were full of baloney—NO—more like, *"B.S..—and there's the door!"*

"I mean, let me tell you, the day the Black Panthers came into the Capitol— there was *smoke* coming out of his ears because we took him out the back way—out of the Assembly Chambers, and through other offices—just to divert around these people; which made The Man *mad!*"

I was there but I wanted Dale to tell the details. I asked Dale how that decision was made.

"It was just a very *touchy* situation," Dale responded.

"These guys showed up in the Capitol Building with *guns!* Long rifles, shotguns, *you* know, short guns—pistols. These were *REAL* weapons." "Yes!" **"Absolutely!"** "I mean, it was just—it was—it was—." "He didn't have any kind of confrontation with them before we ducked him out!" "No!" *"No!"* "I think he *saw* them down the hall—is all—and that's the closest we ever let him get to them. And he *didn't* like that. He didn't like being told what to do in a situation like that." I mean—I think he thought—*'Look, I'm who I am, they can't do this to me!'* "Not cocky! And I don't blame him at all. I can fully understand the personal feeling that he had, but our concern was just ONE—*His Safety!*"

I asked Dale to recall RR's feelings about the *respect and honor* he had always felt for the institutions of our government. That this type of thing shouldn't be happening.

"Oh Absolutely!" "Absolutely, that's true!" "And, face it—things were just— *TENSE!"* "That stuff was going *downhill* a little bit!"

"It was an affront to everything that was taking place that day! It was how to be non-respectable, disrespectful and antagonistic to authority, and have the public accept it."

"Essentially, you had to be very careful how you dealt with those things, because of the *public outcry*—since there was an element of *free speech* involved."

"So, we had a *mad* governor on our hands!"

Please explain how you were trying to weave him through the offices—and he wasn't interested in vacating the premises.

"Sure" "Sure!"

Did you depart the building?

"No" "No!" "There were other ways around—you'll see us in the A.P. photo, here, of Governor Reagan, Art and I coming off the Gov's personal elevator into his office. Anyhow, it was a revealing picture. I mean there was *real anger* on Ronald Reagan's face!"

RR was *"mad"* that our security team took him out and around the trouble spots—but he, nevertheless, listened to and heeded the authority of those of us entrusted to protect his and his family's lives.

"Oh, yes, he sure did —from the law enforcement standpoint. "He sure did— he sure did! Art was with him that day—you have to remember that the governor, I think, had tremendous respect for Art Van Court."

I reminded Dale that I had brought Art out of L.A.P.D. early in Campaign 1965/'66 on his days off and vacations.

Later, he became *full time* Security Chief thru a special dispensation and early-retirement from L.A.P.D., thanks to L.A. Mayor Sam Yorty, a maverick Democrat, along with the Chief of Police—and thanks to the people that Art had around him, during the campaign, prior to RR taking office. One of these was L.A.P.D. Motor-Officer Chuck Ward, whose story appears in this book.

"And *you,* C.P. were confronted with a few things like this, at that time—right? I gave a resounding, 'Oh Yes!'

Dale continued, "It wasn't new to him—that he didn't *know* what was going on. And so, when those guys in *security* made a decision—he gave in and accepted that decision—but he didn't *like* it. *You* know, you were there, he didn't like those things.

"Then there was the *Knife Incident.* That was the time when a fellow came into the office complex, and we got a call from Jackie at the Reception Desk in the main lobby (her story appears in this book)—that there was a young man out there who had been 'hanging around' for quite a while, and was of a suspicious nature. We went out to talk to him. In fact, I think Ed Hickey (former U.S. Secret Service) was there. I think it was Ed and I who went out to talk to him—and got him off in the corner. He was wearing a long top-coat—this young African-American fellow. So, we got into a rather calm conversation, trying to find out what he was—what it was he wanted there and everything, and in feeling around the guy's top-coat—as we were just standing there with him—took that knife out of his belt, in the back, and it was as *large* as a butcher knife!"

Then Mrs. Rowlee brought out a photo of the actual knife.

"It was *that* knife! It's a *chef's knife*—it came out of a hospital where he worked, over in San Francisco."

He'd come over 'to visit the governor' all the way from San Francisco—without an appointment, I asked?

"Yeah." "And I'm sure he had greater things in mind. Subsequently he was turned over to the State Police and they took him and booked him. But that was in the early days. A little bit of fun."

Dale's cynicism showed through just a bit here.

How did Dale feel the governor reacted to his job?

"The early days, Curtis, were really—they were *great times*—because of the nature of the situation. Every time, in those first few weeks, that I'd pick him up—it was RR and me in the car, *alone*—and down to the office we'd go. There were many private conversations. When I say *private*—I don't mean that he was divulging anything to me that he wouldn't divulge to anybody else. It was just that there was *nobody else* there. It was *personal.* And, so—it was just a *fun* experience!"

"He treated me as one of his staff people and talked to me. He would talk very, *very* matter-of-factly, about what may have occurred in certain situations. Some of the issues of governing."

RR would ask, *What do you think of this, that, or the other thing?"* Reagan would say. *"This happened yesterday, and so-and-so said, such and such. do you think that's true?"* "And this was not a *façade*. I think this was a genuine interest on the part of Ronald Reagan that just showed an interest in what somebody else's thoughts were. And I really treasured that! I thought *that* was a choice opportunity. I remember they'd gone through a lot of budgetary stuff; which *you* know was in his face right away."

"He looked at the office as being a very, very substantial and powerful office, except that it was *encumbered,* to a great degree, by things that were already in place—that he couldn't get around. It would take time to do something different."

'There were legislative impediments,' I recalled.

"Yeah!" "And this was one of them—it was just amazing to him—that he had so little immediate power to do things—to see something that was *absolutely* wrong and he couldn't do anything about it because it was legally in place." He would ask a number of us to go check out something and see if we couldn't change it or fix it, wouldn't he?

"Oh Yes!"

And we'd have to come back with a report and pass it on up through to the Executive Secretary, who was the Chief of Staff, and report as to why it couldn't be done.

"That's very true."

Well, Dale, those times in the car were *special!*

"A lot of times—they were very *personal* times. I mean—it *was*—they *were*—he would just talk about family things taking place—because we had a lot to do with the family. The kids were small then; Skipper and Patty. I came and picked up Patty one night and took her to one of her first dances. Well, you'd have to (I had to) talk about that to The Man—RR asked, *"Well, how did it go?"*—and things of that nature. It was just pretty interesting stuff."

I told Dale I know how I was treated by him—like part of the family—like a family member. I asked Dale how he felt he was treated. *"Extremely well!"* "I very much felt that I was treated like a member of the family." *"Very much!"* "When they left Sacramento, they included my wife and I in a dinner party at the Executive Residence with Ed and Ursula Meese, Bill and Joan Clark and Mike and Carolyn Deaver. That was all. That was a tremendous thing! They didn't need to include us; the other three families were the ones who were at the top and made things happen. My wife, Bonnie, and I were treated exceptionally—I thought *I* was treated *exceptionally well!"*

"If there was a member of the family that was a part of that contingent, it was Barney. Barney's closeness with Governor and Mrs. Reagan, that was legendary, insurmountable in comparison to anybody else's. It was, aside from the fact that he was on the Highway Patrol; *a whole different thing!"*

* Willard "Barney" Barnett will be discussed later in this interview.

I knew Dale had spent more time than just about anyone, other than Nancy Reagan, with RR during those first eight years and I felt the outside world would be interested in what Dale, a devout Christian, had observed about RR and his relationship with God. He spoke of some of those *intimate* moments, Reagan's mannerisms and his demeanor. Some of which we, who were privileged to be there occasionally, witnessed ourselves: Dale, pensive, deeply thoughtful, and obviously very respectful of the Reagan's privacy, began: "Curtis, these were quiet times. When we traveled in the Limo, immediately the speech cards would come out of his pocket. It may have been relative to the event we were going to where he was just going over his speech again and revising the cards—but in doing all of this, there would be times where I could see him back there and he was very contemplative. I mean, if he were going over his speech and was changing the cards, the hand was always moving. There would be times and he would just be sitting there and was very contemplative. And when you said what you did, Curtis, that it was evidenced that he prayed a lot in his life, even on horseback—I think he did. I think it was evidenced by the fact *that* was very possibly what he was doing. It was times like that when he wouldn't write—he'd just be sitting there, pen in hand, cards in hand.

He was not doing anything, I asked?

Dale went on, "No, but I don't think this was a man whose mind was ever a blank."

I interrupted and said, 'But sometimes, when he closed his eyes, Dale, people and the press would accuse him of taking a nap and dozing. I didn't find him to be dozing when we were together. He loved his naps and Nancy wanted him to have them.'

Dale jumped right in and said, seriously, "Almost always, it seemed to me though, Curtis, his naps were purposeful. Sometimes, if we'd be out of town, in the early days, there were times when we were in the same suite. I had one bedroom and he had the other and he'd go in there, take his shoes off, lay down on the bed and take a nap. To sit on a plane and take a nap, I never saw that much. Sitting on a plane and heading someplace to an event—he was always working on what he was going to do (when he got there). It was just working and re-working."

I then pinned Dale down on the speech-cards issue. You said he "revised" and "revised," Please elaborate.

"Oh, he had his cards and he'd obviously cross things out and write in something else—he was *always* working things over."

Dale then agreed to talk about Dr. Billy Graham:

"My first knowledge of Billy Graham may have been just before I was in high school. The little independent church that we had attended in Illinois, our pastor was gone for some time, and Billy Graham came from Wheaton College and filled the pulpit of our little church there for a period of time. May have been three or four weeks or even a couple of months. Our pastor evidently had knowledge of Billy Graham or he would have had someone else come. He was not a known entity then—but he was great and very much enjoyed by the people of our small church; fifty to seventy-five people."

"After Billy Graham left Wheaton College (he graduated in 1943) and I went into my high school years while Graham joined the Youth for Christ organization (founded for ministry to youth and servicemen during WW II). He would come to Chicago for Youth for Christ meetings. And we in our high school youth groups would either get on the train or pool up in a car and head for Chicago for these Youth for Christ meetings, which were very popular with high school kids from an evangelical church. That was quite a distance, ninety miles, to go hear Billy Graham speak, usually on Saturday nights."

Then, years later, Dale recalls his encounter with Dr. Graham in the Governor's Office.

"I had the opportunity to meet Billy Graham, early in the first administration, he came to the back door (the private entrance) to the Governor's Office. We were standing there chatting by RR's study. I reminded him of the times he came and preached at our little church and he remembered the times—he had no reason to remember me. This occurred during the first time Billy Graham was there. He had been invited by the Reagans. I don't remember how many times he came to the office after that but he was there a number of times. Billy Graham was never an oppressive individual. As I have said to you before and you reminded me of it, Curtis, I don't see how *anybody* could be in the presence of Billy Graham and *not* be challenged as to what their *faith* was. The Man could not have spent the number of times he did with Billy Graham and not answered him as to whether he had a personal relationship with Jesus Christ."

Wednesdays were our riding days with RR. Dale recalled some fun 'escape' times when just the two of them rode, alone, after the horses were moved a little closer to the Capital and the Reagan's residence.

"We'd ride along the horse trails along the backside of Haggen Oaks golf course. Before the development took place the horse trails went right along the fairways of the golf course and off into the trees alongside the course. Mostly the ubiquitous White Oaks and Live Oaks indigenous to the rolling California hills."

"One day, out on the golf course I saw a friend of mine, Bill Merrifield, who at that time was the Auditor of the State of California and he was golfing with his son. So we rode over to the edge of the Fairway, they recognized who we were and I introduced Bill to the governor who realized it was the first time he had ever met the governor. This was not an elected office. Bill was one of the governor's appointees, and had been for a number of years, but it was his first opportunity to meet Reagan.* Those were fun times!"

"Our conversations on horseback covered a broad range of subjects and very *human* things. Nothing was out-of-bounds—you had the freedom to ask anything you wanted to ask; say anything you wanted to say (during these special sessions). Reagan had a comfort in riding horseback; it was *very* relaxing to him. He felt much more relaxed and would talk about anything he wanted to talk about. These were good times!"

"These rides weren't necessarily always on the schedule. It would come up pretty quick." He'd look in at me and say, *"Come on, I've gotta' go, I've gotta' get outa' here---let's go ride!"*

"It was an immediate thing. We had a break in the schedule, we'd jump up, run out of the office and head out to where the horses were kept and go for a ride."

"Remember when the horses were kept on the Breuner Ranch up towards Grass Valley and when it was farther away; then it would require more planning."

* (There were hundreds of recommendations passed up through various selection committees and winnowed down to qualified persons who eventually were appointed to fill key positions in the agencies and departments. Obviously, this was one who didn't interface with the governor like some of the other applicants / candidates and subsequent appointees. He may have reported to someone like the Director of the Department of Finance)

During the last year of Governor Reagan's second term Dale took a seldom exercised opportunity with his boss to help his fellow officers of the California Highway Patrol by quietly lobbying his riding partner, the subject of executive protection for eight years and friend, RR, to sign a bill increasing the retirement of CHP officers. 1974 Assembly Bill No.3801, passed by the Senate and signed by Governor Ronald Reagan, August 27th 1974 Dale was privy to several meetings including one meeting with some of RR's key advisors at Reagan's residence in Pacific Palisades. I asked Dale who attended that meeting.?

"Art Van Court, Lyn Nofziger, Ed Meese and *me*—no one else!" No one from the Highway Patrol. No, this was a private meeting. This was one of the things that was the topic of conversation—the CHP Bill. Essentially, we were all lobbying for that bill."

"From my viewpoint—there wasn't much about Ronald Reagan *not* to like. There may have been some idiosyncrasies—but nothing that one would dislike." *"No!"* "Not for me, he didn't have them."

Dale and I agreed RR was a citizen politician, because he certainly didn't come from the normal ranks of the politicians that all of us had been used to. So I asked Dale what he thought the *essence* of this man was.

"It always appeared to me that he had very strong personal and genuine feelings about things. And he *functioned* on those feelings. Certainly—I'd watch him. I was far more in a position to just *watch*, all the time, than ever to be a contributor. But, I think he was a relatively *good listener*—and I think there were times when he just *played* at being a listener, because of the source—and I think that's a necessity."

"I know—even at Cabinet Meetings—ones that I would happen to be around or attend, for some reason or another—if he had a bent towards a certain direction, he was pretty hard to change. It appeared to me he just had *strong* feelings of his own, and if you were going to change those feelings, you had better have something extremely legitimate to counter whatever his particular bent was. And he functioned that way."

"But, to say that I never saw Ronald Reagan get mad over an issue, would not be true, because I have. But RR would *never* lose it—but he could really "kick-the-boot"— and show—*genuine anger*—and rightly so—in the circumstances that were involved."

"But, he sure functioned on his *own*—his own philosophies, his own attitudes, he was very genuine about that. I think he was a very *forthright* individual—and forthright to a degree. He was not outspokenly forthright."

The Standard definition of the word *forthright* 1974 Webster's Deluxe Unabridged = *honesty, straight forward & direct*-Dale's meaning, also a correct definition = *Openness.*

"But, if he didn't speak it, he still could be stubborn to it because, *'You're not going to change me, because—I'm on the right track—and—you're on the wrong track!'*

"He believed in his convictions and he would stick to them. I don't recall instances—I'm sure that there were times when he succumbed to somebody else's *pushing* in a given direction, but if he had a certain strong feeling about something—

that's the way he was—that's where *he'd stay!* I wasn't there *every* moment—to see that it *always* took place that way. But the things that I was privy to; *it certainly was true!*"

'But you saw him when he wasn't necessarily "on point"—ready to march in to give a speech to five hundred or a thousand people.'

"Very much so. He was very relaxed preparatory to it."

"And it was always interesting that these guys, especially staff researchers, including Lyn Nofziger, would spend a tremendous amount of time putting together a speech for him—that he would then sit in the car, or on the plane, as we were going somewhere—wherever—and he would be *changing it!*"

"They had a great feel for how he would say something, but still, Reagan would conclude, *"That's just NOT for me"*—and do his own thing and write—print it out in his own hand—his own little cards for that speech, and change whatever they (the others) had put in there. It was always interesting to see him—he never just took something somebody else said or wrote and then said, *"That's fine!"* *"I'll say whatever you say!"* or *"I'll just go with it!"* "He was his *own person*; I think very much so. And, that's not to say he wasn't influenced. I think he was influenced a lot by the group of advisors that he had, that were all friends of his out of L.A., The Kitchen Cabinet. I think they had a strong influence on how he felt about things, because they were of like mind. And I think that's why the influence was there. I think his strong associations, it seemed, were with people that felt the way *he* did. I'm talking about Holmes Tuttle, and Justin Dart and the others—whether it be them, or the guys that he really appreciated in the legislature. They were the guys—that a lot of times he differed with. And other times they were on the same side of an issue. They just went in different directions. So, just the fact that somebody else was a Republican, didn't necessarily mean that they *all* had the same feelings Ron had."

You know his detractors, many times, said that he was basically just an *actor*, and he couldn't do much more than read a script, I told him. "Yes, but I don't think that's true at all. You remember, Curtis—it was good to be positioned to where you were just a *listener*, because you could hear all sides coming in."

Dale continued, "Ronald Reagan really had strong ideas about things! I mean, they were *his* ideas and he wasn't afraid to express them. There were times when he would say, *"What do you think about this or what do you think about that?"*

"I'll tell you, I was a victim of something like that one time. We were talking on the way in to the office, and he asked me about something, and then, when we arrived, he went into a cabinet meeting. In fact, one of the cabinet members—I don't remember who it was—came out of the meeting and said that the governor had come in there this morning and said, *"I was talking to Dale this morning, and he said, 'This is the way this particular thing is happening.'"* "And that's what he was going by—he was the kind of guy that—he believed people—*if* you gave him a reason to believe in you. And this had something to do with State conduct, or issues, and something having been in state service for some time—I forget exactly what it was.""Oh well, this cabinet officer or secretary—he or she asked me just *what* the conversation was. And it was not an out-to-lunch thing—and it wasn't a real significant thing, either, but nevertheless, that's the way it was with people—Reagan respected stuff, but he didn't change his mind over what you had to say. If he was asking you about something, it was usually to add to whatever it was that he had in his *own* mind. *"*

I asked Dale to tell me his personal feelings about Barney Barnett, since he had made a statement about Barney being close to the family and *trusted,* as well as how he, Barney, *transcended* all of that.

"Barney became as close as the most *trusted* family member to the Reagans."

Barney came into the Reagan family operations the moment The Man became governor in 1966, and remained after RR left the Governor's Office, during the years in between and after he went into the White House; even after Barney retired from the CHP. He answered the calls for *"help,"* companionship and friendship as the Reagans discovered their beloved Rancho Del Cielo with the stunning ocean-view sunsets, in the oak-studded hills above the orange and lemon groves of Santa Barbara and made plans to purchase the ranch.

Ron and Nancy needed a dedicated, friendly, well- known and *trusted* security person with a law enforcement background, having defensive-driving skills, who could work with the U.S. Secret Service, to assist RR and NR in Southern California as well as on the many trips to the ranch to cut wood, repair fences and care for the place. It was an easy, pleasant camaraderie for the two outdoorsmen.

All of us working on the Governor's Staff as advance-men, communications or security, met and worked with Barney all the time. Barney came from the same unit of the CHP as his "back-up" and colleague, Wayne Waddell—and Dale Rowlee.

Barney, with his red-cheeks and ruddy complexion, stocky, medium-build and light, reddish hair could have been mistaken for the caricature of a Boston or New York Irish beat-cop.

Under his belt and filling his log-book were years of open-air experience on the smoggy, whizzing, many-times traffic-clogged highways of large California cities in all aspects of crime fighting, vehicle operations, accidents and motorcades— sprinkled with periods of Executive Protection for visiting dignitaries.

Dale remembers Barney

"I'm sure his first contact with Governor Reagan and his family was no different than anybody else's. But Barney, probably in a very short time, confirmed in their minds that, in respect to who he was and, in his relationship with them as a family, that he *belonged to them.*"

"I don't care who you talk about on the Governor's Staff —I don't think that Ronald Reagan had as much, or any more, *trust* in the confidentiality of any individual; than he did with Barney. Reagan felt that whatever—*whatever* took place between him and Barney, was between him and Barney—*only!*"

It was the same with Dale. Dale's humbleness wouldn't let him think that his relationship measured up to that of Ronald Reagan's with Barney—but I *know* that it did.

"I was *confident* that he felt that way about Barney. And Barney was that way." Dale went on reminiscing, "Barney would share incidents with you, but, to his death, I doubt he *ever* told a tale or *anything*—that could be construed to be of a personal nature—about Reagan or his family. Even the kids. He wouldn't! You couldn't get a word out of him in respect to those kids. And those kids *deserved* some words, you know. But not from Barney. Yeah, he was that kind of a person."

"And he *fought* with the fact that a lot of this was *very* disturbing to Aggie; with his wife—with his home life. It didn't help his home life *a bit!* And, understandably so. I can understand where Aggie was coming from. Because somebody was capitalizing on the time of the man that belonged to her. Barney was *a very ordinary guy.* Yeah, he was like a New York Irish cop. And—he could be very tough—*very tough!* But—his *integrity* was *impeccable.*"

That may be why the Reagans asked Barney to accompany them as Dale's colleague and roommate on their 1972 "Around the World Goodwill Tour" at the behest of President Nixon.

Chapter Fourteen
THE ARCHITECT

Stu Spencer

"He was probably the best candidate I've ever dealt with." "I've dealt with a lot of good candidates, but he was *exceptional.*" "Why?" "Number one, he had a *core*, he had a *sense*, he had a *belief-system.*" "His *ego* **never** got in his way.!"

Stu Spencer could best be described as 'direct,' 'tell it like it is,' 'no nonsense', not as rumpled as Nofziger—but of medium height, wispy graying hair, gravel-voiced, eyes squinting as if he were out in bright sunlight, under-dressed-casual, tennis garb, plain-spoken, with a 'Give 'em Hell Harry' attitude; and with the keen instinct to know what was good and what was bad for his candidates. For Reagan, Stu could pretty well call the important characteristics of an event, a 'hot' issue or a particular RR demeanor or response towards a speaking combatant / opponent or situation—in an almost *prescient* way. It was in his *bones!* In Spencer it was an innate, intrinsic characteristic of his entire being, and few people around RR possessed it, other than his wife, Nancy.

Winning the Kitchen Cabinet

"It was after he was elected governor, and they held two special elections in northern California, one in Contra Costa County and one in Monterey. It was important to the governor that he win those things because they were both pick-ups in the State Legislature, if he won 'em. There was another one, the 'barrio' race in the Central Valley."

"We went to Contra Costa and we had about a ninety day campaign, and I was runnin' out of money, so I came south, went to the governor's house—he had the Kitchen Cabinet there. I told them what was goin' on in the campaign, what our chances were."I said, 'We're gonna' need another forty thousand dollars.'

"Nobody in the group got too excited about my request—so, I finally said, 'Okay, I've got an eleven o'clock plane back to "Frisco"'—I'll go back and do the best I can. As I'm walkin' out the door of the Governor's House, Holmes grabs me and asks me, 'How much do you really need?' I said, "Forty thousand." Holmes Tuttle said, 'Okay, you've got it!' "So, now I'm happy! I go out and get into my car—start to go down that short, (steep, tight, overgrown with lush foliage) driveway—Ed Mills comes out the front door, and he grabs me as I'm getting in the car and rolling the window down—he says, 'How much did Holmes commit?' I said, 'Forty thousand!' "Ed grimaces and shouts 'Oh my God!' "But Ed was smart enough to know Holmes was talking to me and had made a commitment—but he wanted to know what it was—'cause he was the guy who had to go raise it. Oh, gosh, it was a classic. (he laughs) And, we won it, and the next one, too! These wins were helpful to the governor. Sure!"

"It was at the time when Bob Monaghan had become speaker; he lasted for two years. In the next election we lost two seats we shouldn't have lost and then we had (Robert) Moretti as speaker."

Spencer recalls Reagan as a candidate

"On a scale of one to ten—he was a *nine!* I've never seen a ten—that's why I said, he was a nine. I've handled hundreds of issues and candidates; mostly candidates. He was probably the *best* candidate I've ever dealt with. I've dealt with a lot of good candidates, but he was *exceptional!* You always think about, why?"

"Number one, he had a *core,* he had a *sense,* he had a *belief-system.* Very important to being a good candidate. I don't care what the belief-system is, Liberal or Conservative, whatever; he had a *system.* The other thing is, from the standpoint of management—his prior profession was very helpful. He was an actor. He understood what direction was. He understood what his role was and what our role was and what other people's roles would be in the campaign. That makes it simple. His *ego* never got in his way. He had an ego—every good candidate has to have an ego—but he didn't let it get in his way, at all!"

"He had weaknesses, as a candidate, but those weaknesses were compensated by a good staff and by his *wife.* His biggest weakness was *personnel.* He *never* fired anybody in his life. As I have said to many people, since; it had dawned on me early; that Nancy was the *personnel director.* Her trepidations were: 'Do they have their own agenda or are they going to operate with Ron's agenda?' "A valid question."

"That's the first measuring stick she gave to people. Secondly was how he dressed, and how he did this and how he did that and a lot of things that were really superficial, but they were *important* to her."

"Taft Schreiber told me, after we took on the campaign in 1965, he asked me if we could go have lunch." I said, 'Okay.' "Taft had been Ron's agent, along with Lew Wasserman, for a lotta' years." Taft said at that lunch, 'You know, you're going to have to fire a lot of people!' I said, 'What do you mean?' He said, 'Ron never fired anybody in his life!' He said, 'You're going to have to do it!' "Well, we found out that it was the truth—he was *very* soft-hearted. As when RR was president, I can remember there was a decision made that Peggy Heckler (a former Massachusetts

Congresswoman) should be removed as Secretary of H.H.S. (Health & Human Services) she wasn't doing the job that good, so it was my job to talk to Peggy and I had her over to the Madison Hotel for lunch. I 'walked' all around the subject—a good gal—I liked her." I said, 'Peggy, I really think it's time to move on.' "We went through this whole thing, and finally—she was a smart woman—and finally, at the end of the conversation—she *accepted* it—but she asked for the one thing that we didn't want to happen." Peggy said, 'I'd like to sit down and talk to the president about it.'

Stu went on, "Now, Ron had signed off on it. Everybody else had signed off on it. But we knew him well enough that she'd get in there and start talkin' to the president (he laughs) and Reagan would say, '*Well, I don't know what Stu was talking about—.*'

We both laugh loudly over the standard / typical RR remarks he always used.

"He'd go through this whole routine. That's the last thing we wanted."

By now we are rolling on the floor in Stu's office because we had heard Ron plead innocent so many times, in his quest to paint a better picture and literally 'draw the covers over his head' on this type of confrontation; especially over someone he liked.

I said to Peggy, "Okay."

"And, before she went in, I went in there to The Oval Office and said to Ron, 'Now you'd better back me up—I'm not going to hang out there to dry.' I finally said, 'Give her the ambassadorship to Ireland' "But, he was very *soft* with people and he was great to all of his employees, you'll find out if you talk to people, he couldn't fire anybody and he had a hard time even reprimanding people."

"One of the things that strikes me is that he had a lot of diversity around him .He had people with different philosophies around him—that came from different directions.. We'd get into arguments. Meese and I and some of the others would be having an argument about something—and we'd be on different sides and Ron'd say, "*Okay!*" "*Okay!*" "*You guys go out and just settle it—and bring me back the answer.*" "He didn't want any part of it—the debate—the argument that we were having. He didn't mind standing up to Gorbachev. He didn't mind standing up to Russia. He didn't mind standing up to *evil.* But, within the confines of his 'family' he didn't like all of this argument, the debate, etc."

Reagan considered those who worked closely around him and worked so hard for him, as members of his own extended 'family.'

When asked if Stu Spencer agreed, he loudly proclaimed, "Sure!"

Almost tearfully, Stu recounts, "I remember, I had a tough situation come up—non-political—my parents' *death*—and I got a phone call from Ronald Reagan, and we talked. He heard about it—was told about it—and we had this very *personal* conversation about what I was going through at that point in time. I don't recall that I received any call from any of the other national leaders I had worked with." "No one!"

"Remember the debates with Walter Mondale in 1984? Reagan literally bombed—I mean, he was awful! I forget, it was in Louisville, or someplace. There was a lot of conjecture. They blamed everybody. Some said, 'He was over-prepared.' 'He was *this*—he was *that*.' "I sat in those post-debate meetings and listened to all of this stuff—and Nancy was on a 'tear' about it, of course. My point being that I knew why he had failed. He had *not* done his homework."

"I had gone to Camp David with him that weekend before, and I took the Briefing Book—and he and I had spent a lot of time watching old movies, and when I'd come back over the next morning—I'd see the Briefing Book still sitting where it was, and I said to myself, 'He's not working' "But, I didn't say anything—and he *bombed*!"

"After the debate, everybody—they had all of these (campaign) people —they all started to blame something or somebody else for Reagan's bad showing. Ronald Reagan didn't do his homework and he *knew* it, and he basically said that to me, after the debate." 'Cause he said, *"How'd I do"* I said, 'Oh, you did pretty good.' He said, *"I did terrible!"*

And I said, (he laughs) 'Yeah, because you didn't do your homework!' (Stu laughs again) Reagan says, *"Um Hmm—You're right!"*

"What bothered me was the fact that the press stories were going to blame this guy, White House aide, Richard Darman, and all these other people who were preparing it—and Ronald Reagan, he made his *own* mistakes—he knew it. He wasn't gonna' talk about it—but he knew it. He knew when he was bad. He was such a good performer—he always knew when he was bad."

"One time—election eve of 1980—we're doing a cross-country flight in the presidential race—we're in Peoria, Illinois—I remember that because it was Bob Michel's District, and George Bush, the V.P. nominee, is with us—we're taping at eight o'clock in the morning the final (most important) thing, it's going on national T.V. that night, a half hour of Reagan."

"It starts with Bush, on his left—he's in a chair, Bush is in a chair—the camera's got 'em both—you hear opening remarks—they zero-in —and Reagan's got to carry it. He's five minutes into it—*God* he's **bad!** It's eight o'clock in the morning, if you'll remember he did not like to get started before *nine* in the morning. And Deaver and I just looked at each other and we wanted to stop the 'shoot'—we took him into the bathroom and he was the first one who said, *"Jeez, I'm terrible!"* "I mean, he knew it!" He said something about, *"The chair doesn't fit me—get me a hard chair that I can sit up forward in."*

"Fine, we did *that*—we go back—we start over—we're a half hour late doin' it—then—he shot **one half hour,** *without a stop!* Perfect! Great shoot!"

"The other side of this that fascinated me was watching George Bush's face—I mean he was lookin' at this guy, RR, in awe of what he was doing with that camera—he was almost like making *love* to the camera. (Stu chuckles) God, Bush couldn't do that in a million years! Those skills and those abilities made him a great, *great* candidate.""Communication!" "The biggest job they can do is communicate. In terms of the issues: There's an old saying that the candidate has got to *fit* the district. In his political career he fit / fits *perfect."* (-*ly*) "What he thought—the majority thought. When he said something, Democrat or Republican—they'd go, 'Yeah!' "He's right!"

"Today, I'm not sure he could get elected—on the same basis that he got elected, then, because the country's changed. It would be a tough call, because it's a different country. I'll put it this way, he wouldn't get elected in California; it's a *totally* different state. It has really changed, radically. I say that based on running on the platform, the issues, that he ran on back in those days. He might be flexible enough that he could adapt—I don't know."

"My partner, Bill Roberts, and I sensed that the people of California were ready for change back then—definitely ready for change. If you look at history—a two-term governor is pretty bankrupt for new ideas after eight years; any governor, Republican or Democrat."

"Pat Brown was in that position. The question was: Can this actor, who was a great communicator, hold up under fire? Because there's going to be *fire*, in this campaign!"

"The second part being: Can we bring an acceptance of it with the media—the working press—and not just be treated as a 'B' actor changing professions?"

"Now an original piece of research which we did through McCann-Erickson, the ad agency which his brother, Neil, was in; we saw an interesting piece of data. Ninety-two or ninety-three percent of the women in California really loved Ronald Reagan! That wasn't because he was running for governor—this was before he ran. This was based upon his 'carryover' value from being in the right kinds of movies. The *good* guy in the movies! He may have been with Errol Flynn in the movies, but *he* was the *good* guy. That's important. What's perception is what you are when you start and when you end. So, we had the opportunity, I think, the only time in our career, to express the women's view. We were negotiating—talking to (Mayor George) Christopher at the same time we were talkin' to Reagan—and finally Bill and I assessed the Christopher campaign—Christopher was of the 'old school'—and so we rolled the dice. And people forget—Christopher was the favorite to win the Primary—he was the picked favorite—he was ahead in the polling data and all that stuff. The Democrats thought so little of Reagan, they even tried to cut Christopher up a few times. They wanted to run against Ronald Reagan! They under-rated him as a candidate—which was a plus for us."

"They nailed Christopher on his dairy, his milk-pricing and a few real estate deals. But, the *key*, in the Reagan campaign, in our judgment was—put him in a position where he was viewed as a *viable* candidate by the media—that he was accepted, and not just an actor."

"And, if you recall—if you look back and think about it—how we set it up— Ron gave a speech—which was an excerpt of The Speech, so to speak, with maybe a little twist here or there—but afterwards—we started opening it up to twenty minutes of Q. & A. with the press. We did it in Visalia, in Tulare, everywhere, before we came to L.A.—before we came to "Frisco"—we did it in the small markets."

"We explained that to Ron, he understood that—you open a show out of town before you bring it to Broadway—you work out the kinks. Cause we didn't know how he was going to handle forty minutes of Q. & A. He worked with these other groups—we had Charlie Conrad, the former legislator, who spent two days a week with him, teaching him what happened in Sacramento. But, we basically said, and he was so good at this we'd say, 'If you really haven't got the answer—say,' (tell them) you *"haven't got the answer.* Because people know you haven't been in government and one of the things about your candidacy that appeals to'em is: You *haven't* been in government.!"

"If you've got something to say—say it. But, if you don't know the answer— don't try to fabricate it! And he didn't. So the Q. & A. stuff went great! Many times he said, *"I don't know the answer to that—I haven't been up there—I'll take a look at it."*

"(Dick) Bergholz, (Carl) Greenberg, (Jack) McDowell, (Squire) Behrens, (Art) Hoppe, I could go right down the list—(CA newspaper's political writers and columnists)—after about a month—they started buying in."

I asked Stu if he recalled that he and Bill Roberts had taught us to be, not condescending, but very *polite* to the working press, and we treated them like part of the staff. That came down through the operation to Dave Tomshany, George Young and out into the Advance Team.

"Right!" "Right!" Stu affirmed.

"Bergholz (L.A. Times) could be mean, Greenberg was one of the most honest, correct guys I ever saw—he got it right—he quoted Reagan right. Bergholz was different, but I noticed after a while that Bergholz almost held this guy, Reagan, in *awe.* He couldn't believe what he was seeing—he expected Ron to fall on his face! He expected him to really screw up! And he wasn't doin' it for him. So Bergholz didn't know what to do—so he ended up doin' a pretty straight job of reporting. Bill and I had to make the biggest leap of faith—acceptance of RR by the press, the media. Not an endorsement—*acceptance* that he was a viable, real candidate If he hadn't gotten that—he would never have gotten off the ground. They would have made sure he never got off the ground. That proved he was a hell of a candidate! He took the challenge and he made it happen."

"In 1964, when Barry Goldwater was runnin' he said a lot of things that were controversial. Two years later Ronald Reagan, running for governor, said the *same* things, but he said it nicer—he said it in a manner which was acceptable to the people. So, it's *how* you say something and *how* you deliver it, that's just as important as the content of what you're saying."

Stu Spencer, my long-time mentor and Reagan confidant, summed it all up by telling me that Reagan *never* changed.

"He was the same person *now* as he was *then,*" Stu said. "The *core* values and *belief system* which Ron had in his gubernatorial campaign and during the governor's years, which I mentioned earlier, were so ingrained in Reagan's mind, in his psyche, that he carried them into his later years as president. He *never* changed! He was the same person then as he was more recently, some twenty years later. He was true to himself!"

Chapter Fifteen

PHONE MAN 'EXTRAORDINAIRE'

Bob & Urania Tarbet

"Bob would come home at night and talk about what 'good people' he was working with. He was excited that he was surrounded by 'good people.' It came down from the top—it started with Reagan and Nancy!" Bob's widow, Urania said.

The fact that Bob Tarbet died in the Fall of 1999 greatly influenced my writing of this book. His very special relationship with Ron and Nancy Reagan, his prescience for identifying problems *before* they confronted us and his uncanny knack for solving them *afterwards,* if, in fact, they began at all, set the example for all of us. He also set a strong example for Mike Deaver, who ultimately inherited the responsibility of handling myriad details in scheduling and operations for Nancy Reagan, so well! This, in great measure, was due to Bob's total faith in the "team concept"—which meant that *everyone* on board, on the staff, needed to understand that the Reagans came FIRST and our needs and desires, came SECOND. It was Nofziger, Meese and Clark who set *that* tone, but it was Tarbet who carried it off so successfully, so admirably, and seemingly, so effortlessly. He was the pro, the guy who could 'get it done.' Unfortunately, he never recorded those precious moments.

I thought I was fairly good at execution of 'hot' orders, with a phone in each ear, or at handling critical situations in a pinch—but Tarbet was *better.* He was cool. He quietly accomplished those tough assignments without fanfare, anxiety or adequate sleep; and always maintained his gracious courtesy, all the while setting a superb example for the younger members of the advance team.

When I first met Bob Tarbet, he was the telecommunications rep for the Pacific Telephone & Telegraph Co., assigned to San Francisco Mayor George Christopher to drive and many times to 'trail' the candidate's car, in Christopher's run for governor, in what at the time was known as the 'telephone-car' or the 'wire-car', as it carried the press and media; sometimes the candidate. He also set up banks of land-line telephones in advance of campaign stops so the press could file their stories and the candidate and staff could communicate with the rest of the world.

I watched this man in action when all of the candidates would appear at the same venue, as I traveled the state advancing for RR. I soon realized we needed someone like Bob to round out our team. Especially after having to go to event after event with *our* first communications rep., whose name shall remain anonymous, also on 'loan' from P.T.& T., who spent most of his time 'schmoozing' with our top-level staff people, while phones could not be found and we ran into some real *snafus.* He was always asking us how he could finagle a job out of the new Reagan administration staff , *if* RR won the governor's race.

Our guy spent most of his time, when on the road with us and candidate Reagan, trying desperately to get into every news photo and film clip of Reagan possible, working for his own, personal gain; while Tarbet spent *his* time setting up communications for his candidate Christopher and the traveling press and handling any task that needed doing; so long as it kept him *out* of the spotlight! When Bob and I ran into each other during our months on the 'stump,' before the Primary election, I realized after a few encounters that he was *not* the enemy, even though he worked for our opponent. Surprisingly, if I had a problem or some foul-up occurred, Bob would look at me, watch what was happening, and suggest some simple, corrective measure, remedy or solution, always unhesitating, always quiet, always smooth and unassuming. After he joined the Reagan Team, he was *always* asking, 'What can I do to help you?'

When we plunged into the main general election race against Governor Pat Brown, I had received some 'intelligence' that Brown was going to try to sabotage our efforts and help slow down, if not destroy RR's chances to win by knocking out or intercepting our communications channels and systems. Also, that he was going to place a spy inside our campaign staff.. Several of us went to Bill Roberts, Stu Spencer and Lyn Nofziger and asked if they could arrange for us to have the services of Bob Tarbet—to give us the edge. It worked. Turned out, it was as if Bob was Heaven-sent! He always did this 'thing,' which I could never put my finger on. He *always* remained cool in the face of adversity and smiled as he would give subtle eye signals about a particular problem situation, and all of a sudden—the storm-clouds parted , so to speak, and the sought after opening, the car with the full tank of gas, the solution to our predicament—miraculously was there—He would lead the way, with staff and Reagan in tow—whether it was through the Ambassador Hotel's kitchens in L.A., the passageways of San Francisco's Mark Hopkins Hotel or thru the inner-sanctum tunnels of the L.A Biltmore—he led the way—and soon—we were *free*, outside, on time and off and running to the next campaign stop!

Bob also had the uncanny ability to handle the numerous issues surrounding the political operations, social activities and *official* State functions of Nancy Reagan, better than anyone on the staff. He acted as a personal aide and assistant to Mrs. Reagan as First Lady of California and, in conjunction with the White House Advance Team and the Secret Service, on special traveling assignments. when she was First Lady of the United States. The Reagans knew they could *trust* Bob Tarbet. He never breached a confidence or the multitudes of secrets he was entrusted with. He never compromised his own conscience and character for something that might have been more beneficial to him, personally. Or for something that might have hurt someone else. He never compromised his own integrity!. From the General election campaign until the day he passed away he had become one of my closest and dearest friends.

After Bob's death in 1999, I called several of my colleagues and asked for a few words from each of them, which I might be allowed to say at his funeral. These words embodied the unique spirit of the men and women around Ronald Reagan, in those early political days: From Former Attorney General Edwin Meese III: 'Bob Tarbet was a great friend and I am grateful to have had the privilege of working with him over the years. His great sense of humor and his constant cheerfulness contributed so much to the Reagan Team. We all appreciate his loyalty and tremendous assistance to Ronald Reagan.' —Ed

From Former Air Force Secretary, Governor Reagan's first Appointments Secretary and our honorable chief of the Clandestine Activities Committee, Thomas C. Reed, 'Bob Tarbet helped make much of Ronald Reagan's success possible; from the beginning.' —Tom

From Former Interior Secretary and National Security Advisor to President Reagan, Judge Wm. P. Clark, Jr., 'In Bob's quiet, taciturn way, through his loyalty, integrity, discretion, and trustworthiness, he helped advance the agenda of Ronald Reagan and thence America's Agenda into the future. We shall NEVER FORGET what Bob Tarbet did for all of us! He did such a beautiful job.' —Bill

From Former White House Communications Director Lyn Nofziger, 'Bob was a dear friend, but more than that; he was one of the original Reaganites. He and I and an actor named Ronald Reagan, spent many hours back in 1966 riding around the hinterlands of California looking for votes. Bob, of course, was the telephone company's man on the campaign, but he became much more than that. He became not only the candidate's friend, but also a friend to all of us on the campaign, a friend who was always willing to lend a hand, even if it had nothing to do with telephones. And the best thing is, he and you, Uranaia—and we remained friends—good friends and *special* friends—over the nearly 34 years since that campaign began. With deep affection.' —Lyn

From Nancy Reagan to Urania (Mrs. Robert) Tarbet,

'Ronnie and I were so sorry to learn about Bob's death. Although there are no words to ease the pain at this difficult time, we want you to know that you are in our thoughts and prayers.'

'Losing a spouse is certainly difficult, but we know that Bob lived a very full and rewarding life. He was a wonderful and great friend to both of us and he made a tremendous difference to our staff in Sacramento.'

'Bob served the State of California and our country with great dignity and loyalty and we will all miss him. We hope the warm memories of him will bring you strength in the days and years to come.'

'Urania, please know that we are praying for you and your family at this time.' 'God Bless you.' Sincerely, Nancy

P.S. (in Nancy Reagan's handwriting) 'I'm *so* sorry—we had a lot of good times together!'

Bob's bright and cheerful wife, Urania, with her distinctive red hair, hearty laugh and intuitive nature, Urania Christy Tarbet, later to become a world-renowned Pastel artist and Pastel (the medium) instructor became one of our 'volunteer' assistants; an added bonus we hadn't counted on.

Urania picks up Bob's story

"Bob was very loyal to the Christopher campaign, interestingly enough, Christopher's uncle encouraged Bob to go to work for Christopher, due to Bob's and the uncle's Masonic affiliation. Bob really had a wonderful time with that group of people. They were very gregarious Greek people. But they had known for some time that Reagan was the candidate who was going to have his name on the general election ballot. We had also known Stu Spencer, which made it comfortable for Bob to transition over to RR."

Of course with the 'blessing' of the telephone company.

"Curtis, when the company took your communications person off the assignment and replaced him with Bob, that man, *your* man, was so, so upset with Bob, thinking Bob had somehow 'engineered' his demise."

Bob had nothing to do with it. It was the consensus of the Reagan team that the fellow had to go and the best replacement would, in fact, be Bob Tarbet, I reminded her. "We actually had to move to Los Angeles from San Diego to take the new job," Urania said. "Bob was so thrilled when he was assigned to work for Reagan! He would come home at night and talk about what 'good people' he was working with. He was excited that he was surrounded by 'good people.' It came down from the top—it started with Reagan and Nancy! Because Bob and I were so close, he saw this same, *great* closeness, this love affair, in RR and Nancy."

"One night he came home and said that he had pushed the elevator button and when the door opened, there were Ron and Nancy kissing. And he thought that was just so beautiful—that they were *real* people! That they really cared for each other and worked together."

And, we agreed, he proved it over and over again as the decades went by and Bob and I were still being called upon to assist them from time to time.

"Because they were this *team*—it kept filtering down—and everybody on the staff just found their little *groove*, on the bigger, overall Reagan campaign team."

Urania said that Bob always shared the glory in any endeavor, rather than trying to hog it for himself.

"It was the same thing with the photos: He was always by Nancy's side or at her arm, moving her from place to place. When they traveled together to events whether in Des Moines or New York City, and when connecting with Ron, he never wanted to be in the limelight; so he stayed out of the photos as much as possible."

"I used to go along or advance many of Reagan's meetings, events and speeches. I remember one event at the Century Plaza hotel in West L.A; I sat at one of the tables and helped by handing the guests their tickets. I wasn't paid for that—I was just volunteering, because Bob was going to be there anyway. Before that, many times I went to downtown L.A. to Bob's office and I'd help with mailings. I wrote so many invitations to events for the Reagans. I helped with the writing of the invitations to some events for the Apollo X and Appolo XI Astronauts, in conjunction with someone from the Nixon White House."

I told Urania that was one of my projects the governor had given me, as well; to advance the Apollo X crew throughout California.

"Yes," I remember. "It was also the first time a White House event was given for the astronauts. I absolutely liked what was going on with Reagan and what he was doing, so I not only helped at these functions because my husband was working there—I, myself, saw what this man was doing for our state, and I knew that whatever he was doing in our state, was being watched by other states since it was such an important state, especially when it came to being a focal point for West Coast news. Other states were looking at us to see if they wanted to emulate what we were doing here. (In terms of administration policies) I just felt that whatever Reagan was doing, here, it was like throwing a pebble into a pond; and I wanted to be a part of it!"

Confirmation of Reagan's *FIRST* run for president

"The GOP National Convention in Miami Beach, Florida was an adventure!"

I agreed, it was an adventure, like *none* other. This was under the banner of The California Favorite Son Committee.

"There was so much happening. It was so exciting to be a part of that! It was so wonderful, in thinking about it, I was really a part of history. Lyn Nofziger had brought into our telecommunications center at the (Deauville) hotel, some sort of now old-fashioned, teletype machine—a TWX machine—for transmitting written messages." "Later, Lyn came into the room and asked me to send this message over the wire and as I'm reading it and typing it into this machine," I thought 'Oh, how fantastic!' "What it was—**it was the announcement that Reagan was going to run for president.** This went out to all of the news media— the press—He knew he wasn't going to (really) run for president right then, but it was the *beginning*. This was the very first announcement. It was a stellar moment. Yes! I remember that evening, when I shared this with Bob, we toasted the event as one that was really historical."

Urania and Bob and the 'loaned' P.T. & T. crew, along with the trusted members of Tom Reed's and F. Clifton White's Clandestine Activities Committee, set up an entirely separate wired telephone system from the hotel room-to-lobby-to-room system- inside the hallways, cables hanging out the windows from one floor to another, and up and down the fire stairs where live, well-fed rats crouched in the corners—complete with a commercial PBX telephone switchboard trucked out from California, with all of the levers, cables, plugs, toggle switches and lights making it look like an airliner's cockpit. "I had to keep it operating, with some staff help, around the clock—24/7. I was really pushing myself—we all were!" Urania said.

All of this because there were no cell phones. "I ended up getting pneumonia, due to our comings and goings in and out of the water-vapor air conditioning system of the hotel and the unbearable Florida heat and humidity. We ended up having to give up our tickets to a short Bermuda 'let-down' vacation we had planned for, after the convention, and went straight home to L.A."

"I so admired the people on our security team who were stationed in all of the stairways and stairwells during the entire convention (most of whom were using their personal vacation time and many had paid their own way to Miami Beach to do this for Reagan) since those very dirty fire-stairways were *un*-air conditioned and dripping with humidity. And they were still smiling at the end of the day. I felt comfortable and secure because I would see all of these familiar faces from L.A.P.D. and other departments."

They did it because of their dedication to Ronald Reagan and his principles. We used the fire-stairs because the elevators were crammed with delegates, press and tourists, took forever to arrive and we needed an easy route between our three upper headquarters' floors; and many times, in desperation, we would run all the way up from the basement or the lobby, *UP* twelve to fifteen flights of stairs.

"Indeed!" Urania agreed.

"I remember some interesting little incidents which occurred on that switchboard. One time one of the governor's two legislative liaison people, who came to Miami to do some task or another, called the COMCENTER and asked me 'to deliver a bucket of ice cubes to his room A.S.A.P.' I assured him this was NOT the hotel's Room Service and he'd have to call from the other phone in his room."

Then I recalled a very *touchy* situation, just after we had distributed our new and few, custom-made, high-tech Motorola Handi-Talkies to a select group of Reagan regional floor leaders and delegates, all of which had a direct link to the Mayflower moving van, our Command Trailer at the Convention Center several miles away, we received an angry phone call at the hotel COMCENTER PBX from a friend of the Reagans, a wealthy international tire manufacturing company executive, who was actually bellowing over the phone that he had been 'overlooked' and 'by-passed when the new Walkie-Talkies were handed out .' Then he asked for the director of the operation, and Urania looked at me, pointed to a desk phone and insisted I try to resolve this 'important man's' complaint. I grabbed the phone and he yelled at me too, announcing those famous, key words, used by most self-possessed persons, 'Do you know who I am?' I allowed as how I did, indeed, know who he was and that we had met on several occasions with the Reagans and that he had not been 'overlooked' but that I understood that he was there as a delegate, and scheduled to participate in a number of social events, but not to work 24 / 7 as a floor leader— and besides—we didn't have enough of these HT's, since they had been specially designed and fitted with secret frequencies at Motorola Labs near Chicago, just for *this* convention. This sent him into a *rage*. He said that I 'didn't understand how *important*' he was and that he was 'going to the top with this!' I immediately called Tom Reed and he said, 'Curtis, I'll take care of it.' I never heard another word about it, after that call to Reed (TCR).

I asked Urania if she thought it was true that Bob, with the help of his team, P.T.&T., certain telephone company labs, those of the L.A.P.D. Intelligence Division, the Lockheed engineers, along with Motorola had put together a system for Ronald Reagan which was of the highest technology, quality and capability of anything in the communications field, anywhere.

"Yes!" "Yes, it was; it was the 'cutting-edge. Up till then, it was like a horse and buggy operation."

I asked Urania why Bob emerged as the one person on the staff, after I was given new responsibilities, who was chosen to travel with Nancy Reagan?

"Curtis, she said, I really believe Nancy truly appreciated Bob's character. First of all, he was such a *good* man. He was gentle, intelligent—he was there for *her* and I think she felt this—*that* communication between the two of them. He could just *read* when she wanted to move (out of a particular venue or situation) when she wanted to linger—and they just worked in concert with one another. He was definitely in sync with her at all times. He could tell when she needed to have something attended to—and he was right there for her. You know how she was with food; she ate very little. There would be many times when she wasn't even interested in lunch—and they'd be on the road, running, running—event to event, back home and on the road again—and one time Bob said to Nancy that he was going to pick up some sandwiches and he asked her if she would care for anything." Nancy told him, *"Oh, Yes!" "Today I'm starving."* "Bob asked her what she would like and she replied," *"Oh, just anything."* "Usually, she would only nibble on it. This time Bob brought back a Monte Cristo sandwich—he introduced her to that sandwich and she absolutely fell in love with it—she loved it! From then on she'd say, *"Well, how about a Monte Cristo,* and that just blew Bob away. She usually ate the whole sandwich!"

"Bob never had a second or secret agenda. He gave the Reagans his undivided attention. But when he finally got home, especially if he had been away for a week or two, he was totally exhausted! In fact, no matter how tired he was, I never heard Bob complain; at all. I remember one time Bob came home and he said that Nancy and he and the entire entourage / crew—you were probably there with them—downtown L.A. in the old Spanish Mission de Nuestra Senora de Los Angeles in the famous, crowded and festive old Mexican marketplace and tourist stop known as Olvera Street—it was a celebration of the winning of the California Primary Election in the birthplace of the City of the Angels—and this lady rushed up to Nancy and handed her a piece of Mexican wheat bread—pan (pahn)".

I *was* there and I recalled our 'cues' went up since the operative rule was for the Reagans to NEVER take food from anyone else's hands until it was checked or only if you knew the vendor or giver.

Urania went on: "Bob said Nancy carried this piece of bread for what seemed like an eternity and finally turned to Bob and out of the corner of her mouth whispered to him, *"Bob, would you please get rid of this piece of bread for me."*

It was always the little things that seemed to endear us to the Reagans.

"One time you and I were together and we had to go over to the Governor's Executive Residence on 45th street so that you could give Nancy some information, a report or some something she needed and when we stopped by the mansion at about 11:30 AM, to make the delivery, she said, *"Oh, please stay for lunch!"* It was such a gracious thing to do! I do remember that. When my son, John, was about four or five years old we would be invited to the parties in the Governor's Office and the barbecues at the Executive Residence for legislators and staff, and we would take John with us. He was going through his cowboy stage and would wear his cowboy boots, his little play gun and his cowboy hat, and he wouldn't go anywhere without them. At one of these barbecues, I was so taken by this—I looked over and here was Reagan leaning down talking and talking to John and I walked over and here RR was talking about his cowboy days, *himself*—he was sharing this with John (who has now grown into a fine, tall young businessman and father) because he knew that this was an important thing with John. He asked John if he could borrow his gun for just a minute—he was going to show him something—so John handed Reagan his little toy pistol—it was a toy, a little tiny metal thing. Reagan took that gun, he twirled that gun—I could not believe it—like Roy Rogers—he was so expert at this—and then he came down and he put it in his pocket! John's eyes were as big as silver dollars!"

"My point in saying this to you, Curtis, is that I was so amazed that at these events, it was truly a family event, that Reagan didn't just go around and—'glad hand'—with the adults. He gave his attention—I mean it was total, *full* attention—he gave to John!"

"I was in Italy when Reagan passed away, sitting with several friends watching the funeral on T.V., and I cried and cried. I was so, so happy to see Patti by her mother's side, ever so graceful and attentive—and I think that you and I and all of the people who were there in the beginning probably had the same feeling, in as much as we *knew* that Patti was a very unhappy child, she was a rebel—and it was a delightful sight to see!"

Contrary to what the press and media have reported over the years, the Reagans were very loving parents and included the children living with them in everything possible.

"I remember those backyard barbecues, the legislator's parties, the birthdays, Father's Days, Mother's Day's and all the others at the Governor's Office—they were *always* included," Urania said.

I recalled that the children were always planned for on our blue office schedules, even for picnics in the country, when the Reagans took a brief respite from their duties for a few days off to go ranch hunting in southern California.

"Curtis, Bob was there, along with you and he took dozens of pictures of those trips." (See some of those previously unpublished photos in this book & Vol. 2.)

"I remember once I was visiting Sacramento and was in the office, a little tiny office, where you and Bob were working and someone asked you two to call and make appointments for Nancy Reagan to visit various schools in the area for Patti and "Skipper." I remember I had to do this for you since Bob suggested that, perhaps, a woman would be better speaking for Mrs. Reagan. I then called and made reservations for her to meet and interview the headmasters, dean of students, school reps., etc. Nancy was there, and she made a decision and she chose a school, but the children came home every day." Urania said, "These schools were so carefully screened and checked into by Nancy, herself."

"I'll never forget when Bob came home one night and he told me of one of the most difficult and scariest incidents he had ever encountered. Reagan was governor by then and Bob was driving the communications back-up car tailing the bumper of the governor's black limousine to one of the University campuses, to attend a Board of Regents meeting, in southern California." (Reagan sat on the Board and this was in the middle of the college and university tuition battle, not to mention the air being filled with anti-Vietnam War rhetoric)

"Upon their arrival, the limousine was surrounded by screaming, chanting, spitting, Yes, *spitting* students! They started rocking the limousine, Reagan and Security Chief Art Van Court got out and made it into the building,"

Apparently Highway Patrol Officer Barney Barnett was driving. Variations of this same story have been given by different staff members, but this is the first one from Bob Tarbet's perspective

"As a number of men held the huge glass, double doors of the university meeting hall from being stormed by the angry students, Bob said that mostly wild-eyed girls and college women started spitting on the glass doors and windows and it was dripping in long, gooey strings like wet spaghetti and egg whites, while screaming filthy language at the university administration people inside."

"Bob said the young women were far more belligerent than the young men—like wild animals." She continued, "I almost forgot, when the mob started rocking the limousine—Bob immediately drove his telephone / wire car around the back of the building and one of you opened up a back door to let him inside the hall."

Before the ordeal was over, when it was time for the governor to leave the building after the Regents' meeting, someone indicated we were going out the front door, when in fact, we made a bee-line for Bob's four-door Mercury parked at the rear of the building—alas, the crowd obviously had scouts watching both exits and some heavy, but very agile students, who vaulted onto the trunk or hood, climbed to the top of the car, the roof, jumping up and down like little children on their parents' bed-mattress'.

As the governor's party opened the door and saw the previously well kept, shiny Mercury—instead, now they saw a battered car with the top completely squashed in, nearly to the seat backs.

When the smelly, jeering crowd parted for an instant, burly Art Van Court hustled the governor into the back seat where they both sat hunched over, mostly lying on the floor, like sardines for the speed-run off the campus. According to Urania, Bob described their departure in the flattened Mercury as 'an *escape!*' Bob told her that as soon as the escapees reached the safety of one of the tranquil neighborhoods surrounding the campus; he stopped the car and he, Van Court, and Reagan, all gave a 'Heave-Ho' and together pushed the top up a few inches, from the inside, so they could see well enough to drive."

"Meanwhile, Barney, who was in radio contact with the squished refugees, made arrangements to meet them close by and switch the governor and Van Court into the limo." Days later, it seemed funny, but Bob admitted that things got a little scary there for a while. It certainly wasn't what the new Governor of California had planned to do that day; but he wasn't the least bit intimidated. The problem was, most of the time, he wanted to confront and engage in discussion with the demonstrators. It *was* scary!

Chapter Sixteen

BROWN BAG
CAMPAIGN BEGINS

Dave Tomshany
Assistant Campaign Director,
Reagan for Governor Committee &
Spencer-Roberts Consultant / Field Operations

"Nothing phony about the guy, anywhere, anyway, anyhow—it was just that he was totally *human*—typical Midwestern upbringing—this guy, people could relate to easily!"

Tomshany was hired by Spencer-Roberts during the 1963/'64 Nelson Rockefeller for President campaign in California for $600.00 per month, the going rate for an apprentice consultant. Later he was asked to accompany Ronald Reagan on a statewide speaking tour where he traveled and literally lived with the candidate during 1965 and early '66, using his own new 1965 powder blue Mustang convertible, mainly because Reagan didn't like to fly. S-R then bumped Tomshany's salary to $850.00 per month and gave him an expense account which amounted to a "brown-bag" budget for both himself and candidate Reagan.

While they had meetings with and Reagan gave speeches to farmers, ranchers, factory workers, chambers of commerce, Republican groups and service clubs, Reagan and Dave stayed overnight in little baking, dusty Central Valley towns along Highway 99 with lots of noisy railroad tracks, row crops, orchards and cotton fields where the eye-watering, acrid aroma of feedlots and smudge pots filled the air; not to mention their battles with the Valley's notorious "Pea-Soup" fog.

These exploratory trips, on which he would take his turn at the wheel of the little two-seater convertible, sometimes with the top down, left lasting impressions on Reagan, Tomshany told me.

They climbed out of the L.A. Basin, up through the canyons where blow-torch Santa Ana winds lurk and brush fires rampage on the national news. Winding down into the 'Nation's Breadbasket' on the famed Grapevine, after crossing the Tejon Pass, pungent aromas of freshly drilled oil near Bakersfield mixed with the sweet smell of orange blossoms, cooked on working tractor engines; like some cheap perfume weeping through a dance sweat. To confound the senses even more, crop-spraying WW I Stearman bi-planes, with the staccato power of their loud, oversize radial engines, laid down insecticide over the citrus trees, which appeared to be playing hide-and-seek with the thirsty, ever-sucking oil wells. *Reagan thrived on this country and it was obvious, he loved California and meeting her people!*

Tomshany recalled those early days alone with RR and said, "We had many hours together, as we traveled around the state because, at first, the traveling was just Ron and me, mostly."

"Sometimes Nancy, once in a while my wife, Mary, would go along to the local events, the four of us. Different car. But you get to know a person a lot. He'd talk about his mother, I'd talk about my mother. I'd talk about our swimming stuff— lifeguarding. And, we'd get to a place—and if we had a few minutes of extra time, and maybe there were a couple of kids over here or there throwing a football—*he'd* throw the football to those kids. I was a lifeguard when I was in high school and on the swimming team in high school—a lot of those Midwestern things that I saw in him were reflected in *my* thinking of him and me together. We had a lot in common in that respect."

"And the Depression Days and stuff like that were more prominent in his mind, but, never-the-less, when his family was having hard times, mine was too—and I was old enough to remember when the banks closed."

"One time we had taken a trip—going up to Paso Robles —and we had a meeting with the Republican Committee there—just the two of us on this particular trip. When we traveled we'd stay in a motel just like anybody else—many times these were like old auto-courts from the 1940's. He'd check in—I'd check in—he had one room—I had the room next door—something like that—NO SECURITY—NO NOTHIN'—!"

"No off-duty policemen helping out, no Advance Team or staff aides or Special Assistants or employees—NADA—ZIP. It was just one of those crazy things!"

"This particular place we stayed in—I think it was called *The Motel*—it supposedly was the *first* motel ever called or named a *motel* in the whole nation. I think it was in 'San Louie' (San Luis Obispo) —either there or Paso Robles. But, anyway, we went to this Republican meeting, in the evening there, and after it was over, about six-thirty—something like that—well there was nothing else on the agenda—so, we were sitting in the bar—I usually had a couple of drinks, but he, all he would have is/was mostly just one glass of wine. and that was *it*. Anyway, this friend of mine—I'll back it up to his story a little bit later. We had just noticed that the high-schoolers were headin' out to the stadium for a football game. So Ron said, *"Let's go!"*

"So we went out—(he laughs)—just the two of us—we sat there in the stands like everybody else. We didn't know a soul. We sat there and watched the whole football game, and everybody's sendin' programs over to be autographed and all that stuff—but never-the-less—it was fun—Ron didn't mind doing it. Anyway, we watched the game and finally, when we left, we got in the car and went back to the hotel where we were staying—the inn—*The Motel*—and as we walked in the door, that was the first time I had met Dave Rowe."

"Dave was a former, long-time, friend of Bill Roberts and Bill had previously lived in Paso Robles and had known Dave and his wife. Dave was an advance-man like yourself, Curtis. Dave was telling us about how they're going to have a big parade in the morning in Paso Robles, a town of about 5,000 people."

Typical of how the early campaign "happened" upon serendipitous, ready-made events for Ronald Reagan.

"They figure they're gonna' have twelve thousand people showin' up for this parade."

So Dave says, 'Hey ,do you think Ronnie would like to ride a horse in the parade tomorrow?' "Of course, right there, Reagan's ears perked right up and he says," "*Oh, we get to have a little ride in the morning, too?*"

This was known as Campaign Scheduling by the "seat-of-your-pants." The campaign "Play Book" was many times modified in the early stages and the candidate was very agreeable and adaptable, in *most* cases; unless it involved the dinner hour, Nancy and the end-of-the-day and *bedtime!*

Good Fortune or Good Luck, many times, plays a part in a good campaign, besides having a *GREAT* candidate. In the 1966 Reagan for Governor Campaign, one good opportunity after another seemed to present itself, which gave us an exciting *edge* over our opponents.

Tomshany continued, "There was a guy by the name of High Blythe, I think was his name, who had a horse ranch in the area and since Dave Rowe and Bill Roberts were old friends, I trusted Dave and his judgment, so he called High Blythe and says, 'Come on down here—I want you to meet somebody.' "High came down to the motel and he and Reagan talked—he says, 'I've got a great horse I'd like to have you ride in the parade tomorrow!' "And so, Ronnie says, "*What time does it start?*" High says, 'Oh, nine o'clock, something like that.' "Well, anyway, Ron really enjoyed that thing—that meeting—anytime you could get him on a horse—he felt right at home. After he rode the horse in Paso Robles, after we left the parade—we took off to go inland. We came to a town that nearly got wiped out in an earthquake, years later."

"Coalinga, a little tiny place where the earthquake had occurred. Reagan was scheduled to speak to a high school group. There could have been a real *turning point* in the whole campaign at that time. The normal scheduling plan called for about an hour nap in the afternoon preparatory to an evening speech."

Tomshany said he "couldn't remember if Ron had a nap that day or not—but that things turned 'sour' during and after the speech. That was his lifestyle, the way he wanted it; to rest in the afternoon; Nancy insisted on that, as well." It was a good thing and allowed RR to get ahead of the 'power-curve.'

Tomshany went on, "He made the speech in the school, the press were there, and during the speech he referred to—The *Vietnam War*. Now, up to that time nobody was calling it a *War*. It was a Vietnam *Conflict*. The *Gulf of Tonkin Resolution* was in there somewhere. They were also calling it a *Police Action.*" (as in the Korean Conflict or War)

"As we left the auditorium and went back to the motel, just to get ready to leave town, Jim Wrightson of the Sacramento Bee and a reporter from UPI were there to meet us. Ronnie was especially tired that day. I don't think he got much sleep the night before. In that meeting with the two reporters—just the two reporters, Ron and myself in this room—they got him sidetracked on Farm Labor issues—on a position that was *NOT* his true position and the UPI guy—well, first they got him on using the term—*Vietnam War*—that's what he called it—a "*War*"—and they were going to write their stories on that! Then they got him to talk on the farm labor issue—on the position—the position that was *not* his. And, as you recall, I took him to a bunch of labor meetings with AFL/CIO-types. Hell—he made a lot of points with those guys! Farm Labor was a big thing in those days, as you know." (Caesar Chavez was stirring things up in Delano at that time)

"But Reagan's position, spoken in his speech, was not his *actual* position—and he could see and I could see where it was going—and the UPI guy was ready to run out of the room with the story—because he had a big story that was going to blast Reagan on *labor.* Just about that time Jim Wrightson from the Sacramento Bee, whom I didn't think was necessarily a good friend of ours." Jim says, 'Now wait, let's clarify one thing—'and Reagan came around to his correct position. And the UPI guy lost his (negative) story! And Jim really did Reagan a favor, there. Afterwards he told me," 'You've got to watch this guy!' "But RR was just tired, you know, and that can happen with anybody. It could have been a major *turning point!*"

"After leaving there, we still had that problem dealing with the *Vietnam War* situation. I was talking to either Fred Hafner (SFO Office Mgr., for S-R) or Bill

Roberts in L.A. and I said, 'What are we going to do!' 'We've got to find a way to put Reagan "in bed" with Lyndon Johnson on that one'. And we found *one* statement. That did the trick!"

"Where Lyndon Johnson referred to it as— *The Vietnam War*—and, so, we were off the hook!"

"Otherwise, RR would have been a 'war-monger,' like Goldwater was portrayed. This became known as 'The Coalinga Statement' and it worked out O.K. for Reagan. Especially in the morning news, where they were talking about 20,000 Americans— at that time—that *never* returned from there!"

With some help from his early companion, advance man & scheduler, Dave Tomshany, and a friendly reporter, Reagan was able to navigate through some 'rough water' on a key issue in his rigorous campaign for governor in 1965 and '66—and, as Dave says, "This was just *one* trip!"

"You do know I was the *first* political person Nancy Reagan ever *fired*!"

"I was fired, after the Primary Election, because supposedly one of her socialite friends called me one evening at the Wilshire Blvd., Headquarters and she insisted that Ron and Nancy come to their private party—and I said, 'No they can't!' And it went on and on—I was probably on the phone for half an hour—just trying to say 'NO!'—every way I could—including the fact that they were going to be *gone*— they were leaving on a vacation—there was just *no* way they could be there at that party. It is interesting to note that this 'friend' was not close enough to Nancy to call her at her home and make the arrangements, herself. I remember she then called Nancy and said that I had been 'insulting' to her. And so Nancy said, *"We're going to get rid of Dave."* "Of course—she wanted to get rid of *everybody*!"

"She wanted to get rid of Eileen Fontana the telephone / PBX operator—you remember—when Nancy was calling me one morning—she called about six or seven times trying to reach me—and I was in a meeting with Stu—and finally, N.R. called back and put the call through to Stu's office—and Eileen forgot—we had the old-style PBX switchboard—and Eileen had forgotten to pull the plug or throw the key / lever, down below, and she says, 'Oh, the *bitch* is on the phone again!' "And then dropped her!" "Nancy called her right back and said, *"Well, I hope I didn't destroy your day!"*

Stu Spencer said, later, Nancy Reagan never confronted him about Eileen's impropriety or even mentioned the comment obviously made out of utter frustration. Eileen stayed on. Dave was re-assigned to other S-R campaigns.

"I got in *big* hot water with her another time, too. When Ron and I went to San Diego—we drove to a meeting down there."

"Earlier in the campaign, Bill and Stu invited Jane Wyman to come into the Spencer-Roberts offices in L.A.—the former wife—you know—you understand— just to have a little chat with her and tell her that we're just not going to say more than we have to about *the divorce*—and Wyman was agreeable and everything was fine. All she wanted to do was stay back and out of it. But not so for Nancy. Anything to do with the former wife was a sore spot, very early-on. Later on it changed a little bit."

"Anyway, Ron and I, went down to San Diego. He spoke at the Republican banquet in San Diego and the press, of course, were there during that time (RR was followed by teams of press & media everywhere he went) and by the time we drove back, generally three hours to his house in Pacific Palisades; she met us at the door. She was *LIVID*—because Jane Wyman's daughter, Maureen, had *introduced* Ron, her father, at this San Diego banquet and speech."

"Now, I had no idea who Maureen was before that day—and all of a sudden it's *his* daughter from the previous marriage and—*OH, SHE WAS LIVID!* I think she chewed me out for, probably, fifteen minutes!"

I had brought along a copy of Edmund Morris's book, DUTCH, and turned to the chapter entitled "Dark Days" Page 339 RE: The incident recited by Morris where he claims Reagan walked out of the Negro Republican League/ Assembly forum and debate with Mayor George Christopher and William Penn Patrick (no relation)—"*IN TEARS!*"

This was an event I had personally advanced for Tomshany as part of the campaign schedule.

Here is Dave's response: "The Negro Republican Assembly (The California Chapter of the National Negro Republican Assembly) Candidate's Debate event was held Saturday, March 5th, 1966 at 3:00 P.M. I took him there—to the Miramar

Hotel in Santa Monica—and right off the bat we got off on the wrong foot. When we were checking in at the door—they said, 'That'll be ten dollars.' I said, 'I'll pay my ten dollars.' 'Oh, and ten dollars for *him,* too!' I said, *'He's* the candidate, (one of the speakers)—you invited him and you're going to charge him ten dollars?' 'Well, I'll pay, but, I hope you're collecting from the other candidates too.'

"We went in and it was a mish-mash from the start (aspersions were cast on Reagan's alleged prejudice / bigotry and they got (real personal)—Christopher was needling Reagan somewhat and William Penn Patrick was there and he needled and goaded him worse than anybody."

"Anyway—when Morris, says, 'He, Reagan, strode off the stage in tears.'"He was **NOT** in tears—but he was—well—his Irish temper ***was up!***"

"Boy—when he walked out—he was furious!"

See Dave Tomshany's Synopsis, Chapter II, entitled: "Barbs & Blowup," in his book, ACTOR TO POLITICIAN, The Reagan Transition.

"Reagan lost his cool. He jumped to his feet, threw down some note cards, and proclaimed loudly,"—*"I resent the implication that there is **any** bigotry in my nature. Don't anyone ever imply I lack integrity. I will not stand silent and let anyone imply that—in this or any other group!"*

RR strode up the aisle muttering, *"Sons of bitches!"* referring to Christopher and Wm. Penn Patrick.

I witnessed this from the back of the room. Morris got his facts wrong!

"And RR came out and Bill Friedman (off-duty L.A.P.D.) Ron's driver and security person was there with us—and so as we got in the car," Ron says, *"Let's GO!"*"Ron and I were in the back seat. Well, we had no place else to go but his home, which was about a fifteen to twenty minute drive from there."

See Dave Tomshany's Synopsis, Chapter II: "He was boiling with anger and turmoil as we motored towards his home. I knew for sure that Reagan had not *one ounce* of bigotry—you get to know things like that when you spend as many hours together as we had spent. He was very much closer to saying, "TO HELL WITH POLITICS!" during that twenty-minute ride, than at any time during the entire campaign for governor. We drove to his home in Pacific Palisades and I knew the press was going to be tough on him, so I suggested, 'Let's get a hold of Bill Roberts, if we can.' "I got Bill and Bill says, 'I'll get a hold of Nofziger.'—who was on the team then and actually in the audience at the Miramar—Nofziger called back to the house from his car phone to say he would meet all of us there."

Lyn had witnessed the entire episode.

"Soon after he arrived, Nofziger convinced Ron and Nancy of something they had already almost decided—to return to the event. Nofziger drove Reagan back to the hotel in Santa Monica to attend the follow-up cocktail party with Black leaders and try to 'mend fences' with the press."

Tomshany stayed back at the house long enough to have a 'double shot of vodka' and I, Tomshany's advance man, stayed at the event to take the pulse and prepare for candidate Reagan's return.

Reflecting on the flap Dave said, "As far as the press is concerned—this could have been a big turning point in the campaign—it could have wiped it out—all you've got to do is have Negro Republicans bashing you in the newspaper; but it worked out fine."

"Because Ron and Lyn went back, the other candidates having left, and the press were not too bad. It was just a bad headline, the next day. The story itself wasn't that bad."

"One item they (the press & biographers) didn't report anything on was during the Campaign *Kick Off* January 4th, 1966. Reagan did a twenty-eight and one half minute film—stand-up / sit-down film—it wasn't a video—it was a film, in those days, that we used on the 'Kick-Off' —he did it in *one* 'take'—twenty-eight and one half minutes—which was just ideal—just perfect for a thirty-minute spot—for a film allowing for commercial breaks—that's unheard of—most candidates and actors require a dozen or so 'takes' if it's never been done before. I've had candidates, believe it or not, who've tried to do a thirty-second *radio* spot—reading it—and have to do fifteen 'takes' on *that*."

"He was incredible!"

Dave Reminisced

"I took him on his *first* commercial airplane flight in recent memory. This was apparently Reagan's first flight after his WW II days, since Ron had decided *never* to fly again, if he could help it. He preferred taking the train or driving. Remember, this was a big issue during the campaign. He *wouldn't* fly! How could this man be governor if he's not going to fly? And, you can't cover California unless you fly! So, sure enough, I booked him on a flight. He and I went on United Air Lines. We got on the plane and because there had been so much 'noise' about it beforehand, the pilot got on the intercom and said, 'We've got a distinguished guest aboard— Ronald Reagan!'" Dave laughs. "We got up to San Fran and we expected to meet one key reporter, Art Hoppe, of the Oakland Tribune."(long-time political satirist and Reagan chronicler).

"We walk into this room at the airport and every TV channel in the Bay Area is "*on*" (lights, cameras, audio & print are there & on). "He handled himself beautifully! That took care of the airplane / 'no flying' story real quick."

Dave then opened up his *Original* Daily Log Schedule Book producing the actual tickets, motel room receipts, 'chits' for lunches and dinners amidst a pile of brittle, yellowing and faded brochures, programs, menus, flyers and daily schedules from the actual events Ron had addressed. (See photos in this book)

Mary Tomshany many times accompanied her husband on some of those statewide trips in order to get to see Dave more.

She recalls what the trips were like and especially what RR., the candidate, was like.

"One time some central or northern California rancher had a huge barbecue for RR and Tim (her nickname for Dave) and I had flown up early—and Reagan was coming up later—we were going to the local airport to pick him up When we got there, there were lots of people around and I stood way in the background, at the back of the crowd. The plane touched down and taxied over to the waiting throng of well-wishers and local dignitaries."

Mary said, breathlessly, "The door opened on the airplane, and Reagan stepped out—he looked over the crowd—and he went down those stairs."

It had to be one of Western Air's Lockheed Electras or the Amerine Turkey Farms' DC-3 *"Turkey Bird,"* with air-stairs.

It's true! Reagan flew, during many months of 1966, in a lumbering, noisy but always reliable, glimmering silver transport with windows; normally used by one of his poultry- farmer supporters, Mervine Amerine, to fly *live turkey poults.* This truly was a *"seat-of-the-pants"* grass roots campaign. See Chapter One, FLIGHT OF THE TURKEY BIRD."

Mary continued, "And he made his way, practically crawling, through the crowd—over to *me*—and here were people everywhere, plus official greeters (V.I.P.'s & volunteers)—things set up for his arrival—stanchions and ropes to guide his walk through the crowd, a sound system, bunting, flags, etc."

"He went right by them," Dave laughed.

"Right down the steps he came towards *me*, Mary said, and I was so frightened and surprised—I went up against the fence behind me and Ron said, *"What's wrong, Mary?"* This is what I thought, 'What's he coming over to me for?'"

Typical of RR—who always recognized a friend in the crowd—even those who actually worked every day for him and were 'on-duty,' so to speak.

It was indicative of his intrinsic good nature and politeness.

The best way to explain this phenomenon is to say: RR felt like we were all part of his 'extended' family and that's the way he treated us. When he saw Mary, or any of us, at functions where he was appearing or speaking—it was like we just *happened* to be there *coincidentally* or possibly we had come to deliver some urgent report or, many times, we brought news, notes or information from Nancy, his sweetheart.

As far as Mary's uneasy feelings about Ron's 'surprise'—we had been taught by Dave Tomshany, Stu Spencer and Bill Roberts, and especially Lyn Nofziger, that our theme and our position as advance-men was to be invisible—available, doing our assigned tasks, but anonymous and in the background—*not*—hogging the cameras or the 'limelight' in *any* way! Thus, Mary T., who heard this 'drumbeat' every day thought, 'Not me!'

Reagan's personality, his inherent gracious nature, was such that he became uncomfortable when people around him—the staff—did things for him. He simply did not *expect* extra service but was *always* grateful for it. Mary went on, I thought, 'What's he doing coming over to me?' "I backed up to the fence and he asked me what was wrong—then the mayor of the city or one of the official greeting party came up and said, 'Oh no—come through here, back up—'" "Reagan was just so congenial—a perfect example of manners and etiquette—he smiled at me, then he turned and went back over to meet the official greeters," Mary recalled. She and Dave said in unison, "Once a friend, *always* a friend."

"That's the way he was!" "That's really the *essence.*"

WORN-OUT OLD CARS, TRAINS; THEN THE "TURKEY BIRD"

Mary went on, "Before Reagan flew, he would travel on the train. One day Tim called me and said, 'You'll have to come to the station and pick us up.'" "And so I ran around the neighborhood—we lived in a neighborhood with a bunch of kids and I had three children, ages seven, five and four, still living at home—*little* kids! So I thought, 'I'll just drop them at the neighbor's real quick and I'll drive down there to Union Station–downtown L.A.. I went everywhere and no one was home. No one could take care of my children."

"So, I put them in the station wagon, a nine year old and tired '57 Mercury, I said, 'Lookit—you three kids sit way in the back—don't talk—don't breathe (loudly)–don't *say anything*—just stay way at the back—we're going to the train station downtown!'"

Reagan and Dave had traveled to northern California and back on the train. Mary had taken a wrong turn on the wrong freeway and ended up being late and was a bit rattled when she arrived. Dave (Tim) agreed to drive and Reagan got into the front seat with him. Mary sat in the middle seat and the kids were in the way-back (third seat).

"We were driving along, driving along, and Tim was talking and all of a sudden Reagan turned around and said," *"What are those kids doing back there?"* *"Come on up here!"* "And he started telling them stories."

"And he put each one of them on his lap! "They were pretty young, but they didn't make a sound! They all sat there like little statues."

Mary said she was 'just taggin' along' to help out. Dave said there was 'just no other place to go to get help or assistance in a pinch.' He agreed, it was a 'seat-of the-pants'—'shoestring operation,' in the beginning.

An example of this no-frills, low-budget campaign follows: Dave told this story, "I had met Ron at a train or plane and picked him up to bring him home to The Palisades. We were standing in the driveway talking, at his home, in front of the car—and suddenly he feels this *hot* water—the radiator had sprung a leak and was squirting water all over his suit—He got *hot*—*(he* laughed)—and said, *"It's squirting right through the grill!"* Reagan low-keyed the wet suit and said it was, *"No big deal."*

Mary Tomshany, who was reluctant to be taped, finally decided there were some stories she thought were interesting and should be told. Mary recalled:

"I was with Tim several times when he'd drop Reagan off at his home in The Palisades and something about it was *so* wonderful. The front door would swing open and Nancy would come out—and I always thought *that* was like Loretta Young's '*thing*,' when she used to open the door and walk in—on her T.V. show. Nancy always greeted him at the door and I always thought that was so beautiful and romantic"

Dave said he could *never forget* her vigorous, warm embrace and kiss whenever she greeted Ron.

"One time Tim and I, Bill Roberts and Nancy and Ron had dinner together at a Mexican restaurant (they loved Mexican food) before we took them to the train station. It was another trip on 'The Owl' for Tim and Reagan." Mary recalls, "This was so cute—Reagan was by an open window and Nancy was there, on the outside, hugging and kissing him as the train started moving slowly down the tracks—then it picked up speed—with Nancy now running alongside to keep up and to keep kissing Ron."—reminiscent of American Service men going off to WW II—Roberts said, as he pictured Nancy *disappearing*, 'God, I hope she knows the platform ends down there!' (We all laughed.) Then Mary added, "She stopped in the nick of time."

"On one trip on the inexpensive sleeper, The Owl, Dave remembered, Ron had this compartment and I had this smaller *sleeping thing*—a sleeping chair in some sort of alcove—people coming and going, etc—like sleeping in a hallway, sitting halfway-up, with a curtain around me. In the morning, we got up and had breakfast and before we got into San Francisco,." Reagan said, *"Well, that wasn't too bad—sleeping there!"*

Dave had kept quiet about his little cubicle until Ron asked about his accommodations.

"Of course, Ron loved trains—with G.E. he'd travel around the country—he'd have two or three days by himself—to read, relax—whatever—and, if he had been flying in those days, he couldn't have done that. And that's why he liked it. He said, *"From now on, when we travel, YOU get a compartment, just like mine!"* 'I told him I didn't have trouble sleeping, but it was cramped.' He said, *"You get one, just the same!"* "And that shows this *human* side of him, too. He wasn't going to have *anybody* take a lesser position."

"We were at Knott's Berry farm, in Buena Park, south of L.A.; Orange County."

Political conservatives Walter and Cordelia Knott had created and developed the Boysenberry. They ran a roadside berry stand, pie shop and 'famous' chicken dinner restaurant and made enough money from these, plus their Ghost Town and original Old West Mining Camp and stores—to construct an exact replica, in red brick, of Independence Hall in Philadelphia; to express their patriotism.

The Knott family loved Ronald Reagan and were always offering to hold functions or public events to introduce more people to RR and allow him a forum to speak on conservative issues; as they had done with Senator Barry Goldwater, when I was with him.

Dave said, "This day we were at the Berry Farm for lunch and, in those days, they had those nice, collegiate-looking young girls, who did all of the serving in their restaurants, We saw them that day, also. We ate lunch inside and had parked the car right outside the door. As we were getting ready to leave, got into the car and were trying to figure out where our next stop was on the campaign trail,—all of a sudden—here were about seven or eight of the young waitresses—the girls—all with their noses pressed to the glass windows—looking out—and I waved for them to come out and meet Reagan. They all came out and shook his hand. Typical gracious attitude of this man. They brought menus out and he autographed them for the servers; who were thrilled to meet him!"

On the day of the start of the Watts Riots, August 13th, 1965, Dave and Ron had been scheduled to go to San Bernardino, and make several public appearances.

This was the same day Dave Tomshany took delivery of the brand new 1965 powder blue Mustang with the marshmallow convertible top, which he and Ron both drove nearly 16,000 miles, mostly throughout southern and central California in their search for serious voter interest in RR's potential candidacy in 1965 and early '66. Today, the car is on display at the Ronald Reagan Presidential Library in Simi Valley, California.

The order of the day in the State Capitol during the Watts Riots was chaos and indecision. Governor Pat Brown was on vacation in Greece where he was receiving blow-by-blow and burning-block by burning-block descriptions from his Chief of Staff about the destruction going on in the inner city of mostly South Central Los Angeles.

Businesses from store-fronts to warehouses were burning or being looted or both and private cars, as well as police cars were being commandeered, turned over and burned, by groups of lawless individuals in the mostly Black section of L.A., on the edge of downtown.

As Dave and Ron left town they could see columns of smoke rising from several locations in the center of the sprawling 'City of The Angels.' Fear had spread across southern California, but, because of their previously-made commitments and with the 'blessing' of Stu Spencer and Bill Roberts, Reagan and Dave decided to chance the trip by taking a freeway along the foothills of the San Gabriel Mountains, which would keep them *out* of the riot zone, in South Central L.A. Trepidation was evidenced by Dave's and Ron's concern over the security of the Reagan home in Pacific Palisades, home to numerous film industry celebrities, radio and television personalities, and wealthy business people, several miles West from downtown L.A. and few miles West of Beverly Hills and Bel Air, towards the ocean. Dave said they had seen the police officers on 'lookout' on the bridges over the freeways as they were leaving town.

Dave also questioned whether anyone would show up at the several events planned by anxious Republicans out in the San Bernardino area, some forty miles to the East of L.A. However, this was the large county where Reed Sprinkel, a highly organized civic leader, had been recruited to be the co-Chairman; and who was also interviewed for this book.

"We had several events in the San Bernardino area and could see the smoke plumes rising from South Central L.A. as we headed out there," Dave continued. "That day the news media and police were telling everyone (in the area south of downtown) on the radio and T.V. "STAY HOME" "DON 'T GO OUT!"

Some surprising and funny things happened as Dave and Ron went about their schedule and made their way back to L.A. on that fateful day.

"Reagan was speaking to the Lions or Kiwanis Club at The California Hotel in 'San Berdoo.' (San Bernardino) As we walked into the lobby of the California Hotel, here was a bunch of older folks sitting there watching a Ronald Reagan movie—'Cattle Queen of Montana' with Barbara Stanwyck—anyway, we walked up behind these older fellows and one of the guys says, 'Look at that—My God—it's *him!*' Of course, Ron always greeted everyone warmly, and he did with them, as well. They were shocked."

"He made his speech and met with some of the local Republican Party people there and then, that evening, we went to the college stadium, which held about three thousand people, where he was scheduled to give a speech at 8:00 P.M. We got there about fifteen minutes till eight—we drove in, just the two of us in the shiny new powder blue Mustang, with the top down and drove around the track once. Except for about twenty people—the stands were empty!"

"Meanwhile, the radio in the car and T.V.'s at the hotel were telling everyone to 'STAY HOME' 'DON'T GO OUT!' "Because of the Watts Riots."

Dave said Reagan looked over at him and said, *"Maybe we should dig out* (on the dirt track) *and then leave.!"*

Dave turned to his co-pilot and said, 'Well, give them a few minutes more.' 'Give 'em a few minutes.' "And just like a *miracle,* all of a sudden—the stands were nearly *full!*"

"We drove back around the stadium one time and parked and—they filled it up—pretty much." "It was *amazing!*" "Reagan gave his speech and we got out of there. Of course, on the way home that night, we were just scared *shitless*—because his house might have been targeted, as this thing developed. We took the San Bernardino freeway to the Harbor, down to the Santa Monica and up to Sunset Blvd. and over to his house. We could see the *fires* all around, smell the smoke and hear 'everything'—entire blocks burning, explosions, sirens, gun shots, and helicopters overhead, etc."

They arrived back in Pacific Palisades to find Nancy and the Reagan household intact and unscathed—the major part of the rioting having occurred several miles to the south and east.

As the requests for Reagan to meet, greet and speak to various organizations increased, time became precious and the questions and key state issues became more defined and complex.

Dave remembers that at some point during the transition from the 'brown-bag' lunches and auto-court motels to a more sophisticated and professional campaign structure, in the winter of 1965, BASICO, Inc., under the direction of Dr. Stan Plog with assistance from Jim Gibson, were employed by the Reagan for Governor Committee to research and present facts on key issues effecting the citizens and on the minds of the voters of the State of California. Also, to present synopses on the operations of key state agencies and departments This will be fleshed out in greater detail in the interview with Dr. Jim Gibson in his chapter entitled: THE CREATIVE SOCIETY.

Reagan was asked to speak to women's and men's clubs, civic organizations, chambers of commerce, Rotary, Lions, Kiwanis, and numerous community service clubs both large and some very small and even do walk-thru's at large and small businesses, and manufacturing plants, both north and south.

He called the luncheons and dinners, *"The rubber-chicken, mashed potatoes & peas circuit."* Reagan was received, it seemed, like a folk hero or a rock star wherever we went with him.

"I remember I took Ron out to a women's club in Diamond Bar, southeast of L.A., and there were five hundred women in this low-ceilinged room and just the *two* of us. We were the only males there. And, I am telling you, the *NOISE* in that room was just *unbelievable*—there was all the latter of the silverware, the cups on saucers—and that *talking*—all the higher-pitched voices—*shrill!* Oh, it was so bad—we got out of there—and we just couldn't believe how pleasurable it was to get away from all that noise! I think that's when my ears—my hearing, went bad!"

Lower-voiced men do it differently—like in a sports bar on Super Bowl Sunday, screaming—'DEE-FENSE!'—'DEE-FENSE!' When asked how Reagan was received Dave said, "OH, MAN!" "MAGNIFICENT!"

"This time we were at the Beverly Hilton Hotel, speaking to one group and we ran into this lady while walking through the lobby. She represented some other group, an association of professional women, probably more *liberal* than conservative, meeting there at the same time. She said, 'Oh, Mr. Reagan, would you come and say a few words to *our* group?'"

"Well, you remember, not wanting to pass up an opportunity and having a few minutes open on the schedule—we said, "O.K!.""

This spontaneous re-scheduling sometimes would happen *every* day, when some group found out RR was in the vicinity.

"We walked in to the back of their meeting room—the room was filled with professional women—they looked around and looked around, saying and muttering little things like, 'Oh boy, here comes a *political* speech.' We went in there and Ron gave them a short talk about his concerns—I mean not more than *five minutes*. It was the most *incredible* thing! He had 'em in the palm-of-his-hand! They loved him!" George Christopher, William Penn Patrick, Warren Dorn—all of those guys—they'd get up and they'd speak for *hours*—and talk and talk—they'd drone on and on and on—no substance—lousy delivery!"

"I took him out to a Republican campaign workers' meeting in Alhambra, one time, just the two of us. We got there late and stood in the back of the room waiting for the other candidates to get finished—it went on and on and on and they'd get a little mild applause—the audience consisted of political people, office staff, paid and volunteer party people, mostly precinct workers. During the speeches by the other candidates for governor, we'd listen awhile then we'd walk outside into the lobby. When the last one spoke—Ron and I were still outside the room. Occasionally, we would peek through the door, and Reagan was going to go in as the final speech wound down." I said, 'Wait—wait!' "And through the crack in the door we could see the last one finish speaking. I said, 'Wait!' The applause went— *You* know—Dave gestures with his fingers and his hand heading down towards the ground—and then I said, 'O.K.!' 'GO!' "We opened the doors—he walked down the center aisle—then it hit—MAN—DID HE GET THE APPLAUSE —TEN TIMES BETTER—*just for walking in*! Ron gave them FIVE MINUTES and that was the end of the speech!" "That was *IT*." "What a difference!"

"Then there was Senator Thomas Kuchel (K e e k e l)—when I was running his campaign in CA. I'd say, 'Tom, quit talking about your friend, Earl Warren (ultra-liberal), to Republican groups.' I said, 'Get in there and give a short—*this* and *that*—you know—I'm *against* this—and I'm *for* that—they'll love you.' "He would *NEVER* do it! I had a camera crew—a very expensive camera crew—follow him around the state for seventeen days straight—to try to make a simple thirty second T.V. spot. But, that was typical!"

Dave saved this story for last because he felt it was a major defining moment in Reagan's campaign for governor, when Ron and Nancy realized they had reached a milestone, and they might be able to win the race. Dave and S-R were always warily looking out for stumbling blocks along the way, Dave called them 'turning points.' Well, they were all pretty well blown away after this 1965 Fall tour which ended in downtown San Francisco right in RR's toughest opponent's front yard. This 'turning point' was a positive, unforeseen surprise for *everyone*; opposing candidates included:

The Republican State Convention was held at the San Francisco Hilton hotel from Friday, September 24th, 1965 thru Sunday, September 26th. Early-on, S-R, through their San Francisco offices, with the help of Assistant Finance Director for Northern California, Nita Wentner (Ashcraft) and a lot of eager volunteers, began planning for an event that would set the tone for the rest of the campaign.

Dave explained some of the plans, "We decided on a reception at the hotel to allow as many of the public as possible to meet and shake hands with both Ron and Nancy Reagan. The other candidates decided to do the same thing in adjacent rooms at the hotel's convention facility. Thus the public could wander from one room to the other to get an up-close, personal view, greet and visit with each candidate."

In addition to San Francisco Mayor George Christopher, there was Chairman of the L.A. County Board of Supervisors, Warren Dorn, U.S. Attorney Laughlin 'Loch' Waters and Wm. Penn Patrick, an eccentric businessman and political gadfly who flew his own, surplus F-86 Sabre Jet.; all candidates.

Dave said, "We mailed out 20,000 invitations to the public in certain, targeted areas, to come and meet Ronald and Nancy Reagan. We offered cookies, coffee and some soft drinks, juice, etc."

"This reception was to be the culmination of a tightly scheduled three-day run into Central and Northern California, with stops all along the way," Dave said.

Ron and Dave departed the Reagan's Pacific Palisades residence on Wednesday, September 22nd, 1965 at 8:15 AM in Dave's own little, sometimes cramped, shiny new, powder blue '65 Mustang convertible, heading out through the mountains north of the smoggy L.A. Basin on the 'old' Grapevine to connect with Highway 99, the straight ribbon of asphalt that ran through every San Joaquin Valley town and burg. And, of course, this being harvest season, it was clogged with huge hopper trucks loaded to the top with crisp, white onions as big as baseballs, with their pungent, unmistakable aroma.

Oranges, peaches, apricots; even cotton in some and sugar beets in others.

With Ron taking his turn at the wheel some of the time, the candidate and his compadre zipped along past groves, plowed fields, canals and thousands of acres of row crops in the "Nation's Breadbasket." San Francisco is 450 miles north of Los Angeles.

"Ron was the scheduled speaker at a Republican fund-raiser that evening in Modesto, and then we overnighted at a motel there. On Thursday, September 23rd, RR was the speaker at a United Fund luncheon in San Jose at noon, then in the evening at a Constitution Day Celebration in Los Altos and overnight in Berkeley across the Bay Bridge from San Fran. On Friday, September 24th, RR was speaker at the Berkeley Breakfast Club, then across the Bridge, we traveled again and down the peninsula to Palo Alto in time to appear as the speaker at the California Employment Agency's convention at noon."

"Next, off to San Jose where he boarded the 'Happy Train,' filled with excited Republican faithful, for the trip into downtown San Francisco and the GOP State Convention."

A grueling schedule, since RR had to be on his 'toes' and 'on point' *every* minute.

The planned Reagan Reception for the invited public was an evening event, and it was getting dark as the people continued to gather.

Dave Tomshany vividly recalled, "Ron and Nancy stood on a small platform in this banquet room and the well wishers stood in long, long lines that snaked out down the hallways, into the hotel lobby, onto the side walk, into the street and around the corner! We turned out an estimated FIVE THOUSAND (5,000) people, (See Nita's original invitation & memo) just patiently standing around drinking coffee and eating cookies in these long lines—waiting to meet and shake hands with Ron and Nancy."

"And I kept them coming, one after another, after another, until we finally had to cut it off after a couple of hours." "It was *unbelievable!*" "I decided to check on the turnouts at the receptions of our opponents. I remember that Loch Waters' and Warren Dorn's receptions were attended by only a few people. None of the other candidates had *anyone!* Even George Christopher, the Mayor of San Francisco should have had a *few* people. Not!"

"Later, I was standing near the entrance to our reception room when Warren Dorn came over to see what was happening, he stood there for a few seconds as he viewed the crowds, then looked down and said, *'MERCY, MERCY, MERCY!'* "

After searching for a couple of days, I located Warren Dorn on Tuesday, October 9th, 2001, at his home in the ocean front community of Morro Bay, California, where he became mayor after he retired. He not only remembered the incident—he told me he had decided, then and there, that he 'didn't have a *snowball's chance in Hell* in that election!'

Dave then continued, "After the line was finally cut off and the handshakes were over, Bill Roberts and I and Stu Spencer and a couple of other staff members accompanied RR and NR up to their suite. In the elevator, on the way up, Ron proclaimed, *"Gee, if I'd had you guys promoting me while I was still in the 'other' business (motion pictures)I'd still be in the other business!"* "We all laughed."

"This was Ron's and Nancy's defining moment. They finally *knew* that there was serious interest in RR's candidacy."

"Soon afterward they made a definite decision to run for governor. The only casualty of the event was a very sore hand and arm for Nancy. After being treated by a doctor in L.A., she had her arm in a sling or brace for about a week."

Dave Tomshany said that there was *no comparison* between Reagan and *any* other candidates he had ever worked with. "Ron could assimilate material, information and facts—then deliver them to the audience, through the camera, with confidence, concern and good humor; in a concise, simple and interesting manner," Dave said.

Probably the foremost reason he could do it, notwithstanding his extraordinary skills at delivery; he passionately believed in his subject.

Chapter Seventeen

L.A. COP GIVES UP DAYS OFF
& VACATIONS FOR YEARS
TO HELP REAGANS

Chuck Ward

"It was a labor of *love*."

Chuck Ward was a quiet, soft-spoken, serious but affable L.A.P.D. motorcycle officer who frequented some of L.A.'s finest restaurants and often Paramount Pictures Hollywood studios. He readily proclaimed that he was a "movie nut." He enjoyed the southern California sunshine and it's lifestyle. Ward was *always* a law enforcement officer, on or off duty.

When he was not in uniform, he was a nattily dressed, debonair, gentleman in his crisp grey suit and long black trench coat. He loved his country and wondered where it was headed and where California was headed under its present leadership, Governor Pat Brown. He had his share of heroes, among the people he had met. His barber at Paramount Studios was "Vince"—Ronald Reagan's favorite barber.

One day while getting his hair cut at the studio, in walked Ronald Reagan and the two started up a conversation that would lead to a decades-long relationship whereby RR would ask for Ward, personally, to accompany him on various trips and engagements throughout his career. Ward's *first* encounter with RR was at Shelter Island in San Diego at a California Motorcycle Officers Convention. Reagan was on a vacation.

Ward said, "I walked into the bar—and I saw Mr. Reagan standing, talking to a man and a woman—they were just kinda' standing there laughing—and as usual, he, RR, was drinking a Coke—*really*—and so, they left—and he was kind of by himself, and there was hardly anybody in there—so I walked over and introduced myself—and told him that I admired his acting—but I also admired his politics! I told him that if he ever decided to run for office—this was in the winter at the time—that I'd like to work for him; *gratis*—just *volunteer* my time—whatever position he could use me in. And he said, *"O.K. Uh, yeah."* He said, *"If you see anything, get a hold of me."*

"Anything, meaning an announcement—if he said he was going to run—you know—the whole bit."

Chuck Ward and I had worked side-by-side for years but I wanted him to explain his duties while at L.A.P.D. and how he handled his job providing *personal protection* to Ronald Reagan.

Chuck began: "We had the Traffic Enforcement Division which were 380 motorcycle officers of the L.A.P.D., covering the city."

"I usually worked Hollywood area—either Sunset Blvd., Hollywood Blvd., or Wilshire Blvd., and, I had been a movie-nut since I was five years old. My dad, when I was four or five, took me to see THE JAZZ SINGER. I always got my hair cut by Vince there at Paramount Studios. I knew a lot of people there—I knew Y. Frank Freeman, who was the head of Paramount—I knew Wally Westmoreland in fact he was a good buddy of mine. Anyway, I was getting my hair cut one day and Mr. Reagan came in all by himself—and we were talking—and I told him where we had talked before and he said, *"Oh Yeah."* And he recalled where he had met me—down at Shelter Island—and I said, 'I hear rumors—is anything going to go on?' And he said, *"Well Maybe."* I said, 'I still want you to remember that I want to work for you—in whatever capacity.' "I saw him a couple of times there—back in 1965 at Paramount—where we were both getting haircuts. Then one day, a couple of months or so later, he comes walking in and he's with another fellow, and he says, *"Oh, Chuck, how're you doin?"* And I said, 'Fine, how are you doing?' And he said, *"Well, I think I'm going to do it!"* He said, *"I want to introduce you to this gentleman— he's going to be my security—his name is Bill Friedman."* He said, *"You guys probably know each other."*

"Well, we didn't. Different divisions and a large department. He turned to Bill and he said, *"Chuck is security with us whenever he's free—he goes with us wherever."* "And that's how this relationship started."

Reagan didn't know much about the background of Chuck Ward, but he trusted the man whom he had met, briefly, over the past year with that innate, inner sense. "Up to the November when he ran—I took five weeks off from L.A.P.D. for vacation time, to go with him."

"We went everywhere—I was in San Francisco with him—San Diego— everywhere. Yeah, we flew—and my seat partner a couple of times was Roy Rogers— and Clint Walker—Ray Bolger—we were riding around to campaign stops in jockey Johnny Longdon's motor home. One time, when we were down in Orange county, there was Chuck Connors and Clint Walker; talk about feeling like a midget with those guys around you. I did personal protection—stayed with him all the time. It was funny—he always rode in the front seat and I rode in the back seat—Freidman was driving—Bill and I got along fine. Reagan was an *ethical* man. *Honest.* The kind of a guy you could trust—anywhere—anytime!

"Like former Attorney General and Governor, George Deukmajian (for whom Chuck later worked, on the payroll, in security). Reagan and he were similar— *realistic and honest!*"

"Who was that big shot in San Diego—he got into a little trouble down there—he was a big money-man—owned a lot of property? I was in a room, about this size, in the hotel—and the guy wanted a position—with the governor—with the administration."

Chuck began to describe an individual who was a well-known figure around San Diego and whose behavior many of us had heard rumors about before. He always began his name with only his *first* initial. Chuck told of being an eyewitness, and helped put *truth* to some of those rumors. In the process RR's character and integrity soared even higher.

"I heard him offer Mr. Reagan *lots* of money, not just for Reagan, but for the 'cause'—the administration—the whole bit, and Reagan said, *"I don't play those games!"* " He turned it down—flat!" **"I was the only one in the room, besides Reagan."** "You'd know the name—this guy was a real big-shot; he got into a little bit of trouble somehow."

'He got into a *lot* of trouble in San Diego,' I told Ward. This man was known as a pushy, overbearing, eccentric wheeler-dealer, with just a tad more class than John Gotti.

Chuck continued: He just flat out said, **'Hey, I've got twenty thousand here.'** "I mean it wasn't chicken-feed. It wasn't just supposed to go into Reagan's wallet— it was to go for a 'cause' —he wanted a position on some board or commission!" Reagan told him, *"You can't buy anything from me!"* "He, this big-shot, wanted a 'spot.' "Reagan would have *none* of it!"

"I heard Reagan swear, once. This was the only time I heard him swear.""We were in the car—and we were going down to this college. There's a group of colleges"

'The Claremont Colleges?' I asked.

"Yes!" "He was looking at the paper, or something, and all of a sudden RR said, *"Doggone it."* Then Chuck asked, "Do you know the newspaper columnist,

Maryanne Means? She still writes—used to be a young, good looking kid. She had interviewed Reagan—then he told her something, *"off the record."* Well, she published it! 'He used the expression,' *"That no good bitch!"* And—I'd never heard him say anything but maybe—*"darn"* He said, *"That no good bitch!"*

He said, *"I know for a fact that she and John Kennedy stayed all night together—shacked-up."* I think he then said—*"on one of our main battleships and it's against the Constitution, it's a violation of the U.S. Constitution, for that to happen."* *"I ought to publish—THAT!"*

"Because he was really ticked about whatever she wrote about and printed that was "off-the-record,." he was upset, because he expected her to keep *her* word—like he would."

I asked Ward how Reagan treated him personally and if he issued orders to him or was demanding during their travels.

"He treated me fine! Just like I was a friend." He never said, *"Do this—Do that!"*

"He never issued *any* orders. No. No! From my personal experience, and I don't know how he was as president, but he was very easy to work for."

Chuck Ward was not involved on a full-time basis after Reagan became governor, since he hadn't had enough time with the L.A.P.D. to retire—however, he was called back time after time for special assignments by Governor Reagan, himself, for such events as the 1968 GOP Convention in Miami Beach, where he simply worked *gratis* during his designated vacation periods, basically, using them up for any personal or family holidays he could have taken.

Ward reported to Ed Meese, RR's new Chief of Staff, at the Convention. He was the *only* one there in uniform, among many L.A. cops in plainclothes, assisting with security and acting / operating as liaison with Reagan's "Kitchen Cabinet."

We know that Reagan trusted his security chief, Art Van Court, but somewhere in his psyche, and this could have come from Nancy, he wanted his own style of "back-up" plan and thus engaged the quintessential 'copper', Chuck Ward, to provide an additional measure of protection for himself and the family; outside of the office bureaucracy.

Chuck Ward contemplated the effect that RR had on his own personal life as he carried these experiences into his future years. The kind of impact Reagan had on his thinking and his direction: "I don't think you could be around the man very much and not become more enlightened. My admiration for him just went on and on. There was *never* a moment when I thought, 'Gee, I wish he hadn't have done this or had done that.' "

"In the Reagan organization everyone was pulling together—it was a *team*, I think, and no matter where you were on the totem pole, so to speak; it didn't matter!"

Ward said that everybody was always friendly and some became his good, long-time, personal friends.

An example was Judge Wm. P. Clark Jr., "He was always friendly. He didn't care what you were, your socio-economic station in life, you were *on* the team!"

This, of course, filtered down from Reagan himself and permeated the staff.

Having been involved in the personal protection of both Senator Barry Goldwater and Ronald Reagan for a number of years, I knew what my mission was, but I wanted to hear what Chuck Ward believed *his* was, so I asked him what he was prepared to do—*if* some threat should come RR's way?

Chuck said, "I was always armed—and we'd take it from there. I could sure intercede real fast. If he were to be in the line of fire—it was just automatic—I'd get him out of there—push him down on the floor—or whatever."

Then I asked him, 'Then you would have put yourself in harm's way?'

"That was the understanding, I think, of any good security guy—that's your job! You've got to protect the *principal*—take care of the *principal*—and worry about yourself, later."

Ward said he didn't have any problem with that.

We, in that special group, were ready to take anything that came our way—to protect this rare and incredible man, Ronald Reagan, who had miraculously come into our lives; we found we *loved* him like a brother.

Ward repeated, "No Problem! None at all! **No, Uh Uh! No—Never!**" "Actually, it never crossed my mind—this being a problem. Even though I wasn't paid—I was there because I *wanted* to be. This was *entirely voluntary.*"

CHAPTER EIGHTEEN

ADVANCING REAGAN

Buck Ware

"The *essence* of Ronald Reagan—Courtesy—Integrity—Congruency and Practical Intelligence." "In private, even after long days on the campaign trail, he was always the *same* person everyone saw on T.V." "Profound *decency*."

Buck Ware came to us out of the 'blue' so to speak, not because he was a friend of some insider or relative of Ronald Reagan, but because he was determined to help the man become governor and kept on pushing until he connected.

Buck recalled, "The first time I paid attention to Ronald Reagan was when he gave a Speech on T.V., The Speech, at Dodger Stadium in Los Angeles, for Barry Goldwater in 1964. My dad and I just stood in amazement—we couldn't sit down—as Reagan spoke—feeling that here was a *real* leader. I don't know what the time-lag was before we heard anything else, but the next thing I heard was an announcement one day on the radio by Cy Rubel, chairman of the board of Union Oil Co., in L.A."

Rubel became one of RR's Kitchen Cabinet members and a friend of Holmes Tuttle, I reminded Buck.

He quickly responded, "Right!" "Rubel said they were forming The Friends of Reagan Committee; to help Ron run for governor. So a few minutes after I heard the announcement , I picked up the phone and called Union Oil Co., asked for 'Cy,' and back in those days, they just said, 'Yes Sir' and put you through," he laughed.

Buck said Rubel didn't know him from a bale of hay. "I told him I had a resort that handled big company picnics, group gatherings and events and any time Reagan wanted to use it—it was *his!*"

Buck's resort consisted of nearly five hundred acres, almost two miles long, with tall, shady Sycamore and mature Cottonwood trees, along the Santa Clarita river. It had huge freshwater swimming pools and was located in the "Canyon Country" north of Los Angeles. Like Reagan, the rancher / outdoorsman, chopping wood and fixing fences, Buck did many of the same things while running his Soledad Sands Park resort. From drilling wells, chopping wood, painting buildings and fences, maintaining tractors and equipment and installing stages, podiums, lighting, sound and communications systems; he did it all. Buck did the work necessary to run an outdoor public recreation-oriented facility; sort of a combination state park and Knott's Berry Farm. When I met him, he had what was considered a Type "A" personality. Buck was an aggressive workaholic and a stickler for details. He quickly became the one person we could count on to do everything necessary to make any event at which RR was going to appear seem to go together like clockwork; smoothly and efficiently.

Sending Buck out to advance a tough event was, in some ways, similar to the late 1800's / early 1900's in Texas; when *one* Texas Ranger would be sent to a troublesome town where law and order were badly needed and through common sense and a lot of tough, as well as friendly, persuasion, order was restored.

Buck continued, "Mr. Rubel said, 'Okay!' to his offer to use the resort for the 1966 Reagan for Governor Campaign. I don't know whether it was before or after the Reagan picnic, at which some eight hundred people showed up, but I went down to the RR headquarters on Wilshire Boulevard in Los Angeles, and *you* were the person I was told to meet with. I told you about my skills with group gatherings, communications, crowd-control and my flexible work hours."

I told Buck I remembered. He had said his hours were 'wide open!' Buck said, at that meeting in the beehive of activity in the hot, dusty old headquarters building in L.A. (no A/C then), some forty years prior, 'You tell me when you need help and I'll be there!' "Yeah!"

"You were the guy I reported to. I met Sandy (Quinn) and Arthur (Van Court), and we started advancing the candidate—with those bus trips all over southern California."

Buck said he then had the opportunity to meet the man who took his call "out-of-the-blue," Cy Rubel, during his first actual meeting with Ronald Reagan at an intimate fund-raising reception at the home of Bob's Big Boy hamburger founder, Bob Wian, in Toluca Lake, near the home of Bob Hope and Universal Studios. By this time Buck had made a 'sort of' open-ended commitment 'to help Ron run.'

Buck said, "Everybody, except for a very few of the staff, were so centered on Reagan, were so dedicated, so clear and so clean—so purposeful—it was a joy to show up at six in the morning or five in the morning or whatever time was necessary. The second time I met Reagan in person was at the park, for his event, the picnic. This was the result of my phone call to Cy Rubel and my subsequent trip to the headquarters to make arrangements with you, Curtis. This was the first time I was involved with Ron for any length of time—on a personal basis. I think the event consisted of all of the GOP candidates. It was a large rally. As far as I remember, it came off very simply / smoothly / easily."

I asked Buck to go back to the times when he first worked with RR from a distance and then later to when he was working very close to Ron; as the campaign went into high gear. What was your analysis after an examination of him I asked? Your view of Reagan? You first saw him speak at Dodger Stadium on behalf of Sen. Barry Goldwater, right?

"Yes. It was the first time I ever really paid attention to him, other than seeing him on the G.E. Theater."

"One thing that impressed me, Curtis, it really stuck in my mind—by that time I had owned the park about four years or so—I had developed an awareness of what people were thinking by watching their body-language. When I watched Reagan walk and move and talk—and laugh—and so forth—it just impressed me profoundly! What a congruent person. He was never, in my point of view, he was *never* a politician. I would never assign such a lowly term to a man like Reagan. Everything about Reagan's congruency and from everything I saw in the staff; the staff was a reflection of his *integrity* and it made it so easy to just absolutely respect everyone that I worked with there."

I asked Buck how Reagan responded to him. Did he talk to you? Did he converse with you? Was it cursory? How did you react?

"One time, after the general election, we had a dinner party in Sacramento at The Firehouse restaurant; that was a very special place for all of us. I wound up riding in the car with Reagan and Bill Friedman, and the subject came up that I was a high-speed-reader at that time, and on a flight between Sacramento and L.A., I could very carefully go through one hundred to one hundred-fifty pages of reading material, and Reagan was kind of interested in that. Reagan was sitting in the front passenger seat and each time he spoke to me about it he rotated in the seat to have eye-to-eye contact—and that kind of integrity and presence—especially the word *presence*—-really impressed me. Watching him all through the campaign, his presence with other people just endeared an unusual respect."

Buck compared RR to other candidates whom he had seen, who just sat there, muttered 'uh-huh's' and yawned. Ron used Buck to read, as he did many others of us on the staff, to assist him in reviewing, categorizing and collating into different groups State of California Legislative Bills and research material, which he then read and initialed or signed. Sometimes there were stacks of letters RR had written to citizens who had sent him their personal thoughts. Just candidate, Governor-elect Reagan or Governor Reagan and one of us, reading, signing and boxing, as the little Jet Commander flew along at 400+ MPH, some 30,000 feet over the mountains, valleys and towns of California.

Then I asked Buck: 'How did he treat other people, Buck?' 'How did he treat *you?*'

"Oh, absolutely courteous and congruent—he was a fine person to be with—especially in elevators! Every time we'd get into an elevator, he'd have a joke." Buck laughed. "He was always very respectful; I never heard him say anything that couldn't be put in the newspaper. The way he talked with us was the way he talked in front of the T.V. cameras. There was only **ONE** person that I ever saw. The same person! It didn't matter what the situation was, it was the *same* personality. He only had one face that I ever saw. It think it is safe to say, I was in private situations—enough of them with Ron—I probably would have seen it (if he had changed for the circumstances) because I pay attention to people, Curtis."

"It was so busy election night, in the Biltmore hotel, Phil Battaglia, Reagan's southern California campaign chairman, asked me for a look at the little photo album I had put together on our hectic, bustling campaign activities, each photo with a whimsical caption below it."

It pictured most of the traveling campaign staff, including our bus driver and security team along with many members of the traveling press and media. Buck had given a select number of the albums to members of the inner circle staff, along with Ron and Nancy Reagan. (Many of those photos appear in Vol. 1 & Vol 2. of this book)

Buck said, "Phil and Ron are laughing uproariously over one of the pages."

No one's position or title was spared the tip of the jokester's (Buck's) spear.

"It was so busy on election night, the Fire Marshal should have kicked half of the people out of the hallways; It was wild! Anyway, I showed Ron the book, he looked about two pages into it and he said, *"Oh, save this!"* "It was after the count was in and the election was assured. We knew that we were going to meet the networks at ten o'clock for a press conference in the hotel—and Ron said, *"Save this and give it to me about three minutes before we go On Air."* "So for two or three minutes, while we were waiting for the countdown to go live On Air, Ron and Phil were just laughing their guts out over those pictures! It just took them into a joyful moment and put them into the best possible mood for facing the nation."

I asked Buck if he had ever flown on the "Turkey-Bird" the legendary 1966 Reagan Campaign DC-3 air transport plane.

Buck said he had never flown on the "Turkey-Bird," then added, "The closest I got to it was one day when the airplane was about to leave Santa Monica airport, *you* had mentioned that they didn't have any food on board, and did I have 'any ideas on getting some food on board for the traveling-party?' I called the main office of Kentucky Fried Chicken in Culver City (a couple of miles or so from the Santa Monica airport).I told them that we had the Ronald Reagan campaign plane filled with staff and press heading to northern California and the fellow at KFC said, 'what time do you want how many meals?' It was soon delivered onto the tarmac with the KFC rep carrying meal after meal out of the back seat and the trunk of his car; we loaded them up onto the plane and the reports came back later that, 'It was the best airline catering we have ever had!'"Do you remember, Curtis, a handsome guy, an anchorman on KTLA television in L.A. He was a flyer who had about half a dozen vintage airplanes he kept at the Santa Paula airport, north of Los Angeles, in the orange groves. He was frequently at the Santa Monica airport when the DC-3 was coming in. He was really intrigued with the "Turkey-Bird."

" He was really getting laughter out of the idea of pulling out the seats and carrying live turkeys—wash it out—and load in the next president of the United States."

This reporter / anchor person had no idea of knowing that RR would go anywhere in politics, perhaps even the Statehouse, but he did know that this good looking vibrant actor who was constantly speaking his mind about conservative issues, did *not* want to fly in the best of times, and certainly not in what could be termed a 'rickety old puddle-jumper.'

"Man, you had to almost wear ear-muffs to stand the noise of her take-offs! I was privileged to ride back and forth in the Jet-Commander from Santa Monica to Sacramento quite a bit during the Interim-government period (when RR was Governor –elect between November 1966 and Midnight, January 2, 1967) "I felt that my greatest contribution was to be present, ready and capable of anything that was asked of me. I remember one time, it was either you or Art Van Court, told me that Ron inquired who was advancing some location they were going to—and he was told that I was doing it—and the message that came back was, *"Good, I know it'll go smooth."* I never really had any conversations with him because I felt he was so busy, which he always was, and I felt that I didn't have anything in particular to contribute."

"The paramount theme, created and practiced by Lyn Nofziger, Phil Battaglia, Sandy Quinn, yourself and the other staff members was: We don't jump in front of the cameras, we don't get in the way of the candidate (except for security reasons), but we assist the candidate and don't 'bend his ear' for trivial conversations when we are alone with RR, which might distract The Man from his *thinking* and his *writing*. I was keenly aware of it!" Buck emphasized.

That theme was promulgated, primarily by Lyn, I told him.

"One of the enjoyable things which occurred when we arrived at a hotel or event site for a speech, was to sit at a table in the back of the room with Nofziger. He was always mentoring us younger guys, giving us pointers, explaining who was who and how they (the press and other candidates) were working, what their M.O. was."

'The dynamics of the scene and the people,' I told Buck.

"Yes! He was always such a gracious gentleman to us."

I asked Buck what he observed and what Reagan's relationship was with an Almighty Power.

"I don't remember him ever addressing it—just 'walking' it," Buck said.

"As I said before, I never heard him mention spirituality, praying or whatever; I didn't know about the depth of his relationship with prayer, until reading Peggy Noonan's book, WHEN CHARACTER WAS KING. The prayer circles that surrounded him; many of which he probably didn't know existed—but the effect is *there*. To me, when somebody starts telling how great their religion is; they *ain't* got it! The one's who really get it, are the ones who walk it, talk it and breathe it, without ever mentioning it. This shows a quality of leadership and integrity that you can't help but respect as coming from a very profound source. One of the things that I particularly enjoyed, two or three times when I would be riding in the car with Ron and Bill Friedman, on the way back to RR's house in the Pacific Palisades was, just about the time we were to turn off from Sunset Boulevard to go up Ron's street, Bill would call the house from the car, to let'em know we were coming. We'd get up there and Nancy was *always* on the front porch—and I remember a couple of times, when Ron got out, they were *smooching* so good, so much; we turned around to look at the shrubbery. They were the epitome of lovers, anything that anybody has ever said about Nancy, in a critical manner, to me is insignificant compared to the steadfast loyalty she had to her husband!"

"There was nothing untrue, insincere or pretentious about it! She was just highly focused on supporting her husband; which I think is a tremendous quality! At the President's funeral—(Buck now is weeping)—when she bent over the coffin, I broke down—(he is now crying audibly)—I hadn't cried that hard in—(his words were lost in tears and sobbing)—I have a memory—that when I go back into great moments of the past—all of the *emotion* is there. I can't just 'rattle' it off—without the **emotion** coming forth."

We both were now crying audibly.

"Do you remember, Curtis, during the campaign we went to the L.A. Produce Market about four o'clock in the morning?"

"Oh Yes!"

"That was before I started carrying a camera. The reason there was so much security out there (downtown L.A.) was to take care of the rabble-rousers (potential demonstrators per advance intel from L.A.P.D.) We were out on the sidewalk in front of the appropriately named: L.A. NUT & FRUIT CO. And standing right in front of the sign were about twenty protesters; they were really 'Hippies.'"

Did you advance any street parades? I asked Buck.

"I sure do remember the Mexican-American Day Parade in East Los Angeles!""There was tremendous enthusiasm and I remember the shouts of 'YA BASTA!' 'Enough already'—of the Pat Brown administration!"

Reagan the well-seasoned equestrian rode a horse in the parade and surprised and delighted the friendly, cheering crowds.

"I was not a political person at all, until Pat Brown made a complete ass of himself over Caryl Chessman, the notorious 'Red Light Bandit' and rapist in L.A.!"

Brown had stayed the execution of Chessman in another of his very liberal moves as Governor, during the 1966 campaign.

"The thing that impressed me so much about the Reagan staff, during and after the campaign for governor, was the very apparent absence of egos. The reactionary mind is always going to be self-serving, and I just don't have any recall of but one person, of seeing anyone who was there in anything (any endeavor) other than selfless service to a man whom we knew was great."

I asked Buck why he thought Reagan was '*great?*'

"I worked about the same number of hours as you did, Curtis!" He laughed. "After I left you guys at night (at the end of the 'work-day') I'd drive an hour up to the park and an hour back the next day. Reagan did not show me one iota of ego. He was a loyal servant. There was some real, visceral hatred for Reagan when he was governor; mostly from liberals—I was nauseated by the blind hatred I saw and heard. I ended my friendship with five different, really prominent people in the New Age community, including Edgar Mitchell, the astronaut." (former astronaut 1966-NASA-Group 5)"

Buck, what is the essence of Ronald Reagan, in your mind, your beliefs and your knowledge; after forty years of reflection on this man?

"I didn't fully appreciate him. I just didn't have the intellectual tools, the language, the metaphors, to understand him until I had read two of Ayn Rand's books, ATLAS SHRUGGED and THE FOUNTAINHEAD. The philosophy she expounded on in ATLAS SHRUGGED clarified and explained why I had been so deeply attracted to Ronald Reagan, and Walt Disney, as well. Two 'peas in a pod'— with a wonderful philosophy of life."

What do you think this man brought to the table, Buck?

"Integrity!" "Consciousness." "The word *decency* doesn't sound big enough, but it is somewhere in the vicinity of it.." "Profound decency." "He was an *intelligent* man—Oh, My God, Yes!" "During some of the briefings, the departmental briefings, that I sat in on in Sacramento, during the transition government period; people would make their presentations, expecting that—'he's just an actor'—Ron would be making notes and he'd come back with an hour of profoundly deep, significant questions and he'd help people explain what they were really thinking; without influencing them but just to bring out the best in them. There is the *key* thing: He brought out the BEST in people. Reagan's *presence* and his *qualities* are just as much alive in me today as they were then!"

Chapter Nineteen

THE PRESS PHOTOGRAPHER

Dennis Warren

"I never saw a real hatred for Ronald Reagan."

"I was very much impressed with him then—because he was *so* likeable!"

Dennis Warren was a nationally-recognized, full-time, freelance and UPI-Capitol Bureau photographer who watched Ronald Reagan evolve from G.E. Spokesperson, thru his candidacy for governor to the presidency and chronicled on film some of his greatest moments. Warren was called "The Nikon Nightrider," the title of an article about Dennis, by Bob Sylva which appeared in Sacramento Magazine December 1978.

"After Reagan spoke to the crowd on the Capitol steps, in April 1968, where he was received more or less—politely—after Martin Luther King's memorial, there was a young black kid and a young white kid, about seven or eight years old, and he grabbed onto'em, and he and the staff and the security people all went back to Reagan's office—and somehow I got in on it too. Here's one of the photos. He gave them some jelly beans. He had a jar of jelly beans (actually Jelly Bellys ®) on his desk, but he didn't have anything to put them in. He got into his waste basket and found a manila envelope—it was clean—he put the jelly beans into that and gave it to the kids, and I shot a few pictures of them."

Pat Ingoglia asked, "Dennis, did you have any *one* fond, memorable moment with Reagan?"

Warren responded: "I was seventeen years old. I spoke with Reagan for the first time after he finished giving a speech at Sacramento High School in October of 1963, where I stood in the orchestra pit watching my very large, reel-to-reel tape recorder and holding the microphone, just steps under the stage where Reagan spoke. He was introduced as:

'One who some people say will be the next governor of California, Ronald Reagan.!' "And that was surprising. When that was said that night, it really made a mark on me. Looking up at him I remember he looked just as young as he did on T.V."

"After he spoke, they had a reception for kinda' like the hard-core people in the cafeteria at Sac High where people were standing around talking in little groups with punch and cookies and I remember going over and talking to him and someone mentioned 'airplanes' and he said, *Well, ah, ah, back many years ago, I was about to get on an airplane and a little voice came to me and said not to fly—and I have not been on a plane since—and I will not go on a plane again!*" "And I thought, well there goes our gubernatorial candidate—how are they going to run a campaign with just busses and trains? I was very much impressed with him, then, because he was just so likeable!"

"For the most part—of all the things I have covered—I covered nine national political conventions, four were Democrat, the rest Republican—I've covered almost *every* major anti-war demonstration in the sixties, except the one where they shut down the Pentagon—but I was at the one at Nixon's Inaugural when they had sixty or eighty thousand people on the Capitol Mall and it was just a sea of people with the Washington Monument sticking up. I was in Boston covering the peace marches and then L.A., and then during the anti-nuke things—the Nuclear Freeze demonstrations during the '70's, when Reagan was still popular and all and the People's Park thing, in Berkeley."

"Generally speaking, I don't think I ever saw any *real hatred*, by his enemies, for Reagan; except maybe at People's Park."

Check out Dennis's UCB demonstrations, Sacramento Capitol and National-Guard-on-riot-duty photos in this book.

"When, the fellow who was shot by the National Guard troops, and another fellow was blinded, in Berkeley during the initial riots in People's Park, then they were pretty anti-Reagan, but, comparing this to the same types of events—Lyndon Johnson, I mean, he was *viciously* hated. Maybe because he was one of theirs and he had screwed them over, I remember at the Democrat Convention in '68, the crowd outside the Hilton was going, 'FUCK!—FUCK!—LBJ!' They finally stopped it because they realized it was not going to get on T.V. and they picked up this, 'The whole world is watching' chant. But—**I never saw a real hatred for Ronald Reagan.**"

"Anybody, I think, who really saw Reagan on T.V., or in person, at the very least they—felt he was popular and felt, (aside) [I can't do their thinking for them, but] 'If we riot against him, it's going to help *him*.' "An example was when he went to the University Board of Regents meeting in Berkeley—they lined his pathway—but they just were *Silent!* Usually they would jeer and then they were silent."

This was one of the times RR turned to the crowd, with his forefinger in front of his mouth, and simply said, *'SSSH'* "What an ice-breaker!"

"I seem to recall that—it was a feeling of, 'This is a good way to protest him.' 'He *is* popular and he's not that bad as a person;' kinda' thing."

"I definitely think he grew in stature with the job as governor. You'd see a different Reagan from one event, press conference or convention speech to another. It was an evolution."

"When he spoke as governor, after six months, he pulled into Omaha, for the Y.R. National Convention, on the way to the Western Governor's Conference, he answered their questions rather well—and he doesn't give made-up answers. He really handles himself well," recalled Warren.

I asked this photographer / more caption-writer than journalist about his personal feelings about Ronald Reagan as an individual. Whether there's depth there, whether there's true character to the soul and to the heart of the man—or whether there is *not*.

Warren hesitated, then said, "I think that I can say, Yes, that there is—in the affirmative—on everything you're saying there, but, I think I can say it only based on what I have read and seen on T.V., over the years and what was reported on him, but not really, as much, from personal experience. When he was with me, he was *always* very friendly."

"The crowds would come alive around Reagan. I remember the **'VIVA—OLE'** shouts started with the Young Republicans during the Goldwater Campaign and it became a *Reagan* thing. A Reagan chant. That's another thing I noticed—more than with any other candidate —was the way Reagan appealed to the Latinos. It really surprised me!"

"Reagan was always surrounded by political enemies and the Democrat legislature and he managed to come out of it—so well—and he was *energized* by it!"

Chapter Twenty

THE NON-HANDLER

George Young

"The press portrayed Ron as a puppet and a *tool* of his handlers." "He simply was not!" "He was one tough *nut* to handle." "He was focused and knew what he believed in—and, what he wanted to portray." "I marveled at how *advanced* Reagan was in his thinking!"

George was twenty-six years old when he went to work for the Spencer-Roberts political consulting firm in 1963 and was number three in command when he first began working with Ronald Reagan as a potential candidate. This was two months prior to Dave Tomshany taking over the formal scheduling of events and the road trips all over California. Then George became the "Organizational Man" in charge of the headquarters.

RR's earliest campaign experiences & a few vignettes

"It was my *initiation* process—and Ron's. It was S-R's too—it was their training period. My wife, Sue, and I would pick up RR at the Beverly Hills Hotel and take him everywhere to various meetings. Sue and I picked him up one day at the hotel (a popular meeting, dining & dancing "hot spot" not to mention the gala balls in the Crystal Room, for Hollywood's movers and shakers) and took RR out to Walter Knott's Knott's Berry Farm family, home in Orange County, in our old Ford station wagon. We drove him to many such events and meetings with key people involved with the "Friends of Reagan Committee," Holmes Tuttle, Henry Salvatori and Cy Rubel. I had *no* assistants! I had *no* soldiers. No Advance Team in place at all—just the testing period—getting to know RR and the dynamics of working together."

"We had a lot of *formulas*, political formulas, for the successful operation of campaigns here at S-R. Ron took *some* and *never* bought into others! He was his own guy from the word, 'GO'!"

"It was a Saturday and Ron and Nancy and I were in my car, returning to L.A. on the Santa Ana Freeway. Coming upon the freeway interchange as we neared the downtown area, Ron said, *"The big test is coming tomorrow morning."* Ron said that he was anxious to see the L.A. Times poll which would be coming out the very next morning. I told him I knew of a place we could pick up an advance paper that evening; at the Statler Hilton Hotel."

"We stopped by and, sure enough, the papers were there and much to Ron's *complete* surprise he was shown *beating* his opponent, should we make it to the General Election, Governor Pat Brown!"

"Ron was very skeptical about whether the Times would give us a fair shake, because they were obviously leaning towards George Christopher. With smiles on their faces, they gave a little *'gasp.'* I think that is the first time they allowed themselves to think," *"We might win!"* "This seemed to be the first time they got confirmation that he might *win*. I was just happy to be there, for a *first!* That was a nice time to be there."

"I marveled at how advanced Reagan was, in his thinking. The normal, old way, of running a political campaign would be for the consultants (S-R) and myself to craft the constituents and voters into various *blocks* with titles and categories for each. They were also called Special Campaign Divisions; such as those entitled: Hispanics or Chicanos, which some wanted to be called. Ron got into some *ugly* fights with Stu Spencer, who was used to using those terms, over Ron's desire and determination to eliminate them from his campaign vocabulary. Spencer grew up in East L.A. and was not being derogatory. But, Reagan felt the terms were too *divisive* in our society and he wouldn't use them."

"When we went hunting for some key people in the Mexican-American community or, as it was being called then, the Hispanic community; we located a very popular medical doctor by the name of Dr. Francisco Bravo, who not only liked Reagan, he was involved in all aspects of the ethnic life of the community." However, when the press release was written, and issued from the campaign headquarters, the Hispanic physician was referred to as: "A Prominent East Los Angeles Doctor."

"The press portrayed Ron as a puppet and a tool of his handlers. He simply was *not!* He was one tough *nut* to handle. He was *focused* and knew what he believe in and what he wanted to portray."

George's comments prefaced a three hour taped-interview and gourmet dinner prepared by his wife, Sue, at the Young home in California.

"*Warmth, honesty* and *sincerity* exuded from the candidate, out on the campaign trail, wherever we went, whatever group he spoke to, whomever he met with, whatever we did," Young said.

"It was his *inherent* good nature. In retrospect it is evident, due to the dynamics of presidential politics, Ronald Reagan could never have made the Great Leap into the presidency without first serving so well as California's governor."

"Ronald Reagan was a different kind of candidate. I was in the political management business for twenty-seven years. I had run a congressional campaign, on my own, the year before I went to work for S-R and had met Bill and Stu and they said, 'Why don't you come over and set up office, right out of our facility—we think we've got some work for you.' "We joint-ventured a few things and when their fortunes took off and they needed a lot of help; I became part of their firm. "

"We had a wonderful relationship! I was very surprised when they signed the Reagan Exploratory Committee effort. We had been, more or less, philosophically positioned in the *moderate* side of the Republican Party. We'd done Tom Kuchel's (Keekel's) re-election for U.S. Senate. We'd done Nelson Rockefeller's California primary campaign."

I told George, 'We called Rockefeller *liberal*, George!'

"Yeah, I know, but I called him *moderate.* The story around the shop was—that we had been given this opportunity to work for Reagan because Barry Goldwater told him," 'I wouldn't do anything in California without those guys on my side!'

"So we just had a very early effort in 1965—when we organized a little program called, The Friends of Reagan, which was principally a fund-raising source and a way of floating the trial balloon to see whether or not this was what everybody wanted to do. Most of the main people were the same as the members of The Kitchen Cabinet. Cy Rubel was the chairman, with Holmes Tuttle, Henry Salvatori and Justin Dart; people like that."

"They were important people in the community and they gave money and they raised money. And other people who gave money looked to them for leadership."

"We did a lot of things to raise money at S-R. It was never easier than raising money for Ronald Reagan. It sort of spoiled me! In all of the twenty-some years that followed, I was never able to find another candidate with that much *charisma!*"

"I mean, we did things like—we would mail to the Republican voter name list in an assembly district—one to every household—and ask them for money and tell them—it would be a letter from Ron saying, *"I'm thinking about this run for governor—and—I'm wondering if you could help.* And the money would just flow in! It would just *flow* in!"

"Frequently in small amounts like ten, twenty—thirty dollars. But, sometimes five hundred or a thousand dollars. He's the ONLY candidate that I have ever been associated with who was able—on a 'cold' list—to raise more money than it cost to send it! A lot of these 'professional' fund raising efforts are based upon your 'prospecting' the list, you find the donors, then you go back to them—and back to them—and back to them—and maybe on the third or fourth go-around—you finally break even."

"Well, we were making money the *first* time—with Reagan! It really was a remarkable thing. He just *had IT!* People liked him! He stood for what they wanted."

"People right now don't remember how hungry Republicans were to win an election; because we had so much success!" I told George, I'd never forget him saying, "The money *poured* in!" Young smiled, said, "Yeah! It did! With the staff doing nothing but opening envelopes with checks and making deposits, all the time. Kathy Davis was one of those in the S-R offices—she would just sit there, open the mail, and they would start stacking the checks up—on the desk—and they would stack them by denomination. And every day they would type up a little report, with everybody's name and the amount of money on it. It was *big!* It was pretty exciting. And I was so young that I didn't realize how unique it was!"

"Bill and Stu—they were scratching their heads saying, 'My God!' "We haven't ever seen *this* before. Now I can scratch my head and say, 'WOW, I've never seen that *since!*' I truly have not!" "No!" "No!" "Not in all the years of managing campaigns. Not on a 'cold' list. basis On proven lists, you can make money on it. Not a 'cold' list."

"In the very early days there, I was the third man in the firm—and it was a three man firm—with a couple of ladies, including Kathy Davis, who went to Sacramento to become RR's first personal secretary, so it became my responsibility to take Ron places."

This was in the earliest days of the exploratory effort.

"Occasionally, when it was Ron and Nancy, I would bring my wife and Bill and Stu didn't mind that. Sue is not a super-political person. She tolerates it because of *me*. She got along well with the Reagans. We would go and we were kind of like their *companions*. It wasn't like a *staff* relationship. I had no advance assistants helping me. No 'soldiers' out in the field. We had *no* literature to hand out—and that was kind of the attractiveness of what Ron was doing. Because he was saying, *"I'm here to find out—do you want me to run?"*

"He wasn't 'hard-sell'—. Later on—we developed 'sign-up' envelopes—'sign-up' cards—but I'm talking about September and October 1965."

"We did a speech one night over in Glendale, and the press were there, and somebody was doing some sort of an investigative approach to their story—as to why Ronald Reagan would be speaking in Glendale—and he entered the interview with a pretty determined attitude—that Glendale was some kind of a *racist* community."

"He asked Ron why he would choose Glendale to give a speech—'because of it's racist reputation.' Looking back on it, I see now, why he was such a good candidate. Because, he didn't have any *coaching* from Spencer-Roberts—or from me—he just immediately attacked the premise of the question. Which is what I've been coaching candidates to do all these years, afterwards. He wasn't going to answer it." He just said to the reporter, *" I don't think that Glendale is a racist community, what facts do you have to base that on?"*

"Republicans were pretty defensive at the time. If you recall, we hadn't won anything (races) for a long time. And the press was pretty successful in positioning our candidates in *losing* postures. They just turned Barry Goldwater into a *devil*. A *monster!* Yeah!"

"They were quite successful. And we did a lot of things in the Reagan campaign— to protect ourselves."

I reminded George what he had said earlier, "—that Ron's demeanor was *not* defensive." I told him this story: 'Remember what happened in the '64 Goldwater campaign, the Goldwater traveling staff, including the press, were handed little brass lapel buttons that looked like an Arizona cactus, and it had the initials from top to bottom, E.L.P. on it for Eastern Liberal Press?'

It was funny for about three minutes, but the sad part is, in my opinion, it was a *defensive* move. It turned the press, even more, against Barry. I asked George to follow-up on his comment that, 'Ron Reagan was not like that.'

"No." *"No!"* "He was such a good candidate. There's a myth that a lot of people believe: That somehow we coached him and *manufactured* this candidate *'product.'* In the way he approached things. And that really is *not* the way it happened."

"I'm not saying that we didn't make good political and campaign decisions for him—because I think we did. But, in terms of the advice we gave him about how things should be conducted and how he should conduct himself—he took what he wanted—and frequently Reagan said, *"Well, that's not the way I'm going to do it!"*

"Stu and Bill and I would make proposals for him to consider and, just in traveling, the general 'rule' is that a candidate's speech should target one, two or perhaps three issues—and just repeat those over and over and over, developing a theme in the campaign—making sure that the theme is attractive to a majority of voters. Eventually you become identified with it, and so on—and then you *win!"*

"When you are dealing with a candidate who is—limited—it's the best formula for success. *You* know—Ron would have none of that. He wrote his own stuff—he would put his ideas down on those index cards, he would bring them—everywhere—it was like shuffling playing cards. He'd use a paragraph here and a paragraph there—and sort of assemble his speech—'on the fly.' "

"I made a list during the campaign—he had twenty-one subjects—that he would rotate through his speeches! He would frequently only use a dozen or so, in any given speech, but you *never* knew which dozen—he was sizing up his audience—I suppose thru skills that he used in the entertainment business."

"Experience had taught him that if one subject worked, then you would go to the next one and the next one. So, each speech was a little different and it drove the press 'crazy' because we wouldn't give them advance copies. Certainly, in the beginning, they didn't believe that we weren't writing his material. Spencer-Roberts had this 'larger-than-life' reputation of being able to *manufacture* winners. So there was this whole *myth* that we were doing this for Reagan when, in fact, we were doing a lot of good things—but we weren't doing *that!"*

Earlier, George talked about RR not wanting to categorize people in various ethnic Groups. He expounded on that further: "This came later, this was after the primary election. Remember, we were putting together a special effort for the Hispanic vote. I think we called it Chicano, at the time."

I did, too. 'I remember he rode a horse, on a western saddle, in an East Los Angeles parade. I ran the entire length of that parade, alongside his horse, as added security, after doing the advance work and met my advance pick-up team at the other end.'

"There was a major *breakthrough*—a "mover" and "shaker" in the Demo ranks, an Hispanic leader by the name of Dr. Francisco Bravo. He was the practicing physician I mentioned earlier. He had organized a number of very successful, political, grassroots efforts in East Los Angeles. And—had *never* backed a Republican, before! And, for reasons that were never made clear to me, he had decided that he was willing to consider Reagan—but he had a number of demands. They were stipulations about wanting to be able to carry through on promises that he would make vis-a-vis money, and commitments and candidate-time—which was a responsible position."

Rhetorically George said, 'You (Bravo) don't want to go out and use your reputation and then be left 'high and dry' by the campaign.'

"And the way we did it in those days was we had Chicanos for Reagan, and there would be somebody who would be chairman of that committee. Or, we would have Democrats for Reagan, and there would be a chairman for *that* committee. "BUT—Reagan would have NONE of that!" "Even though, we explained, 'This works!' 'This is the way to get elected' This was a fairly well-seasoned concept.*"

Reagan simply said, *"No ETHNIC identification!" "NO ethnic identification in my campaign!" "NO ethnic committees!" "Period—that's it!"*

George said, "I thought, Bill and Stu will talk him outa' this. They couldn't! That was Ron's attitude in the early, '60's. That was his *advanced* thinking. "Bill Roberts made a really strategic withdrawal on that issue and came up with a way to satisfy Dr. Bravo's needs and Ronald Reagan's policy, and Dr. Bravo was eventually appointed as a Statewide Vice-Chairman of the Reagan for Governor Committee."

"No *ethnic* identification! We created bumper stickers for him with the slogan: YA BASTA! Which meant 'Enough already'!!! Reagan was very much his *own* guy. Self-Image is so important. When you get a candidate with a *great self-image*—it's worth a lot."

At the 1968 GOP National Convention in Miami the U.S. Secret Service, which was newly assigned to guard the potential presidential candidates' every move, took over the personal protection duties from Reagan's staff and in the process tried to plan every moment of the candidate's life from where he slept to each and every move he made, who he was meeting with, and, in some cases *why*. Actually, they wanted to know the layout and *need* of going to the meetings—especially large-crowd events—to minimize danger to The Man.

Some of the Secret Service staff were abrasive and belligerent, others polite and considerate. It was quite an upheaval from our normal operating procedures. One of the good things that came out of this metamorphosis of our security operation was the fortuitous inclusion of Ed Hickey, S.S. Personal Protection detail agent, who was assigned to the inner circle of the Reagan family protection and, after we returned to Sacramento, retired from the S.S. and was asked to join the governor's staff.

George recalled, "My instructions were, 'Don't tell them what you are doing' so I didn't interface with them at all."

George mentioned that the '68 Convention was one of the most exciting times of his life—when he was at the Miami International airport and this whole Reagan meeting, greeting and high-energy hoopla came off the way he had hoped and planned all of those months before—and it was also one of the most *tense* times in his life. This was a lot to shoulder for a mild-mannered 'Clark Kent' sort of guy, who was more at home in his office in L.A. than out on-the-ground in the 'eye of the hurricane.' This was so typical of *any* appearance or series of very public events with RR. Due to his charisma and crowd- appeal, if we added some sharply dressed Reagan Girls and a band; it became *pandemonium* almost every time.

Then he talked about Senator Strom Thurmond, and I didn't want to lose that.

"Oh, well, this is all hearsay on my part. Because I was very focused—I had two jobs to do, and I did 'em. Naturally, after they were concluded, we were looking at the results and wishing we had won, but the consensus of the people who usually knew the *real* answers to those questions was that we were on the verge of *turning* the Southern Delegations, and that it was the personal appeal of Strom Thurmond who stepped in and—held back the 'tide'—and held those Southern Delegations for Richard Nixon."

"I don't think Strom had any negative feelings towards Ronald Reagan—he just had a commitment to Nixon and felt it was Nixon's turn—and acted accordingly. And was convincing enough to make the difference. But—if those Southern Delegations had started jumping—I mean—the votes were so close in so many other states—that just a five or ten percent swing of delegates moving off of Nixon—to Reagan—would have tipped them and we would have had one of those fabulous American stories—but it didn't happen."

EPILOGUE

(Art Van Court & Curtis Patrick collections)

When I was first introduced to Nancy Reagan by Peggy Goldwater, in the fall of 1964, at the Coconut Grove in Los Angeles, after Reagan's stellar delivery of THE SPEECH, I was twenty-six years old. Etiquette and decorum, were paramount in my family, as I grew up. Copies of Emily Post's and Amy Vanderbilt's renowned books on those subjects were prominently displayed on both my grandmother's and my mother's dining room sideboard buffets, in amongst the fine china dishware and old-world silver serving dishes. Proper social graces were ingrained in me and my siblings from an early age. The words that flashed into my mind at that first introduction to Mrs. Reagan were 'class' and 'respect.' She fit right into my model of how a successful lady in the upper echelon of Los Angeles society should look and act.

Nancy carried herself with an air of confidence, perhaps enhanced by the fact that she was married to such a vibrant, recognizable, likeable man. From the moment I met her, I liked her. She called me, personally, after our first meeting and several months later, I went to work for the consulting firm, Spencer-Roberts & Assoc., representing her husband. She always treated me, as if I were a welcome member of the family.

Even though I was assigned to handle advance work for their first campaign for governor, it was as natural as if she were my mother or my Aunt Peggy for me to ask if there was "anything I can do for you," whenever we'd meet. Occasionally, she'd take me up on my offer and I'd end up driving her Ford Ranch Wagon to the market in Brentwood near their Pacific Palisades home for some last minute groceries, or, I'd drive my own car to pick up Skipper or Patti at their nearby schools.

One of Nancy's cars, a bright red 1970 Ford Ranch Wagon, in its original condition, is in the underground storage facility of the Ronald Reagan Presidential Library in Simi Valley, CA. It seemed she always drove a middle-America type station wagon.

I can remember Nancy being called on the spur of the moment by her husband or Bill Roberts or Holmes Tuttle, announcing an unscheduled dinner or get-together to plan campaign strategy and on my way back to the Wilshire Boulevard Headquarters I would accompany her to Bloomingdales or one of the other coutures in Beverly Hills to pick out a dress or some outfit to brighten up the occasion. Together, we'd carry the packages back to the house, unload the whole lot with the help of Ann, their house-keeper, just in time for Nancy to be ready for the evening's activities.

These were hectic times and they called for extra hard work, lots of patience and little rest. I was happy to accommodate them in any way possible to get the job done to insure that Reagan became the next governor of California. Most of my colleagues felt the same way; we worked together as a team. The best part was, the Reagans appreciated every-thing we did for them—so it was easy!

Sometimes the Reagans were just entertaining close friends and Nancy needed to pick up some overlooked essentials, She'd do that herself. She was a wife and a mother and did everything she could to make her family happy and proud of her. Their home was modest, not pretentious, a beautiful, comfortable, warm, friendly and peaceful place to be.

Every moment we were with them, those of us who were close to the Reagans could clearly see that to Ron, Nancy was articulate, pretty, intellectually stimulating and sexy. One of her major assets was, and still is, her keen sense of decorum, correctness and social protocol; so important to her husband's career. Nancy was chic and impeccable while entertaining kings and queens, potentates, artists, musicians, fellow actors as well as "captains" of industry, or just friends and acquaintances. She made them all feel comfortable and welcome. As you were reading the preceding chapters of my many colleagues, you saw how they made us feel like part of their family, rather than employees or just faceless staff members. Their attitude towards us was truly amazing and it engendered strong loyalty!

When Ron became *Governor* Reagan and Nancy his First Lady, some of her finest hours were spent comforting wounded Vietnam War veterans who had just returned from the disease-infested buffalo swamps and jungles of Southeast Asia. Military men and women in hospitals all over California, as well as their families and loved ones, were the beneficiaries of Nancy's generosity and caring nature. She made telephone calls, wrote letters, or simply spent a little time holding the hands of those in need of some special attention and she did it without fanfare or a desire for recognition, never allowing the press to accompany her. We were all incredibly proud to be a part of her life!

As others who know them well have said and as we found out later on, 'It was apparent that Ron's failed marriage, years earlier, hounded him inwardly.' He would have turned heaven and earth to avoid another Hollywood marriage from going "on-the-rocks." What we saw in Ron and Nancy Reagan was a strong contradiction to that dictum. I saw that they were consummately loyal to each other and deeply committed to one another's happiness and well-being 24/7. We staffers became an adjunct part of that love affair; making every effort to keep those two in communication and connected, again. As Nancy Clark Reynolds so aptly phrased it, "They were totally *entwined* into one another."

Ron had the greatest respect for Nancy and her judgment, but he had no problem speaking up, if necessary, when there was a disagreement. Most of us respected Nancy's devotion to Ron and knew it to be truly genuine. In fact, it was *infectious.* Some of us grew to love Nancy, as we did RR, (our "nickname" for him amongst ourselves) and would have done anything for her. To the best of our ability, we made every effort to do as much as we could, but it was often a challenge trying to pull rabbits out of *every* hat. At the end of the day, you had to admire her and appreciate her goals. Nancy Reagan had a depth of character which many people never had the opportunity to see.

Negative stories, whether in gossip-columns, news or feature sections of daily newspapers or in the media about either one of them cannot dispel the true, loving, generous thoughtfulness that Ron and Nancy expressed to one another in their mannerisms, body-language, demeanor and courtesies in their everyday lives. In addition, Nancy's book, "I Love You, Ronnie" revealed the very personal love notes, some of which I carried back and forth many times while Ron or Nancy each added another layer of love in a new line or phrase. This was no affectation! The naysayers were, as Lyn Nofziger used to say, "Full of Baloney!" Nancy Reagan wasn't perfect but she frequently suffered criticism due to her always insisting that RR be put *first* ahead of everyone else's desires and needs, including her own.

Nancy provided valuable, thoughtful, and sometimes controversial input on many subjects; especially her fairly accurate insight into the character of staff members, which was almost prescient. Her input was a direct, no-nonsense statement which needed to be addressed, reviewed and given consideration. However, in the *final* analysis, and perhaps contrary to the beliefs of many, the business and political decisions of the State of California that effected its citizens were determined by Governor Ronald Reagan.

Found in Volume 1, Volume 2 & Volume 3

*Behind-the-Scenes Revelations,
Glimpses, Anecdotes & Vignettes
From 49 Diverse people,
Their Personal Relationships With
Ronald Reagan and How Their Lives
& His were Changed Forever!*

Curtis Patrick

For Latest Updates go to:

www.curtispatrick.com

www.reaganwhatwashereallylike.com

ABOUT THE AUTHOR

Portrait Innovations, Henderson, NV

Curtis Patrick was introduced to Ronald and Nancy Reagan in October 1964 by Peggy Goldwater, wife of U.S. Senator Barry M. Goldwater, (R) AZ (Patrick was special assistant to the Senator during 1964) on the night of Reagan's delivery of his most famous early political expression, entitled by the media and his supporters as simply: The Speech, "A Time For Choosing," given on Goldwater's behalf to try to "jump-start" his failing presidential campaign. Patrick was overwhelmed by Reagan's honesty and sincerity. He asked Nancy to call him if Reagan ever decided to run for governor.

Patrick had been a student at the USC School of Journalism, having changed majors from Business Administration, and was learning the real estate business after hours. His life then took an unexpected turn, when his mother was divorced from his alcoholic stepfather, and he was forced to leave college and help his mother, younger brother and two younger sisters save the San Fernando Valley orange groves, ranch and flower business, where the family had been raised. Thus, at the age of twenty-three he was engaged by the United States District Court in Southern California to oversee the operations of the ranch, provide security and protect the assets of the estate.

Later, Nancy made that call and Patrick became Reagan's first advance-man and part of his statewide scheduling team with responsibilities for communications, transportation and back-up security. He helped put together a security operation for the campaign, working with members of the Los Angeles Police Department (L.A.P.D.), several of whom he had met during his youth on the ranch.

During the general election, Patrick supervised the thirteen-member Reagan Advance Team, under the direction of Spencer-Roberts & Associates and Richard Sandy Quinn; he worked closely with Nancy Reagan and Reagan's "Kitchen Cabinet."

After Reagan's landslide victory, he asked Patrick to join him in Sacramento. The governor first appointed Patrick as a Staff Secretary for Special Services and later Special Assistant to the Executive Secretary (Chief of Staff) and finally Special Assistant to the Governor.

In 1968 Patrick was asked to head a secret team of Reagan loyalists engaged by RR's Appointments Secretary, Thomas C. Reed ((later U.S. Air Force Secretary), Communications Director, Lyn Nofziger (later same title in the White House) and political legend, F. Clifton White—to create a high-tech communications command center and clandestine rolling field-office, planning-room, operations and strategy center—carefully housed inside a brand new 45 foot Mayflower moving-van semi-trailer, complete with the huge, shiny green, square-rigger, Pilgrim's sailing ship logos. The new home-to-be for Reagan's National Field Operations-convention floor-delegate management team, with state-of-the-art air conditioning by the Lennox Corp., was designed to give RR an advantage in fighting for his delegates and fending off hostile moves, primarily by the Nixon, Rockefeller and Romney forces. Now that the persons who were attached to the super-secret Skunk Works at Lockheed Aircraft Co., in Burbank, CA. have passed on, their involvement in assisting us in Miami Beach, *gratis,* during their vacations, can now be divulged. Their part: to sharpen our electronic anti-eavesdropping systems with high-tech electronics.

Then, the whole outfit was driven nearly 3,000 miles to Miami Beach, Florida, to the GOP National Convention, where it was positioned outside the convention center against a solid concrete wall with a movie-set style loading dock painted on the side of the building, so RR's opponents would think the Reagan " house trailer" was obviously coming in just as soon as the moving van finished "unloading" its cargo. Not only the opponents but the press and media as well, believed it to be true. (see attached photos) It was near Nixon's doublewide mobile home provided by the Florida Citrus Association.

Inside was an electronic command post with twenty stations for trusted field directors who could simply reach for a cornucopia of the latest high-tech Handi-Talkies, radio-phones and hard-wired, secured telephones, as well; to locate *key Reagan delegates* in the swing states and try to hold them to a second ballot vote for Governor Reagan.

Patrick moved to the state of Nevada in 1972 and continued to keep in touch with and handle special assignments for the Reagans and staff colleagues. He became active in politics, was elected State Chairman of the Nevada Republican Party, was a successful political, government relations / land use consultant, real estate broker and investor. Patrick wrote campaign plans and press releases for dozens of successful candidates and ballot issues. He headed up numerous committees and organizations, including the business community's Master Plan Steering Committee for the southern portion of the Nevada side of the contentious Lake Tahoe Basin for the Tahoe Regional Planning Agency, the T.R.P.A.; for six years. Patrick was President of the Tahoe Sierra Preservation Council, a 3,500 member group of Lake Tahoe California and Nevada property and home owners who proposed legislation to protect private property rights, as well as, the pristine quality of Lake Tahoe. He helped to preserve and develop Historic Glenbrook (1872) on the East Shore of Lake Tahoe—into a Victorian village.

He was a Trustee and later became Chairman of the Board of Trustees for the Tahoe Douglas Fire Protection District & Bomb Squad, for more than thirteen years and, with his wife, Joan, was instrumental in establishing the Nevada State Republican Legislative Caucus, later becoming the Republican Assembly Caucus and the Senate Leadership Caucus.

Patrick was a Volunteer firefighter in the Carson Valley in Douglas County, Nevada and rose to the rank of Assistant Chief of the Sheridan Volunteer Fire Dept.

He and Joan live in Henderson, NV., close to their children, grandchildren and great-grandchildren. For the past eleven years Patrick has been engaged in the RR Oral History Project and in the writing of this book, Volumes 1. & 2., to help preserve Ronald Reagan's legacy.

To Curtis Patrick
With deep appreciation. Ronald Reagan

OFFICIAL WHITEHOUSE PHOTOGRAPH

BUY A SHARE OF THE FUTURE IN YOUR COMMUNITY

These certificates make great holiday, graduation and birthday gifts that can be personalized with the recipient's name. The cost of one S.H.A.R.E. or one square foot is $54.17. The personalized certificate is suitable for framing and will state the number of shares purchased and the amount of each share, as well as the recipient's name. The home that you participate in "building" will last for many years and will continue to grow in value.

Here is a sample SHARE certificate:

HABITAT FOR HUMANITY

THIS CERTIFIES THAT
YOUR NAME HERE
HAS INVESTED IN A HOME FOR A DESERVING FAMILY

1985-2010
TWENTY-FIVE YEARS OF BUILDING FUTURES
IN OUR COMMUNITY ONE HOME AT A TIME

1200 SQUARE FOOT HOUSE @ $65,900 = $54.17 PER SQUARE FOOT
This certificate represents a tax deductible donation. It has no cash value.

YES, I WOULD LIKE TO HELP!

I support the work that Habitat for Humanity does and I want to be part of the excitement! As a donor, I will receive periodic updates on your construction activities but, more importantly, I know my gift will help a family in our community realize the dream of homeownership. **I would like to SHARE in your efforts against substandard housing in my community!** *(Please print below)*

PLEASE SEND ME _____ SHARES at $54.17 EACH = $ $_____

In Honor Of: _____

Occasion: (Circle One)   *HOLIDAY*   *BIRTHDAY*   *ANNIVERSARY*

        OTHER: _____

Address of Recipient: _____

Gift From: _____ *Donor Address:* _____

Donor Email: _____

I AM ENCLOSING A CHECK FOR $ $_____ PAYABLE TO HABITAT FOR HUMANITY <u>OR</u> PLEASE CHARGE MY VISA OR MASTERCARD *(CIRCLE ONE)*

Card Number _____ Expiration Date: _____

Name as it appears on Credit Card _____ Charge Amount $ _____

Signature _____

Billing Address _____

Telephone # Day _____ Eve _____

PLEASE NOTE: Your contribution is tax-deductible to the fullest extent allowed by law.
Habitat for Humanity • P.O. Box 1443 • Newport News, VA 23601 • 757-596-5553
www.HelpHabitatforHumanity.org

CPSIA information can be obtained at www.ICGtesting.com
Printed in the USA
LVOW07s0525200813

348714LV00001B/2/P